The Subcultural Imagination

The Subcultural Imagination discusses young adults in subcultures and examines how sociologists use qualitative research methods to study them. Through the application of the ideas of C. Wright Mills to the development of theory-reflexive ethnography, this book analyses the experiences of young people in different subcultural settings, whilst also reflecting on how young people in subcultures interact in the wider context of society, biography and history. From Cuba to London, and Bulgaria to Asia, this book delves into urban spaces and street corners, young people's parties, gigs, BDSM fetish clubs, school, the home and feminist zines to offer a picture of live sociology in practice. In three parts, the volume explores:

*   History, biography and subculture;
*   Practising reflexivity in the field; and
*   Epistemologies, pedagogies and the subcultural subject.

The book offers cutting edge theory and rich empirical research on social class, gender and ethnicities from both established and new researchers across diverse disciplinary backgrounds. It moves the subcultural debate beyond the impasse of the term's relevance, to one where researchers are fully engaged with the lives of the subcultural subjects. This innovative edited collection will appeal to scholars and students in the areas of sociology, youth studies, media and cultural studies/ communication, research methods and ethnography, popular music studies, criminology, politics, social and cultural theory, and gender studies.

Shane Blackman is Professor of Cultural Studies at Canterbury Christ Church University, UK.

Michelle Kempson is a lecturer at Solihull College and University Centre, UK.

Youth, Young Adulthood and Society
Series editor: Andy Furlong
University of Glasgow, UK

The *Youth, Young Adulthood and Society* series brings together social scientists from many disciplines to present research monographs and collections, seeking to further research into youth in our changing societies around the world today. The books in this series advance the field of youth studies by presenting original, exciting research, with strongly theoretically- and empirically-grounded analysis.

The Subcultural Imagination

Theory, research and reflexivity in contemporary youth cultures

**Edited by Shane Blackman
and Michelle Kempson**

 Routledge
Taylor & Francis Group

LONDON AND NEW YORK

First published 2016
by Routledge
2 Park Square, Milton Park, Abingdon, Oxon OX14 4RN

and by Routledge
711 Third Avenue, New York, NY 10017

Routledge is an imprint of the Taylor & Francis Group, an informa business

British Library Cataloguing in Publication Data
A catalogue record for this book is available from the British Library

Library of Congress Cataloging in Publication Data
Names: Blackman, Shane J., editor. | Kempson, Michelle, editor.
Title: The subcultural imagination : theory, research and reflexivity in contemporary youth cultures / edited by Shane Blackman and Michelle Kempson.
Description: Abingdon, Oxon ; New York, NY : Routledge, 2016. | Series: Youth, young adulthood and society
Identifiers: LCCN 2015045220| ISBN 9781138844032 (hardback) | ISBN 9781315730684 (e-book)
Subjects: LCSH: Youth--Social conditions. | Youth--Social life and customs.
Classification: LCC HQ796 .S8845 2016 | DDC 305.235--dc23
LC record available at http://lccn.loc.gov/2015045220

ISBN: 978-1-138-84403-2 (hbk)
ISBN: 978-1-315-73068-4 (ebk)

Typeset in Times New Roman
by HWA Text and Data Management, London

FSC
www.fsc.org
MIX
Paper from
responsible sources
FSC® C013604

Printed and bound by CPI Group (UK) Ltd, Croydon, CR0 4YY

For Kate Blackman, long may you shine.

For Matthew Pratt, whose encouragement has been invaluable.

Contents

Contributors

Vihra Barova is Assistant Professor at the Institute of Ethnology and Folklore Studies – Bulgarian Academy of Sciences – and lecturer in Social Anthropology at Plovdiv University, Bulgaria. She has written in the field of urban anthropology, on topics across youth studies, subcultural theory and social inclusion/exclusion.

Shane Blackman is a Professor of Cultural Studies at Canterbury Christ Church University, UK. He received his PhD at the Institute of Education, University of London as an ESRC scholarship student – supervised by Professor Basil Bernstein and Phil Cohen. His books include *Youth: Positions and Oppositions, Style, Sexuality and Schooling* (1995); *Drugs Education and the National Curriculum* (1996); *Chilling Out: The Cultural Politics of Substance Consumption, Youth and Drug Policy* (2004) and *Young People, Class and Place* (eds), *with* Shildrick, T. and MacDonald, R. (2010). He has recently published papers on ethnography, subcultural theory, anti-social behaviour and alcohol and young women. He is an editor of the *Journal of Youth Studies* and *YOUNG: Nordic Journal of Youth Research* and a member of the *ESRC Peer Review College.*

Phil Cohen grew up in post war Bloomsbury. He was sent to private schools which he hated and thence to Cambridge which he liked even less. He ran away to sea, and resurfaced in time to play a part in the counter culture emerging in London in the late 1960s, especially in the London Street Commune movement that occupied large buildings in central London. He subsequently re-entered Academe as a contract researcher carrying out a number of studies of youth culture, school transitions and popular racism. For the past 25 years he has worked as an ethnographer in East London documenting the impact of regeneration and demographic change on the lives, livelihoods and life stories of working class communities in the area. In 2013 he published his memoir *Reading Room Only* (Five Leaves) along with *On the Wrong Side of the Track?: East London and the Post-Olympics* (Lawrence and Wishart). *Graphologies*, a collection of poetry and prose, was published by Mica Press in 2014. *Material Dreams: Maps and Territories in the Un/Making of Modernity* was published by Palgrave in 2016. He is currently research director of LivingMaps, a network of artists, academics and activists concerned to develop a creative and critical approach to community mapping; he is also a research fellow at the Young Foundation.

Rachela Colosi is a Senior Lecturer in the School of Social and Political Sciences at the University of Lincoln. Her research interests are in unregulated and 'deviant' occupations – primarily women's engagement with different forms of sex-work such as erotic dance. Rachela is author of *Dirty Dancing? An Ethnography of Lap-Dancing* (2010, London: Routledge) – shortlisted for the BSA Philip Abrams Book Prize 2011. She continues to research and write about the lap-dancing industry and, along with Professor Phil Hubbard (University of Kent), recently completed an ESRC funded project that explored the impacts of lap-dancing venues on local communities.

Gemma Commane is a Lecturer in Media Theory at the Birmingham School of Media, Birmingham City University. Gemma's academic background is in Media and Cultural Studies, specialising in subcultures, youth, sexual deviancy, identity and urban ethnography. Gemma's PhD, *The Transfigured Body: Fetish, Fashion and Performance*, was a sociological and ethnographic enquiry into female sexual identity in burlesque, fetish and BDSM clubbing cultures. She is committed to social and cultural change and was part of the research team for CITISPYCE (funded by the EU Seventh Framework Programme) at Aston University in 2015.

Eleni Dimou is Lecturer in Criminal Justice and Criminology at the University of Kent, Medway Campus. Her research and teaching interests include critical and cultural criminology, globalisation and crime, Latin America and the Caribbean, youth subcultures, media and crime, drugs and culture, power, resistance and the de-colonial perspective of social sciences.

Anthony Gunter is a Principal Lecturer in Criminology, School of Business and Law, University of East London, UK. His teaching and research interests are in the areas of youth cultures and transitions, race/ethnicity and crime, and ethnography. He is the author *Growing Up Bad: Black Youth, Road Culture & Badness in an East London Neighbourhood* (Tufnell Press, 2010), an ethnographic youth study undertaken in an East London neighbourhood. Since 2011 he has carried out ethnographic research in East London exploring young people's lifestyles and transitions, serious youth violence, policing and community-led Third and Statutory Sector responses.

Robert Hollands is a Professor of Sociology at Newcastle University (UK), and is a former graduate of Queen's University (Canada) and the Centre for Contemporary Cultural Studies (CCCS), at the University of Birmingham (UK). His research interests include urban nightlife, smart/creative cities, the egalitarian arts, alternative urban cultures and cultural tourism. He is a research consultant to the Prague Fringe Festival, and his current research is on Amber Associates, a 40-plus year-old egalitarian film and photography collective based in Newcastle Upon Tyne. He is also the recent recipient of a two-year Leverhulme Trust Major Research Fellowship entitled 'Urban Cultural Movements and the Struggle for Alternative Creative Spaces' (September 2015–2017).

Michelle Kempson is a Lecturer at Solihull College and University Centre. She completed her PhD in Women and Gender studies at the University of Warwick, and her research interests and publication history centre on youth studies, adult education, feminist theory and cultural aesthetics.

Robert McPherson is a PhD research student in the Department of Media, Art and Design at Canterbury Christ Church University, UK. He teaches Sociology, Media and Cultural Studies, Youth Studies, Popular Music and Alcohol Studies, and Qualitative Research methods. His doctoral research is an ethnographic study into young people's alcohol consumption in the Canterbury night-time economy.

J. Patrick Williams is Associate Professor of Sociology at Nanyang Technological University in Singapore. He has published widely in the areas of subculture, identity and ethnography, including *Authenticity in Self, Culture, and Society* (2009, Ashgate) and *Subcultural Theory: Traditions and Concepts* (2011, Polity).

Acknowledgements

Thanks are due to the peer reviewers of our book proposal, the editor of the series Professor Andy Furlong and in particular all the authors of chapters in the book for following our guidance. We would also like to thank David Downes, Paul Rock and Dick Hebdige, who helped along the way. We are also grateful to Debbie Cox, Valerie Kempson and David Kempson.

Many of the chapters in this book began as papers presented at a symposium organised by Michelle at the Institute of Advanced Study at the University of Warwick in June 2013, where Shane gave a keynote paper. We would like to extend thanks to the Institute of Advanced Study, and to all of the speakers at that event who helped to shape our thinking on the connections between reflexivity, research, subjectivity and subculture.

We would like to thank Routledge for their continued assistance throughout this process.

Introducing the sociological and the subcultural imagination

Shane Blackman and Michelle Kempson

The social imagination: towards the subcultural subject

Subcultures are controversial, beautiful, frightening, commodified and liberating. From the spectacular to the personal, subcultures are in the midst of negotiating a process of social change. New technologies enable instant communication pan-nationally, making diversified modes of communication and expression open to many young people and creating the need for a re-examination of what constitutes the subcultural subject in live sociology.

The Subcultural Imagination explores the consequences of the 'reflexive turn' on subcultures research via an interrogation of how collective histories, social structures and personal biographies interrelate to create a set of distinctive subcultural experiences and subjective possibilities. We suggest a re-visitation of C. Wright Mills' work in the *Sociological Imagination* (1959) in order to explore how researchers within the field of subcultural studies are able to respond reflexively. C. Wright Mills asked for sociologists to revisit the methodological choices they made in order to avoid presenting the research field in a vacuum that is devoid of historical and spatial references, and of an understanding of complex processes of historicity that make only specific readings of research fields accessible to the researcher, and that, therefore, restrict the possible conclusions they will be able to draw.

The promise of *The Sociological Imagination* by C. Wright Mills (1959) is built on the aspiration to integrate culture and society, through understanding and explaining social worlds at the micro level of the individual and the macro level of social structures. In Britain, C. Wright Mills' idea of The Sociological Imagination is part of introductory texts for A level and undergraduate sociology students. We note the resurgence of interest in C. Wright Mills work. In 2000 Oxford University Press published a special 40th Anniversary Edition of *The Sociological Imagination*. In 2006 Steve Fuller produced his own *The New Sociological Imagination*. In 2009 the Department of Sociology at Goldsmiths celebrated the 50th Anniversary Celebration of *The Sociological Imagination*. Since 2010 we have seen the creation of the blog from the website sociologicalimagination.org/ with editors and an advisory board, where posted articles celebrated the anniversary of C. Wright Mills' death. In 2015, the 12th Conference of the European Sociological Association was titled: Difference, Inequalities and Sociological Imagination.

Its canonical status is confirmed; the sociological imagination has become shorthand for agency, representing an opportunity whereby people can see their 'private troubles' in terms of 'public issues'. *The Sociological Imagination* is a request: a call for people to use their social imagination to develop a better society. Through making an appeal above and beyond sociology, by enabling people's biographical experience to be understood as part of the history of their societies, C. Wright Mills saw social change as relevant, necessary and possible. At the same time, for the subject area, *The Sociological Imagination* remains a key text because of its motivation within the discipline due its passion, commitment and concern. Kathryn Mills (daughter of C. Wright Mills), in her Foreword to Scott and Nilsen's collection *C. Wright Mills and the Sociological Imagination: Contemporary Perspectives*, asserts: 'Over the past 12 years we've seen a Mills revival in the United States' (2013: xiii). Also, in the Britain, C. Wright Mills' work is defined as a classic study in sociology not as a result of its historical importance, but because it remains a work in process and has been a source of inspiration for a number of established academics – for example, Geoff Pearson's (1975) *The Deviant Imagination*, Paul Atkinson's (1990) *The Ethnographic Imagination*, Paul Willis' (2000) *The Ethnographic Imagination* and Jock Young's (2010) *The Criminological Imagination*. These four key texts are warning us to be on the outlook for the persistence of positivism and the disconnection of theory from empirical everyday reality. Using C. Wright Mills they urge us to investigate how the sociologist seeks to establish humane contact with research participants to collect data and address critically how sociological theory is constructed. Here the imagination is set-up as an alternative or critique against the growth of factual administration in sociological knowledge. Thus Mills' work is identified as creating the opportunity to occupy an alternative space from which to construct a critique of sociological knowledge and methodology.

Although Mills' legacy to sociology is now established, this was not always the case. *The Sociological Imagination* was born into the sociological world where the dominant paradigm of structural-functionalism offered a rather frosty assessment of Mills contribution. John Brewer (2004: 328) states: 'US sociology panned it.' The negative reception related to Mills attack on sociological orthodoxy at both the level of theory and methodology. C. Wright Mills (1959: 34) criticised functionalist grand theory for being 'a clumsy piece of irrelevant ponderosity' and 'not readily understandable'. For Mills (1959: 144) research methods under the dominant paradigm affirmed the positivistic science of society model which dovetailed to corporate capitalism making 'abstracted empiricism as the most suitable tool' to collect quantitative data without an apparent theoretical framework. For Ganes and Back (2012: 400) it was not just the text that produced an unreceptive reaction, they saw Mills' unpopularity resulting from a series of hostile engagements between Mills and American sociologists including, Talcott Parsons, Edward Shils, Peter Lazerfield, Daniel Bell, Alfred Kazin and others. As a result, the book could be seen as a product of its time fighting against the prevailing paradigm; however, we argue it would be more accurate to say it is a product for our time. Furthermore, Mills (1960) put himself on the outside of the sociological mainstream with his critique of American imperialism in *Listen Yankee*, describing his meeting in Cuba with Fidel Castro and Che Guevara. Working under FBI surveillance due to his radical thinking and political engagements outside the safety of the discipline, C. Wright Mills came under personal observation and subject to McCarthyism, as addressed in Mike Forrest Keen's (1999) *Stalking the Sociological Imagination: J. Edgar Hoover's FBI Surveillance of American Sociology*. Romantically, being on the outside of the sociological mainstream means that you are engaged in the myth of heroic struggle. But it was Mills' use of the disciplinary label sociology with the concept of imagination that brought real contestation from American sociologists, who saw it as anathema to the principles of the functionalist paradigm of science, rationality and order.

Mills' release of the sociological imagination put social justice at the centre of sociological theory and method to ask, as Howard Becker (1967) put it, 'Whose side are we on?' As a result, once released, Basil Bernstein (1975: 157) states: 'The sociological imagination should make visible what is rendered invisible.' It was on this basis that The Society for the Study of Social Problems established the *C. Wright Mills Award* in 1964. The first winner of the prize was David Matza's (1964) *Delinquency and Drift*, an investigation into 'the subculture of delinquency', which championed and continued Mills' ideal to bring on the younger generation of social critics. This projected the principle for C. Wright Mills that sociological theory should be integrally related to the study of key social issues including subcultures and deviance.

C. Wright Mills' battle with US imperialism, his personalised attack on American social theorists and his individualistic style to establish a public sociology outside the institutionalised discipline has a parallel with Raymond William's idea of the Cultural Studies Radical Project (Blackman 2000: 46). For both, the ambition was to enable subjective and biographical experience to inform theoretical processes and methodological practices to advance agency. In this sense knowledge is focused on fighting cultural elitism and actively seeking liberation through history, biography and structure. Jones (1972: 3) at the Centre for Contemporary Cultural Studies (CCCS) states: 'Mainstream sociology is dominated by official or authoritarian perspectives at the service of the present organisation of interest and privilege.' Stuart Hall (1980: 20) argues that the CCCS decided to 'break with sociology' because the predominance of functionalist theory had not only displaced the social from sociology but 'its premises and predispositions were highly ideological'. The recovery of sociology for Back and Tate (2015: 135) is where Mills and Hall converge to produce a broader and more inclusive and responsive sociology, in the fight against the conformity of professionalisation. We see the release of the sociological imagination is related to cultural politics, the cultural expressions of marginalised groups, the vitality of historical context and humanistic reflexive methods. Sociology for Mills is a discipline that should be politically engaged and the craft of the discipline its methodology should focus on commitment and humanity. David Matza (1969: 92) identified the sociological imagination as part of the real task 'of humane revision recognising the subjective capacities of … ordinary members of society'.

Being on the outside of the disciplinary mainstream the sociological imagination has been a major influence within the substantive area of deviance and methodologically through ethnography – for example during the late 1960s through the fusion of the National Deviancy Conference (NDC) and the Centre of Contemporary Cultural Studies. Jock Young (2013: xlviii) in *The New Criminology* writes *The Sociological Imagination*, 'is this one of the finest statements of critical sociology, but it is also a work that has had a great influence on the development of the critical tradition in criminology'. The new developments within youth cultural theory, presented at the NDC and CCCS, were brought to fruition by the 'subcultures of imagination and creativity rather than of flatness and determinism, resistance rather than negativism and retreatism, of a world of leisure as well as school and work, of meaning rather than malfunction' (Young 2013: xxiv). The NDC had created the opportunity of an emergent Cultural Criminology, which saw subcultures as possessing meaning, narrative and identity (Ferrell, Hayward and Young 2008). Subcultural theory became critically understood as solving social and cultural contradictions. It was A. K. Cohen (1956: 31) who brought us the original formulation that subcultures were engaged in 'spectacular' delinquency and then Phil Cohen's (1972: 30) analysis argued for the 'distinction between subcultures and delinquency' to be made enabling subculture to be freed from the theoretical pathology of crime.

Subcultural theories, errors, criticisms and schism

The concept of subculture entered sociology at the time when both Durkheim and the Chicago School of Sociology held the ambition of making sociology a distinct discipline. During this period, subculture was also beginning to be shaped by other disciplines including anthropology, biology, criminology, psychology and psychoanalysis. The attraction of the concept of subculture is that it carried disciplinary claims to knowledge and was used to put forward definite answers to social issues. However, the field of subcultural studies has been subject to common errors. This has been compounded recently on the Web through numerous online sites dedicated to subculture. The first error is that subculture was not used in sociology until the 1940s – for example, Brake (1980: 5), Thornton (1997: 1), Jenks (2005: 7), Gelder (2007: 40) and Bell (2010: 159). The second error is that Jenks, Gelder and Bell have argued that the concept of subculture was first used at the Chicago School of Sociology, but none of them tell us who or offer a reference. The third error is the common mistake to argue incorrectly as Andy Bennett (2015: 12) does that A. K. Cohen was a 'Chicago School theorist'; in fact, Albert Cohen was at Harvard doing his PhD with leading structural functionalist theorist Talcott Parsons. The first use of the concept of subculture is by Alfred Kroeber in 1925 (although dating back to 1905) to describe the American Native Indian tribe the Yurok's 'subcultural mythological area'. He worked closely with Edward Sapir at Chicago. The first direct explanation of concept of subculture is by Vivien Palmer at the Chicago School of Sociology in her methodological text *Field Studies in Sociology: A Student's Manual*. Palmer (1928: 73) calls for 'maps of subcultural groups'. She goes on to state that 'Subcultural groups which display variations in the prevailing culture of the land are much more difficult to discover. Investigations seem to disclose, however, that there are certain basic differences in people's mode of life which leads to clear-cut variations in their customs, attitudes and behaviour patterns.' Palmer began her methodological work for this book in 1925 and argued the researcher must be in possession of the 'feel of the problem' (247) and when writing up the study she said, 'the results depend upon the creative imagination of the investigator' (200).

Broadly there have been five major theoretical elaborations of subculture. Each theory contains degrees of relevance and usage in contemporary society. The first, developed at the Chicago School of Sociology, is grounded on examining differences in people's mode of cultural life; the second, the British psychological and psychoanalytic theory of subculture, defined young adults in terms of being defiantly 'subnormal'; the third, the structural functionalist theory developed by A. K. Cohen, theorised subcultures on the basis of being a delinquent gang that were dysfunctional for society; the fourth, the CCCS theory of subculture, defined subcultures in terms of refusal and resistance; and the fifth, the post-subculturalist approach, is based upon a postmodern understanding of culture which is individualistic and fluid (see Blackman, 2014).

The contemporary debate of subculture has been premised on an apparent opposition between the Centre for Contemporary Cultural Studies (CCCS) theory of subculture understood as 'a complex Marxism' and the postmodern perspective referred to as the post-subcultural turn. For Cote (2014: 151) this debate has been a 'lively dispute' because according to Albert Bell (2010: 154) post-subcultural theorists appear to take pleasure in 'deriding the term subculture as problematic, anachronistic and redundant'. For example, Redhead (1990: 25), argues that 'subcultures were produced by subcultural theorists, not the other way around'. Further, Redhead's assertion has been commended as evidence by Muggleton (1997: 201) and Bennett (2000: 24, 2015: 13). Muggleton and Weinzierl (2003: 7) claim, 'The subculture concept seems to be little more than a cliché.' Chaney (2004: 36) asserts that the concept of subculture is 'superfluous'; Sweetman (2004: 92) maintains 'the CCCS may no longer be applicable'; while Bennett (2015: 11) argues that in 'Australian youth scholarship, the concept of subculture still continues to be presented in a relatively unreconstructed and unproblematic fashion'.

The post-subcultural criticism of the CCCS theory according to Christine Griffin (2011: 251) has primarily 'missed, or in some cases actively avoided' any active engagement with the CCCS theory of subculture. For her much post-subcultural work is not merely 'determinedly anti-CCCS' (251) but there is a 'vehemence of much of the more recent critiques of the youth sub/cultures' (249). For Woodman and Bennett (2015: 4) the post-subcultural turn positions itself as the champion of agency for subcultural subjects on the basis that the CCCS 'ignored … the voices of the actual youth subculturalists'; as a result it can then be argued that the 'perceived deficit in the subcultural approach was a primary driver for the ethnographic turn that informed the post-subcultural work of youth studies researchers'. The post-subcultural position conforms to Griffin's (2011) accusation that there is a 'fervent avoidance of too close an association with the reviled CCCS approach'. For example, both edited collections by Christine Feldmen-Barrett's (2015) and Baker, Robards and Buttigieg (2015) primarily 'avoid' engagement with criticism of the post-subcultural position. Where there is an argument developed for example, Woodman and Bennett (2015: 6) uphold that 'youth as a defined set of subcultural practices is also difficult to maintain'. In opposition, it is has been identified by Blackman (2014), Greener and Hollands (2006) and Shildrick and MacDonald (2006) that the post-subcultural turn fails to investigate social and cultural divisions and solidarities experienced by subcultural subjects which influences their participation and performance of youth cultural practices. The post-subcultural disengagement with a collectivist understanding of youth subcultures through their commitment to individualist postmodern ideals means young people are disconnected from their diverse locations in the social structure. Until the post-subcultural position critically engages with its own postmodern postionality it will not be able to understand or critically grasp subcultural subjects' practices and performance within the social and cultural context of leisure and labour.

Patrick Williams (2011: 42) argues that the Symbolic Interactionist tradition anticipated this post-subcultural critique adding, 'Subculture continues to be a useful concept because it remains meaningful in the lives of many young people who define themselves as subcultural.' The schism within sociological studies of subculture has led Paul Hodkinson (2015: 8) to state: 'I am among those who have continued to regard subculture as an appropriate and well-recognised term to describe substantive, distinctive and committed youth leisure or style groupings.' In this book we also advance the usefulness of the concept of subculture. Our aim is not to support the CCCS, but to recognise its value and applicability in relation to C. Wright Mills' ambition to examine individual biographies and histories.

However, any re-engagement with C. Wright Mills calls for a *critical* application of his ideas, and a re-orientation of the 'sociological imagination' for the contemporary context. Rather than mimicking his tendency to polarise the elites and the 'mass public', sociologists now talk in terms of multiple, but interrelated, 'publics' that have complex, multi-dimensional, relationships with societal power structures. The creation of the subcultural imagination allows cultural practices to be interpreted in terms of the agency of each subcultural subject. However, social structures themselves, and the characteristics of specific historical epochs, can also be better understood via an engagement with the behaviours of the individual. The contradictory experiences of inequality in the social structure has been a central causal argument in subcultural studies from A. K. Cohen's (1956) *Delinquent Boys* to Phil Cohen (1972) *Subcultural Conflict and Working Class Community*, where social class acts to generate creative deviant expression as an opposition to mainstream culture. Subcultures have provided young people with diverse platforms to imaginatively solve cultural oppression and have generated alternative spaces for young people to engage in different dimensions of cultural participation to forge and change social class identity.

Shildrick and MacDonald (2006) call for integrated analyses of how structural inequalities shape people's participation in youth cultures. This hints at a broader concern with how researchers negotiate, and respond to, differing subjectivities within the field. The study of subculture is recognised as having a predominantly white male focus (Williams, 2011), and readings of cultural resistance have positioned social class as the dominating social factor impacting young people's cultural tastes (Bourdieu, 1984). However, the development of intersectional modes of analysis that are equipped to address how people negotiate various privileged and subordinate subjectivities simultaneously inspire questions about the intersections between subjectivity and subculture. For instance, several researchers have identified ways in which racial oppression results in the enactment of a specific mode of resistive cultural production practices. Rose (1994: 5) argues that rap music is a 'symbol of rebellion' for black people because it articulates the possibility of challenging black oppression. For Maruta Herding (2013: 184) subcultural preferences are connected to 'multiple identifications', and she argues that the concept of subculture is relevant to development of Islamic youth culture in Western Europe. Previously, the CCCS studies have been criticised for their weak focus on race and gender, through a predominant white and male preoccupation (Nayak and Kehily, 2008). This remains a key problem for Patrick Williams (2011: 45–47) in the rhetoric of post-subcultural studies, which continues to overlook the socially constructed aspect of race and gender. In an attempt to move the debate forward, Rupa Huq (2013: 29) suggests the priority should be on multi-ethnicity in the context of social change in a global context. For us, ethnicity and gender are key categories whereby the construction of identities is shaped via the clash, use, and exchange of symbols where subjectivity becomes constituted through cultural participation. 'Subcultural subjects' may engage in an alternative practice but they still encounter hegemonic tendencies at an everyday level whereby encounters with forms of structural stratification reduce diversity or intersectional oppression can remain implicit. However, social class is important in the shaping of subcultural identities linked to ethnicity, as shown in the emergence of 'grime' youth subculture in the UK suggesting that the interaction between social class and ethnicity-based experience of marginality offer subcultural authenticity (Dedman, 2011).

Similarly, the invisibility of girls within subcultures research provoked McRobbie and Garber (1975: 112) to ask: 'How do we make sense of this invisibility?' Angela McRobbie (1982) was soon to point out that young women negotiate a different leisure space, supported by Christine Griffin's (1985: 187) *Typical Girls*, which argued, 'that the "gang of lads" model is not appropriate for young women'. Roman and Christian-Smith (1988: 16) demonstrate that (male) subcultural studies failed to understand why the experiences of young males could not be generalised to young women. Sandra Taylor (1993: 25) argues that subculture remains relevant in the study of Australian young women, and that this involvement is shaped by class, ethnicity and location. The study of female subcultures became more distinctive in Skelton and Valentine's (1998: 17) *Cool Places* collection with a focus on young women in subcultural locations with chapters on young women's subcultural practices and performance by Dwyer, Leonard, McNamee and Blackman. From here it became possible to identify certain subcultures including mod, punk, Goth, hip hop and dance as possessing more cultural depth, diversity and sensitivity for subcultural subjects to become more closely aligned with feminism. Gender becomes represented in the cultural products of subcultures, enabling women to challenge, and subvert, subcultures that have an apparent hegemonic masculinity (see Connell and Messerschmidt, 2005; Dunn and Farnsworth, 2012; Garrison, 2000; Harris, 2001; Kempson, 2015a). There has been ample recognition within more contemporary research that subcultures sometimes form around marginal subjectivities; the issue of how these subjectivities contribute to the development of established subcultural environments has yet to be tackled in a way that does render them *problematic* within these contexts. Moreover, intersectional analyses tend to prioritise a reading of social relations as being predominantly produced via structural orders, without extensive consideration for the interplay between structure and agency. What we are suggesting, then, is that the contemporary basis for the subcultural subject allows for a critical positionality when faced with a patriarchal subculture.

Subcultures and markets: incorporation, contradictions and resistance

Subcultures celebrate difference and attract attention due to the value they place on authenticity and the negotiation of subcultural value. Thornton (1995) argues that for subcultural participants, there are *authentic* and *inauthentic* ways to behave within the space that will impact upon a person's accumulation of 'subcultural capital'. She references the process of selling out as one such inauthentic practice, arguing that selling music via 'mainstream channels' will result in distrust from within the subculture. Likewise, Kempson (2015b) explores how achieving 'zine star' status within zine subculture when a person experiences notoriety as a prolific zine producer compromises their adherence to the broader subcultural values of equality and anti-hierarchical politics that dominate within this space. This gives subcultures an edge; it makes them real through attachment.

As a result, the market has always expressed a fascination with subcultures. The stealing of a subcultural style by the mainstream is an intended process whereby corporates seek to replenish and enrich their mass products, making them appear more authentic, relevant and exciting. Looking at this issue from the corporate perspective of Harley Davidson, Schouten and McAlexander (1993: 9) argue that the hedonism of the subcultural symbolism requires renunciation because of its deviant power, and capital requires universal wholesomeness for mass consumption. But as Hebdige pointed out (1979: 95) it may be more difficult or even impossible to establish the 'distinction between commercial exploitation and creative originality'. We argue that the key point of access to this knowledge is through the knowing subcultural subject. American corporate companies including,

Levis, Nike, Harley Davidson and others have shown interest in subcultures of consumption to increase their market potential. Subcultures are examined for the potential product attributes, because culture influences consumer behaviour. This means that subcultures have built-in attractions due to their unorthodox, noisy and seductive features, while at the same time subcultures are themselves sometimes influenced by dominant cultural forms (for example Westwood's punk aesthetic). Naomi Klein (2000: 72) speaks about corporate cultures employing 'cool hunters', i.e. young people from the street, to exploit their insights and ideas. The corporates use the structural features of subcultural identity and subcultural commitment to inject and exploit their mass products through the notion of creative limited accessibility, so that the mass product has the appearance of a subcultural product. All subcultures possess different degrees of identified consumer commodities. Some subcultures pursue a more anti-capitalist stance and others cultivate rebel identities. For example, Hells' Angels may present themselves as being in opposition to the norms of consumption or establishment capitalism (and the company Harley Davidson has been actively pursuing members of this subculture to increase brand identity). Nike can be seen as brand leader in the development of sneakerhead culture based on the idea of exclusive or limited editions of trainer shoes, including Air Jordans, Air Force Ones, Nike Dunks, Air Max, Air Yeezy and Convers All-stars bought by Nike in 2003. In 2015, Nike used its technology to launch the new Chuck Taylor II, although there is no mention of the label Nike, anywhere! Corporates including Nike and Reebok seek to build brand identity through appearance of individual or personal relations whereby customers can customise trainers for manufacture (Kawamura, 2016). This takes the form of short runs, rare items and collectors' editions for example celebrated at Crepe City in London: the UK's annual original sneaker event. A related feature of this development is that the price of rare sneakers is vastly above the normal retail cost, which enables middle and upper class youth a solid aspiration to collect these trainers (made possible by their access to parental capital). The style endorsed by the company carries the wider style identity of the more mass produced items, but offers elite subcultural status through product identification and aspiration. Therefore, to what extent do subcultural styles retain transgressive potential? For Hebdige (1979: 95) this is achieved on the basis of 'threat', but at the same time subcultures face trivialisation and domestication so they become 'frozen' in time, and their symbolic challenge is lessened through the corporate demand to extract universal profit. For subcultural subjects at the everyday level, there is a tense contradiction between authenticity within subculture and the use of subculture as a marketable tool to make capital.

Reflexivity and subcultures

The contemporary acknowledgement of the 'reflexive turn' is most often associated with Pierre Bourdieu's work (Bourdieu and Wacquant, 1992) and his endeavour to make sociology a more responsive discipline showing full awareness of influence and positionality. The roots of reflexivity are intertwined with the development of symbolic interactionism through Georg Simmel's Kantian influence and its subsequent take up at the Chicago School of Sociology by Albion Small, G. H. Mead and Robert Park (Rock, 1979: 46). Under Park's (1915) formal manifesto of the sociological urban laboratory the idea of capturing moments and everyday interactions to understand small group formation at micro level is where subcultural studies emerges within an ethnographic and biographical context. The Chicago School researchers were not only concerned with obtaining first-hand experience of the social world, they were also focused on understanding how field studies provided researchers with a deep connection to the subjects of their research (Blackman, 2010). In Britain, this tradition was taken up in the 1960s by National Deviancy Conference and for Paul Willis (1976: 141–142) reflexivity 'takes us beyond' 'techniques of data collection' to 'a theoretical awareness' and the 'status of the method as a social relationship'.

Ethnography, rather than comprising various qualitative research methods (Hammersley and Atkinson, 1995), is a specific epistemological premise that responds to the call for what Weber (1947) referred to as *verstehen* (a deep understanding) of a research field. A researcher's own subjectivity and a researcher's knowledge of their own subjectivity are different entities. Therefore their ability to recognise how their own positionality within a research field can affect that world is largely a matter of ontological premise. It may not, then, be sufficient for a researcher to attempt to identify the impact of their own habitual responses on the research process. If research is the generation of knowledge, then researchers must acknowledge that they can only access partial understanding of their own positionality within the field. This realisation requires the development of innovative methodologies that are equipped to offer multi-perspective views on researcher/participant relations, and on the process of identifying which findings are 'significant'. Furthermore, a researcher must locate their findings 'in context', which involves cultivating critical perspectives on the cultural, historical, geographical and political backdrops of the research. It is therefore apparent, that the process of reflexivity is framed by an expectation that identity will be at least partially constructed through the consumer practices with which individuals engage (Beck, Giddens and Lash, 1995). This has meant that subcultures are often situated in ideological opposition to capitalist economy, to the extent to which 'the global context of youth cultural forms is generally accepted as a given rather than an object of investigation' (Pilkington, 2004: 121). Pilkington, referencing Oushakine (2000), goes on to problematise the construction of globalisation as an integral component of youth cultural engagement, by showing how punks in post-Soviet Russia 'may be engaged primarily as "consumers" rather than "producers"', but that they also 'do not as yet recognize themselves as subjects of that consumption' (123). The 'subcultural subject', therefore, is largely a product of the cultural environment and spatial context they inhabit. This process is not neutral or straight forward because situating a social phenomenon within these contexts means addressing processes of historicity that are themselves entrenched in rhetorics of privilege and hierarchy. Developing an epistemological 'break' with history (often emerging as 'textual', rather than 'contextual', readings of cultural production practices) offers a means of countering the limiting results of this process; however, this approach also has the effect of removing surrounding contexts from the phenomenon under study to the point where the 'objective relations of the field' (Bourdieu and Wacquant, 1992) are obscured. The implications of this point for the study of subcultures are twofold: first, they highlight the importance of situating the data we collect within its broader cultural context; and second, they highlight the importance of developing a *critical* approach to reflexivity that is equipped to question our own 'voice', and the knowledge paradigms from which we draw when 'making sense' of the research experience. The chapters included in this book speak to these objectives in the following ways.

Part 1: History, biography and subculture

For subcultures to have an impact in society, Phil Cohen stays close to C. Wright Mills to argue that a subculture has to be linked to the wider body politic to generate counter cultural practices. He explains that youth subcultures are caught between two forms of modernism: proto and retro modernism where subculture has become a stage to perform a crisis of representation. The youth question for Cohen has become one where young people's practices are no longer specifically attached to them. It has moved to one where the questions 'What is youth?' and 'What is subculture?' have become shaped by what they are made to represent, and this projection is itself a contradictory site for endless commercial opportunities where biographical tension is played out.

Eleni Dimou offers a critical engagement with the conceptualisation of the 'underground' in the context of subculture. Focusing on her ethnographic work with Cuban rappers, she argues for a 'double sided' engagement with both CCCS and post-subcultural approaches in relation to youth cultural participation. Dimou's work draws upon C. Wright Mills' call for sociologists to locate their research within both biography and history in order to demonstrate a means of reimagining subcultural research methodologies.

Anthony Gunter challenges the negative media attention on black young people, subcultures and street life through his biographical research strategies. His urban ethnography is linked to Chicago School studies with a focus on subcultural practices to strengthen solidarity and explain forms of deviance not only within a social and cultural context but also to highlight their value for young people. Inspired by C. Wright Mills' ideas, Gunter's attention is on construction of 'troubles' in young people's milieu to reveal how youth identity is labelled as a 'public issue'.

Part 2: Practising reflexivity in the field

Shane Blackman's chapter seeks to advance C. Wright Mills focus on biography and develop an ethnographic fieldwork strategy defined as the emotional imagination. He uses data from a number of distinct ethnographic studies on young people in subcultural groups to explore two ideas: critical ventriloguy and emotional edgework. Blackman's chapter contributes to methodological debate on the 'reflexive turn' and researcher positionality, which identifies that the power of the researcher is intimately linked to the humanity of dialogue established through shared communication and feeling with participants.

Rachela Colosi discusses findings from an auto-ethnography at a lap-dancing club within the ethnographic frame drawing upon the Chicago School approach to subculture and urban field studies. She argues that her 'insider' status within the club shaped her rapport with other dancers where she employs C. Wright Mills' sociological imagination to develop her research positionality and empathy. The chapter contributes a perspective on how the 'reflexive turn' in sociological enquiry can provide researchers with the opportunity to examine how their own 'status', and the 'capital' they are able to accumulate within the field can shape the research findings.

Robert McPherson's contribution details ethnographic work at a city-centre pub, where he assumed the role of both bartender and researcher. Working within the Chicago School tradition, the chapter explores how a researcher is able to engage with the life-stories of a 'rock 'n' roll builders' subculture, and how they might develop a reflexive perspective on the research process. McPherson's work is at the centre of C. Wright Mills biographical intersection, which deals with the dual responsibility of bartending while researching in order to demonstrate how this 'insider' position might impact researcher/participant interactions.

Gemma Commane's chapter is delivered from within a subcultural context as an inside ethnographer who is caught between advancing the rules, norms and forms of etiquette within BDSM club setting, but feels her empathetic strategy displaced when she encounters a sexually explicit performance which undermines her cultivated reflexivity. Commane understands C. Wright Mills' focus on feeling and questioning of what is deviance as central to how she rebuilt her research subjectivity and emotional response to research participants and the setting of her ethnography.

Part 3: Epistemologies, pedagogies and the subcultural subject

Robert Hollands re-connects CCCS and post-subcultural research frameworks via an engagement with 'nightlife identities'. The chapter offers a comprehensive overview of the 'state of play' in subcultures theory in order to explore links between the consumer-driven imagery of youth cultural participation and 'underground' scenes. He uses C. Wright Mills stance on history and structure to trace his own biographical path into the literature and his empirical work. Hollands also argues that class-divisions within the 'night-life' context remain evident and are largely identified via the consumer choices of participants.

Michelle Kempson's chapter argues for the development of feminist methodology in subcultures research. Drawing upon empirical work into feminist zine production and the surrounding subculture in the UK, Kempson explores the potential of developing 'intersectional epistemologies'. Via critical engagement with C. Wright Mills' ideas on the intersections of history, biography and social structure, the chapter contends that some voices are 'lost' within the subcultures debate when researchers are not sufficiently reflexive about how they collect and 'read' their data.

Virhra Barova engages with post-transitional subcultures in the Bulgarian context. The chapter begins by locating this subcultural environment within the context of post-1989 Bulgaria before moving on to explore the distinctive aspects of the underground scene. She employs C. Wright Mills' understanding that the sociological imagination should join together 'life experience' and 'intellectual work'. The chapter argues that contemporary subcultures in Bulgaria are characterised not so much by imagery but by an ideological cohesion and the desire to locate themselves apart from the mainstream, and from commercial culture.

J. Patrick Williams's work argues for a more reflexive engagement with research into Asian subculture. He looks in depth at the texts produced through two recent studies involving the author and student collaborators. While different levels of researcher reflexivity are visible in the published reports for each study, what the two studies have in common is an emphasis on connecting the researcher's personal troubles to public issues. Williams concludes that the C. Wright Mills' sociological imagination is a key component of his reflexive ethnographic practice, and that this approach has potential in the development of innovative pedagogy.

References

Atkinson, P. (1990) *The Ethnographic Imagination*, London: Routledge.

Back, L. and Tate, M. (2015) 'For a Sociological Reconstruction: W.E.B. Du Bois, Stuart Hall and segregated sociology', *Sociological Research Online* 20(3): 15 www.socresonline.org.uk (accessed: 16 September 2015).

Baker, S. Robards, B. and Buttigieg, B. (eds) (2015) *Youth Cultures and Subcultures*, Farnham: Ashgate.

Beck, U. Giddens, A. and Lash, S. (1995) *Reflexive Modernization Politics, Tradition and Aesthetics in the Modern Social Order*, Cambridge: Polity.

Becker, H. S. (1967) 'Whose Side Are We On?' *Social Problems* 14(3): 239–247.

Bell, A. (2010) 'The Subculture Concept: A Genealogy', in G. S. Shoham, P. Knepper and M. Kett. (eds) *International Handbook of Criminology*, Boca Raton, FL: CRC Press,153–184.

Bennett, A. (2000) *Popular Music and Youth Culture: Music Identity and Place*, London: Macmillan.

Bennett, A. (2011) 'The Post-Subcultural Turn: some reflections 10 years on', *Journal of Youth Studies* 14(5): 493–506.

Bennett, A. (2015) 'Australian Subcultures: reality or myth', in S. Baker, B. Robards and B. Buttigieg (eds) *Youth Cultures and Subcultures*, Farnham: Ashgate, 11–20.

Bernstein, B. (1975) *Class, Codes and Control Vol. 3*, London: Routledge Kegan Paul.

Blackman, S. (2000) 'Decanonised Knowledge and the Radical Project: towards an understanding of cultural studies in British universities', *Pedagogy, Culture and Society* 8(1): 43–67.

Blackman, S. (2010) '"The Ethnographic Mosaic" of the Chicago School: critically locating Vivien Palmer, Clifford Shaw and Frederic Thrasher's research methods in contemporary reflexive sociological interpretation', in C. Hart (ed.) *The Legacy of the Chicago School of Sociology*. Kingswinsford: Midrash Publishing, 195–215.

Blackman, S. (2014) 'Subculture Theory: an historical and contemporary assessment of the concept for understanding deviance', *Deviant Behavior* 35(6): 496–512.

Bourdieu, P. (1984) *Distinction: A Social Critique of the Judgement of Taste*, Cambridge: Harvard University Press.

Bourdieu, P. (1996) *The Rules of Art*, Oxford: Polity.

Bourdieu, P. and Wacquant, L. (1992) *An Invitation to Reflexive Sociology*, Cambridge: Polity Press.

Brake, M. (1980) *The Sociology of Youth Culture and Youth Sub-Cultures*, London: Routledge Kegan Paul.

Brewer, J. (2004) 'Imagining the Sociological Imagination: the biographical context of a sociological classic', *British Journal of Sociology* 55(3): 317–333.

Chaney, D. (2004) 'Fragmented Culture and Subcultures', in A. Bennett and K. Kahn-Harris (eds) *After Subculture*, London: Palgrave, 36–48.

Cohen, A. (1956) *Delinquent Boys – The Subculture of the Gang*, London: Collier-Macmillan.

Cohen, P. (1972) 'Subcultural Conflict and Working Class Community', *Working Papers in Cultural Studies* CCCS, University of Birmingham, Spring: 5–51.

Connell, R. W. and Messerschmidt, J. W. (2005) 'Hegemonic Masculinity: rethinking the concept', *Gender Society* 19: 829–859.

Cote, J. (2014) *Youth Studies*, London: Palgrave.

Dedman, T. (2011) 'Agency in UK Hip-hop and Grime Youth Subcultures – peripherals and purists', *Journal of Youth Studies* 14(5,1): 507–522.

Dunn, K. and Farnsworth, M. S. (2012) '"We ARE the Revolution" Riot Grrrl Press, Girl Empowerment, and DIY Self Publishing', *Women's Studies: An Interdisciplinary Journal* 41(2): 136–157.

Feldmen-Barrett, C. (ed) (2015) *Lost Histories of Youth Culture*, New York: Peter Lang.

Ferrell, J. Hayward, K. and Young, J. (2008) *Cultural Criminology*, London: Sage.

Fuller, S. (2006) *The New Sociological Imagination*. London: Sage.

Ganes, N. and Back, L. (2012) 'C. Wright Mills 50 Years On: the promise and craft of sociology revisited', *Theory, Culture and Society* 29(7/8): 399–421.

Garrison, E (2000) 'U.S. Feminism – Grrrl Style! Youth (Sub)cultures and the Technologies of the Third Wave', *Feminist Studies* 26(1): 141–170.

Gelder, K. (2007) *Subcultures: Cultural Histories and Social Practice*, London: Routledge.

Greener, T. and Hollands, R. (2006) 'Beyond Subculture and Post-subculture? The case of virtual psytrance', *Journal of Youth Studies* 9(4): 393–418.

Griffin, C. (1985) *Typical Girls*, London: Routledge Kegan Paul.

Griffin, C. (2011) 'The Trouble with Class: researching youth, class and culture beyond the "Birmingham School"', *Journal of Youth Studies* 14(3): 245–259.

Hall, S. (1980) 'Cultural Studies and the Centre: some problematics and problems', in S. Hall, D. Hobson, A. Lowe and P. Willis (eds) *Culture, Media and Language*, London: Hutchinson, 15–48.

Hammersley, M. and Atkinson, P. (1995/2007) *Ethnography: Principles in Practice*, London: Routledge.

Harris, A. (2001). 'Revisiting Bedroom Culture: spaces for young women's politics', *Hecate* 27(1): 128–138.

Hebdige, D. (1979) *Subculture: the Meaning of Style*, London: Methuen.

Herding, M. (2013) *Inventing the Muslim Cool*, Bielefeld: Deutsche Nationalbibliothek.

Hodkinson, P. (2015) 'Contextualizing the Spectacular', in A. Dhoest, S. Malliet, B. Segaert and J. Haers (eds) *The Border of Subculture*, London: Routledge, 5–16.

Huq, R. (2013) *Making Sense of Suburbia Through Popular Culture*, London: Bloomsbury.

Jenks, C. (2005) *Subculture: The Fragmentation of the Social*, London: Sage.

Jones, B. (1972) CCCS Perspectives. Working Papers in Cultural Studies CCCS, University of Birmingham, Spring: 3.

Kawamura, Y. (2016) *Sneakers: Fashion, Gender, and Subculture*, London: Bloomsbury.

Keen, F. M. (1999) *Stalking the Sociological Imagination: J. Edgar Hoover's FBI Surveillance of American Sociology*, Westpoint, CT: Greenwood Press.

Kempson, M. (2015a) '"My Version of Feminism": subjectivity, DIY and the feminist zine', *New Feminisms in Europe: Special edition of Social Movement Studies* 14(4): 459–472.

Kempson, M. (2015b) '"I Sometimes Wonder Whether I'm an Outsider": negotiating subcultural belonging at zinefests', *Sociology* 49(6): 106–1095.

Klein, N. (2000) *No Logo*, London: Flamingo.

Kroeber, A. (1925) *Handbook of the Indians of California*, Bulletin 78, Bureau of American Ethnology, Washington, DC.

McRobbie, A. (1982) 'The Politics of Feminist Research: between talk, text and action', *Feminist Review* 12: 46–57.

McRobbie, A. and Garber, J. (1975) 'Girls and Subcultures', in S. Hall and T. Jefferson (eds) *Rituals Through Resistance*, London: Hutchinson, 208–222.

Matza, D. (1964) *Delinquency and Drift*, New York: John Wiley.

Matza, D. (1969) *Becoming Deviant*, Englewood Cliffs, NJ: Prentice-Hall.

Mills, C. W. (1959) *The Sociological Imagination*, New York: Oxford University Press.

Mills, C. W. (1960) *Listen Yankee*, New York: Ballantine Books.

Mills, K. (2013) 'Foreword', in J. Scott and A. Nilsen (eds) *C. Wright Mills and the Sociological Imagination: Contemporary Perspectives*, London: Edward Elgar.

Muggleton, D. (1997) 'The Post-subculturalists', in S. Redhead (ed.) *The Club Culture Reader*, Oxford: Blackwell, 185–203.

Muggleton, D. and Weinzierl, R. (eds) (2003) *Post-subculturalist Reader*, London: Berg.

Nayak, A. and Kehily, M. J. (2008) *Gender, Youth and Culture*, London: Palgrave.

Oushakine, S. (2000) 'The quantity of style. Imaginary consumption in the new Russia'. *Theory, Culture and Society* 17(5):97–120.

Palmer, V. (1928) *Field Studies in Sociology: A Student's Manual*, Chicago, IL: University of Chicago Press.

Park, R.E. (1915) 'The City: suggestions for the investigation of human behavior in the city environment', *American Journal of Sociology* 20(5): 577–612.

Pearson, G. (1975) *The Deviant Imagination*, London: Macmillan.

Pilkington, H. (2004) 'Youth Strategies for Glocal Living: space, power and communication in everyday cultural practice', in A. Bennett and K. Kahn-Harris (eds) *After Subculture: Critical Studies in Contemporary Youth Culture*, Basingstoke: Palgrave Macmillan, 119–134.

Redhead, S. (1990) *The End of the Century Party: Youth and Pop Towards 2000*, Manchester: University of Manchester Press.

Roman, L. and Christian-Smith, L. and Ellsworth, E. (eds) (1988) *Becoming Feminine: The Politics of Popular Culture*, London: Falmer.

Rock, P. (1979) *The Making of Symbolic Interactionism*, London: Macmillan.

Rose, T. (1994) *Black Noise: Rap Music and Black Culture in Contemporary America*, London: Wesleyan Press.

Schouten, J. W. and McAlexander, J. (1993) 'Market Impact of a Consumption Subculture: the Harley-Davidson mystique', *European Advances in Consumer Research* 1: 389–393.

Shildrick, T. and R. MacDonald. (2006) 'In Defence of Subculture: young people, leisure and social divisions', *Journal of Youth Studies* 9(2): 125–140.

Skelton, T. and Valentine, G. (eds) (1998) *Cool Places: Geographies of Youth Cultures*, London: Routledge.

Sweetman, P. (2004) 'Tourists and Travellers? Subcultures, reflexive identities and neo-tribal sociality', in A. Bennett and K. Kahn-Harris (eds) *After Subculture*, London: Palgrave, 79–93.

Taylor, S. (1993) 'Sub-versions: feminist perspectives on youth subcultures', in R. White (ed.) *Youth Subcultures*, NCYS: Hobart, 19–26.

Thornton, S. (1995) *Club Culture: Music, Media and Subcultural Capital*, Cambridge: Polity.

Thornton, S. (1997) 'General Introduction', in K. Gelder and S. Thornton. (eds) *The Subcultures Reader*, London: Routledge, 1–7.

Weber, M. (1947) *The Theory of Social and Economic Organization*, translated by A. M. Henderson and Talcott Parsons. Edited with an introduction by Talcott Parsons. New York: Free Press.

Williams, J. P. (2011) *Subcultural Theory*, Cambridge: Polity Press.

Willis, P. (1976) 'The Man in the Iron Cage: notes on method', in CCCS (eds) *Culture and Domination, Working Papers in Cultural Studies* 9: 135–143.

Willis, P. (2000) *The Ethnographic Imagination*, Cambridge: Polity.

Woodman, D. and Bennett, A. (2015) 'Cultures, Transitions and Generations: the case for a new youth studies', in D. Woodman and A. Bennett (eds) *Youth Cultures, Transitions and Generations: Bridging the Gap on Youth Research*, London: Palgrave, 1–15.

Young, J. (2010) *The Criminological Imagination*, Cambridge: Polity.

Young, J. (2013) 'Introduction to the 40th Anniversary Edition', in I. Taylor, P. Walton and J. Young, *The New Criminology*. Second edition, London: Routledge, xi–li.

Part I
History, biography and subculture

1 From here to modernity

Rethinking the Youth Question with C. Wright Mills

Phil Cohen

Introduction

There is a long history of representations of youth as either a period of careering about or as a form of apprenticeship. Today neither career nor apprenticeship provide a coherent framing narrative, and both have undergone radical transformation in a way that sends mixed and often contradictory life-historical messages. Meanwhile the codes of vocation and inheritance, once marginalised, have made a comeback bid, albeit in perverse forms dislocated from their original spiritual and material meanings. In Chris Dunkley's (2013) *The Precariat*, the central character, Fin, a budding NEET, decides to become a 'chip off the old block' and follow in his Dad's footsteps into contingent labour within the hidden economy, rather than be paralysed by an aspirational discourse which has no bearing on his real circumstances and opportunities. He has apprenticed himself voluntarily to a condition of permanent precarity, and as a member of this shadow workforce he embraces his forced servitude to the whims of the market as a special vocation, albeit one which will probably be registered in the form of a criminal career.

In this chapter I am going to be arguing two things: first, that 'youth' is no longer a discrete and transient stage of life associated with certain styles of 'storm and dress'; it has become either a sign of chronic precarity shared by many age groups, or a transferable physical cum existential attribute, desired above all by pre-teens who have bought their way into 'youth subculture' at an early age and affluent third agers who have invented their own version of the 'adolescent moratorium' as a period of structured irresponsibility.

Second, in order to grasp what is now at stake in the Youth Question, and how these stakes have shifted, we have to take a leaf out of C. Wright Mills' book, and exercise our sociological imaginations. Mills defined the sociological imagination as 'the capacity to shift from one perspective to another – the capacity to range from the most impersonal and remote transformations to the most intimate features of the human self – and to see the relations between the two of them'. He did not think that the sociologists of his day were equipped with the suppleness of thought or subtlety of interpretation required to develop this imaginative faculty, obsessed as they were with quantitative methodologies. Moreover, subsequent generations of social scientists, while they frequently refer to, and sometimes even defer to, C. Wright Mill's mission statement for their discipline, have found it no easier to achieve its goals. Instead, the sociological imagination has gravitated to the visual and performance arts, to the novel and to poetry. Yet such a multi-standpoint epistemology, moving in scope and scale from the abstract to the concrete and back again, is mandatory in regard to the Youth Question.

Bruno Latour's (2005) critique of the sociological tool kit, with its clunky binaries (macro/micro: structure/agency) and reified conception of social causality as a kind of glue binding us together behind our backs, suggests one reason why it has been so difficult to practise what Mills preached. At the same time, the gulf between public and private matters of concern, and the collapse or hollowing out of narratives that connected collective and individual aspiration to each other through struggles of long duration, have meant that the general capacity to imagine alternative social structures has greatly diminished and is confined to utopian or dystopian literature. Yet clearly the Youth Question (the set of issues posed for and by a culture about how it constructs 'youth' discursively as a specific bio-political category and how this impacts empirically on the lives of those to whom it is applied) is a suitable case for the Wright Mills treatment. Here at least biography cannot be divorced from history.

'Generation Rent'

If the Youth Question has recently re-emerged as a hot topic around the notion of 'Generation Rent', this is not just because a particular cohort of young people who had middle class expectations of secure jobs and housing are finding themselves trapped in various kinds of precarious circumstance; rather the contemporary Youth Question dramatises the fact that the life-historical paradigms that hitherto connected biographical trajectories to historically sedimented structures of family, work and community, ain't what they used to be; the principles of periodicity that hitherto defined and regulated existential predicaments associated with adolescence have become as unstable for middle class young people as they have long been for their working class peers. 'Generation Rent' may turn out not to be merely an ethno-demographic construct, a way of attributing political and/or cultural meaning to a specific population, but an element of psycho-geography, defining a certain form of liminality in which states of transient or conjunctural precarity associated with glamourised forms of risk taking become chronic and take on structural and site specific connotations. 'Generation Rent' serves as a generic term for the denizens of urban edgelands thrown up by the impact of globalisation on local housing and labour markets making hopes of lifetime dwelling and jobs redundant.

So are we talking here about a new kind of 'youth subculture', one which embraces NEETS (a person not in education, employment, or training) and wannabe hipsters in a common idiom linked to socially expressive but highly individualistic forms of 'venture capitalism'? If by 'subculture', we mean certain shared codes of dress, music, talk, feeling, belief and life style which evolve in response to marginalisation, and where the dominant narratives of class, gender, sexuality and ethnicity are subverted through a play of symbolic substitutions to create a halo of 'deviance' or insubordination, then the answer is decidedly *no*. We might, for instance, talk about gay subculture, or rather subcultures, organised around certain sexual preferences and their various ways of queerying the gender codes of straight (que patriarchal) society. Equally we might hail 'Chavs' as the worthy successors of skinheads, (not least in their demonisation) and recognise Emo Boys as postmodern Mods. The point about subcultures as sites of self identification is that they advertise, celebrate and fetishise their difference, and indeed often pursue what Freud (1929: 84) called a 'narcissism in respect of minor differences' while their forms of insubordination remain dependant on their 'parent' cultures as their primary reference point, even as they proclaim their autonomy from it. It is only when they become politicised, as happened with gay subcultures in the context of the AIDS crisis, when subcultures depart their real or imagined stylistic ghettoes to engage with the wider body politic, that they become fully fledged counter-cultures, cultures which challenge the hegemony of the dominant codes (in this example, of heterosexism).

'Generation Rent' is not a counter-culture in this sense. It has a different genealogy. It began as a rallying point in the campaign against austerity politics and quickly became a major referent in public debates around housing. It raises issues of civic entitlement, structural inequality, contingent labour and what one generation owes to or can demand from another. The term's resonance addresses the changing status and meaning of adolescence as a distinctive mode of ontological precarity within a life course whose signposts have been radically altered. The fact is that the maps of growing up relayed by all those institutions charged with so doing no longer correspond to the territories that young people actually occupy. This is not just a matter of broken or deferred transitions from family or school, to full time work and independent living, or the changing balance of economic power between different generations. Rather it is a question about how 'generation' as such, is lived as a retro-prospective construct, as both an imagined community in the making and as an invented tradition. Or to put it another way, the Youth Question dramatises a wider crisis of representation in the life course which in different ways affects all ages across much of the class spectrum in the era of late capitalist modernity.

Nothing is more symptomatic of this shift than the fate of the 'youth wage'. A wage form which used to apply to 14–18 year olds, trapping them in blind alley jobs, and was supposed to cover their subsistence needs on the premise that they continued to live at home and were subsidised by the family wage paid to the (male) head of household, has lost its age specificity along with its patriarchal anchorage; today the principle is not only applied to latter day apprentices, trainees and interns but is generalised to most categories of insecure, casual low paid work concentrated in the hidden, pop up and secondary economies. While 'youth' remains relatively fixed as a legal category of dis/qualification, its sociological oscillation between a state of chronic precocity (12 year old school kids who are too sexy for their iPads) and chronic precarity associated with the transition from voluntary to forced contingent labour means that its boundaries are inherently unstable. 'Youth' is not so much a stage in the life cycle as a stage upon which its crisis of representation is performed. But before we can get that shift into perspective we need to tell some of its back story.

Youth as an angel of history

It was Marx who first drew our attention to the dialectic of generations in which biography and history intersect. In *The German Ideology* he wrote:

> History is nothing but the succession of the separate generations, each of which exploits the materials, the capital funds, the productive forces handed down to it by all the proceeding generations. And this, on the one hand, continues the traditional activity in completely changed circumstances, and on the other modifies the old circumstances with completely changed activity
> (Marx, 1845/1970: 57)

Marx, typically, dialecticises the notions of tradition and modernity, without abandoning their anchorage in the idea that each generation possesses a collective biography that gives it historical individuality. Tradition is here regarded as a kind of inheritance or legacy handed down from one generation to the next but it is also, according to Marx, an apprenticeship to the past interrupted by history itself. From this optic, a generation is a special kind of imagined community based on inventing shared traditions linked to formative experiences associated with a particular life/ historical conjuncture (1968, or 1989, for example). It is a retrospective construct even though those who identify themselves in this way may see it in entirely prospective terms. And because each so-called 'generation' is engaged in creating its own traditions to mark its advent as a historical subject, it tends to ignore or reject the invented traditions of its predecessors. There are no 'generational cycles' in history. And perhaps we need to emphasise that 'generation' in itself is primarily an ideological or ethno-demographic construct, which only in special circumstances becomes a social or economic force. When people belonging to particular age cohorts speak and act as if they represent a generation for and to itself, this is usually in order to create a platform from which to mobilise a form of quasi-oedipal politics directed against particular power blocs, especially where these are associated with the exercise of patriarchal authority

In relation to 'youth' and modernity the discovery of adolescence as a distinctive stage of the life cycle is intimately bound up with its association with modernity and the shock of the new. The notion starts by being firmly located within the Romantic Movement, and its cult of 'Sturm und Drang'. What was so stormy about adolescence, and so stressful for the parents of adolescents, was the fact that it marked a hiatus between the position of the young person considered as an object of legal, moral and pedagogic surveillance, and that of the adult, considered as a fully enfranchised citizen of the state, with all the rights and responsibilities that flowed from it. Into that gap were concentrated all those aspects of human behaviour that could neither be rationalised or sentimentalised in the then current schemas of scientific and popular discourse (first and foremost of course, sexuality). Adolescence as a privileged site for the discovery and enactment of desire was important to the Romantics in defining the essential human capacity to transcend mundane existence and experience the sublime. At the same time, adolescence was reconfigured within an enlightenment framework as being a force for progress set against the 'dead hand of tradition'. It was this association which connected youth movements to the process of nation building, and to revolutionary movements, especially in Germany, Russia and the Balkans, movements that sought to overthrow the 'ancien regime' of Feudal absolutism or foreign despotism. It was the power of young people to sublimate their passions in the pursuit of ideals of political freedom, social justice or national liberation, embodied in a democratic state, that made them seem such a powerful force for the rejuvenation of these old societies.

Adolescence was thus produced at the intersection of the romantic and rationalist projects, and fused together elements of ethnic and civic nationalism in a more or less combustible mix. Youth was constructed as a unique nexus of contradiction, oscillating between recapitulation and rupture, the static and the volatile, between what was fleeting and eternal, between the alienation of the individual and the compulsive solidarities of the group. This was the problematic, which Walter Benjamin so eloquently addressed in his early writings in which he rejected the then dominant culture of bourgeois careerism. He was concerned to repudiate history as legacy, the notion that we are all apprenticed to an inheritance not of our own choosing, whether one associated with biological or economic destiny. Even in his late teens Benjamin (1999: 249) is beginning to grapple with the problematic of modernity, which is to issue in his famous characterisation of the angel of history:

> His face is turned toward the past. Where we perceive a chain of events, he sees one single catastrophe, which keeps piling wreckage upon wreckage and hurls it in front of his feet. The angel would like to stay, awaken the dead, and make whole what has been smashed. But a storm is blowing from Paradise; it has got caught in his wings with such violence that the angel can no longer close them. The storm irresistibly propels him into the future to which his back is turned, while the pile of debris before him grows skyward. This storm is what we call progress.

Benjamin is here writing a coda to Marx's meditation on the fact that each new generation makes its own history 'under circumstances existing already given and transmitted from the past and not of its own choosing'. Marx (1852/1926: 23) in the *18th Brumaire of Louis Bonaparte*, continues:

> The tradition of all dead generations weighs like a nightmare on the brains of the living. And just as they seem to be occupied with revolutionizing themselves and things, creating something that did not exist before, they

anxiously conjure up the spirits of the past to their service, borrowing from them names, battle slogans, and costumes in order to present this new scene in world history in time-honoured disguise and borrowed language.

It was through this process of borrowing or bricolage, and through a peculiar mixture of mimesis and masquerade, that the youth subcultures emerging in Britain towards the end of the long post-war used and transformed the idioms of the past in order to imagine a future in which there would be no war, except perhaps between the generations. It was a way of both misrecognising the fact that the war as a totalising experience marking a whole generation, with its traumatic afterblows, was finally over, and of reconstituting out of whatever fragmentary materials lay to hand a magical sense of belonging to a self invented moment of re-making-history-as-modernity. Whether it was a marriage between the Edwardian gentleman and the spiv, or between the boots and braces of the erstwhile proletarian and the shaven heads of concentration camp inmates, these fragile iconographies made implicit claims on modernity while looking back over their shoulder at the past.

In this context the Beat and Hippy cultures of the mid- to late 60s make for interesting reading, or rather re-reading. Were they genuine revolutionary youth movements aiming to overthrow capitalism and patriarchy as some of their political protagonists proclaimed? Were they counter cultures centred on the elaboration of alternative lifestyles? Or were they subcultures in transition, performing the rites of graduation from adolescent revolt to social rebellion with or without a cause? Or were they all three?

For the rationalists, mainly Marxists, the so-called 60s' 'youth revolution' is a cautionary tale. It marks a historical turning point in which the project of political emancipation founded on the industrial working class auto-destructs, the onward march of labour is permanently halted well this side of the New Jerusalem and capitalism goes cultural, or rather 'subcultural', as well as global, and becomes hip. The youth revolution creates a platform for disseminating the hedonistic pleasure principles of consumerism and makes possessive individualism – doing your own thing – sexy, addictive and above all *cool*. Sex and drugs and rock n roll may not exactly be the devils work, but they promote the dispositions of creative self invention, underpinned by a whole culture of narcissism that post Fordism, and the 'just in time' production of the self requires. Playing it cool becomes the motto of a whole 'post' generation, post modernist, post Marxist, post feminist, and post human.

The other, romantic, reading, which is mainly from anarchists and the libertarian left sees 60s' counter culture as a great disseminator of a popular anti-authoritarian politics, a generational revolt against the patriarchal structures of the family *and* the bureaucratic structures of the state, and as such embarked on the quest for new and more direct democratic forms of self organisation. It is also about an aesthetic revolt against the dead weight of elite bourgeois literary and artistic canons and tastes. Rejections then of party politics, whether mainstream or vanguardist, in the name of a cultural avant gardism embedded in everyday life. This version of the counter culture is celebrated as an incubator of new feminism, gay liberation, anti racism, the environmentalist movement, community activism and do it yourself urbanism. As such it prefigures the anti-globalisation and anti-capitalist movements of more recent years.

Each reading tends to privilege some aspects over others as symptomatic. Sometimes opposed but complimentary interpretations are given to the same thing. This ambivalence not only illustrates the intersection of romantic and rationalist views of youth, but reflects the fact that capitalism's subcultural turn simultaneously undermines and renews its trajectories of growth. And it bears on two very different versions of modernity

Why Mods have never been modern: proto-modernism and retro-modernism

In his letter from prison to his wife dated 19 December 1929 Antonio Gramsci wrote, 'The challenge of modernity is to live without illusion and without becoming disillusioned. I am a pessimist because of intelligence but an optimist because of will.' Today Gramsci's famous formula has been reversed. The widespread disillusionment with modernity-as-historical-progress has produced the illusion that it is possible to reinvent the sociological imagination without it being embedded in social praxis. Optimism of the intellect becomes institutionalised in the knowledge economy in the form of blue-sky thinking. Capitalism has thrown up its own cultural avant garde who push at the boundaries of the real and continually create alternative worlds populated by people who never grow old and whose lives are one long adventure of self invention. The sociological imagination has come to power under the sign of the commodity and the consumer fest. At the same time pessimism of the will becomes enshrined as a precautionary principle of the risk society with its penchant for generating worst-case scenarios. Precarity becomes normative under the sign of the Youth Spectacle.

Youth subcultures have provided a major resource and reference point for this move, yielding a florid phenomenology of neo-tribalism that can be relentlessly tracked through social media and 'glocal' music scenes like rap or hip-hop, before gaining a soft landing in post-coded intersections of the network society, not to mention the dance floor. At the same time the Youth Question generates a no less exotic assemblage of cautionary tales whose categories do not cease to multiply, providing ever more fuel for media orchestrated moral panics.

All this has had a major impact on our relation to modernity, or rather two versions of it. The first might be called *proto*-modernism. The past is what is left behind by the present as it progresses into the future as its open horizon of possibility. The past only returns as what has been forgotten or repressed and is retrieved by the intervention of some special device or place of commemoration, where it appears as a more or less teleological principle of continuity – the plan or law or higher purpose which governs destinies and the unfolding of lives in historical time. The capacity to identify and distinguish between progressive and reactionary historical forces relies on this chronotope, which ultimately derives from the Enlightenment. 'Reactionary' is whatever wishes to restore the status quo ante associated with an *ancien regime* of privileged entitlement; 'Progressive' is whatever wishes to advance towards a more just, enlightened and democratic future. This can yield a Whig interpretation of history, which optimistically views the future as an improvement on the present, which is itself, an improvement on the past. Within this narrative frame youth, and especially youth movements, are seen as a progressive force, challenging the dead hand of tradition.

In academic circles this model of modernity is pretty much discredited, although it is alive in popular historiography and autobiography where it sustains collective aspirations and social movements of every kind. It helps builds intellectual, social and cultural capital, and anchors it in place in specific lieux de memoire, including those little archives of souvenir objects, images and texts which are collected as building blocks of autobiographies that will never be written. Under favourable circumstances this narrative does help build the internal resources of resilience needed to sustain struggles of long duration, where defeats can be regarded as only temporary setbacks, blips in the onward march to a better future.

The second model might be called *retro*-modernist, in the sense that it regards modernity not as something to be aimed at or achieved but as something that has never quite happened, is basically unachievable and can only be grasped as a kind of retro-fit. Here the present is experienced and narrated as a series of discrete, discontinuous moments, belonging to an often chaotic synchronicity, split off from a past which never fades but continues to be re-presented and recycled, and from a future which is blocked, occluded, threatening or unimaginable except as catastrophe. History is de-composed, mashed up by a highly unreliable narrator into a more or less spectacular collage of fragments. At one level this chrono-topography involves a profound de-historicising of experience, a radical disconnect between past, present and future; it amortises intellectual, cultural and social capital, which decreases in value over time, and hollows out the cognitive and emotional resources needed to sustain struggles of long duration. Nevertheless it also opens up a space for the sociological imagination, as principles of hope float free from any real embedding, encouraging the projection of, usually, dystopian, futures, or sponsoring various kinds of retro-chic culture.

Retro-modernists are great hoarders of objects and memories. Their do-it-yourself archives, on and off line, create nostalgic evocations of lost worlds of modernity that can always be recycled. In the midst of this flux of subcultural images and events, it is no longer necessary or possible to identify progressive or reactionary forces, since everything is hybridised, at one and the same time a creative and destructive force. Contradiction is sublimated in a facile pseudo-dialectic in which everything is both itself and its opposite. This was precisely what Schumpeter regarded as a general principle of capitalism's development. But this is no cause for celebration. What Schumpeter did not anticipate was that this dynamism, this apparently frictionless acceleration of productivity associated with turbo charged capitalism would engender not only boundless enthusiasm for its boundless possibilities for transforming the world, but a pervasive sense of helplessness and therefore hopelessness among large sections of the population, including those who are its supposed beneficiaries. Now that everyone is supposed to be the author of their own lives, we are being lured into a cruel optimism, which fans the flames of promise, especially among the young, only to extinguish them at the first breathe of reality. This is the generalised ontological condition of the new precariat.

Walter Benjamin was the first to realise that the working class movement necessarily has an ambivalent attitude to modernity. His Angel of History attempts a dialectical synthesis of proto and retro modernisms. Modernisation of the labour process has meant deskilling, and the technological displacement of living labour by dead labour, and as such, it has been consistently opposed by the organised working class. Modernity here simply spells redundancy. But working class communities and their associated youth subcultures have also been enthusiastic consumers of modernity; adults want all mod cons in their homes, even if they dislike the brutal cut-price modernism that shaped so many post war housing estates. The young people who live on these estates want the latest smart phones so that they feel plugged in to the 'network society', even if they remain socially immobilised and rarely leave their immediate neighbourhood.

It could be argued that subcultures oscillate between proto and retro modernist positions. There is a pervasive nostalgia for a once-upon-a-time progressive modernity-that-never-was. And this attitude has especial resonance in popular music. Just listen to the Who, the Small Faces, Ray Davies and the Kinks, not to mention the Jam and the many other bands that have featured in various Mod revivals. Even the Sleaford Mods, whose in-your-face lyrics give voice to the anger of the young precariat, cannot resist evoking the Mods and Rocker riots of the 1960s as the source of their authenticity. The original Mods grab at modernity was symbolised by the way they customised their scooters, turning them from affordances of high tech designer chic into mobile displays of retro-kitsch by the simple device of embellishing them with so many mirrors and chrome fittings, RAF roundels, Union Jacks and other heraldic devices of a bygone age. The Mod scooter becomes a kind of obsolescent Cadillac on two wheels; its sleek functionalist aesthetic submerged under extravagant ornamentation. Modernism goes Baroque.

The Youth Question comes of age

In advanced societies life stories no longer conform to a single 'ideal type'; they are both more individualised, more fragmented and more internally complicated than when their narrative paradigms were transmitted primarily by the family, and its extensions into the moral economy of the local community in the early days of capitalism. Globalisation far from imposing some homogeneous cultural norm of identity formation has simply amplified the relays of difference. Differences of age, gender, ethnicity and class are no longer hierarchised in stable formats of inequality, but interact within a more or less chaotic synchronicity, opening up a space for the subcultural imagination to weave its magical displacements.

Life-historical messages are nowadays distributed by a whole array of secular agencies and media, not solely by religious or moral authorities. For example the role models so vigorously promoted by sports and youth organisations link moral and physical education to the dominant ideology of individual aspiration and competitive achievement. Meantime the advertising and creative industries penetrate the most intimate reaches of autobiography and ceaselessly re-invent the avatars of the ideal consumer self. In contrast the officially authorised narratives of the life course remain highly conservative. For example, the state not only authenticates the socially climactic moments of births marriages and deaths, it not only throws a grid of legal markers of im/maturity over the life cycle, and polices their observance, but, far more fundamentally, it constructs for each citizen the framework of an individualised curriculum vitae. Every institution that is passed through in the course of a life, hospital, primary school, secondary school, youth centre, medical centre, employment, social security etc., records our presence, and its presence is in turn recorded in our CV. These institutions furnish essential references, mapped out in terms of some kind of incremental life course or career and, without them we officially cease to exist. Today patients, delinquents, the mentally ill all have pseudo careers of this kind. The extent to which these institutional co-ordinates are internalised, and become effective self-referential models, may vary. But no one should underestimate how far these statutory story lines have come to construct social identities, least of all for those who have passed through prison, or mental hospital, immigration control or care home. So to pose a question that C. Wright Mills would undoubtedly have asked: how can we relate the social distribution of these narrative frames to the historical individualities of life storytellers? Where can we look for the crucial link between the developmental ideals which furnish normative or stereotypical versions of the life course, including 'youth' and a more hidden curriculum vitae shaped by history's 'other scene'?

Youth life course framework

In my research I have identified four connective frameworks: vocation, career, inheritance and apprenticeship. Their origin and development can be correlated with specific historical conjunctures. For example the rise to prominence of the 'public man' and the professional middle classes in late Victorian society was linked to the establishment of 'career' as a dominant paradigm, while vocation was marginalised and increasingly confined to certain feminine, intellectual or artistic pursuits. The history of these codes is thus bound up with concrete social developments, but it is not reducible to them. The grammars of apprenticeship and inheritance, have taken on a life of their own quite apart from their origins in the indentured labour form, or the transmission of material assets and wealth.

The grid of inheritance originally evolved within a moral economy governed by patriarchal authority. The life cycle is unfolded as a more or less congenital link between fixed origins and destinies. You can only become what you always and already are, by virtue of the special patrimony which has been entailed in your life, from the moment of conception onwards. This closed reproduction of fixed positions may become racialised, or alternatively serve to shore up the boundaries of ethnic identities under attack. But in order to accomplish this latter task the code has to be effectively transmitted to the up and coming generation. In other words it has to be articulated to particular cultural forms of apprenticeship in which life is unfolded as so many stages in the mastery of a patrimony of skill.

Today growing up working class no longer means being apprenticed at an early age to an inheritance of trade or domestic skill passed on from parents or elders in the workplace and community. What now counts is how the dispositions of intellectual, cultural and social capital are entailed in practices of learning, both physical and mental, mediated through the apparatus of extended scholarisation. For those who have to grow up working class without work, and without a language of class to articulate their experience, the code of inheritance can provide a sense of life historical continuity and identity. At the same time, on the other side of the class tracks, its material basis in the transfer of assets not only continues to over-determine life chances, but achieves even higher salience with the financialisation of the property market. Waiting for long living parents to die so the children can inherit their property, and hence be able to afford to buy a place of their own before they retire, has re-animated the whole psycho-drama of dis/inheritance which was such a staple plot ingredient for Victorian novelists in a more Patriarchal age, albeit now recast in a more narcissistic pre- or post- oedipal idiom associated with the rhetoric's of 'Generation Rent'.

Apprenticeship, although it scarcely exists in its traditional indentured form, except in a few highly specialised crafts, has also had a vigorous afterlife. Uncoupled from inheritance, it offers a generic model of peer-to-peer transmission within informal communities of practice both inside and outside the workplace. In the contemporary service economy we find a whole array of coaches, trainers and mentors, who have mastered not only specialised work skills linked to the just-in-time production of peak performance but the values and attitudes of mind and body that go with them. The apprenticeships they offer to their various mimetic disciplines involve forms of living labour which have been abstracted from specific workplace cultures and communities and rendered transferable, often being formally subsumed or translated into the middle class idioms of vocation or career. You can trace this happening in the contemporary formation of young artists and athletes from working class background, not least in the aspirational memoirs they write about their struggles to succeed.

The codes of vocation and career have undergone a similar convoluted process of transformation. Under the imprimaturs of the original vocation code the self is the bearer of a calling which may be moral, spiritual or social in type, but whose existential imperatives direct the young person to cultivate particular gifts, often of an artistic kind, and attune development to a variety of aesthetic pursuits. In this model the adolescent search for identity becomes paradigmatic of the whole life cycle; it is privileged in various humanistic and existential psychologies and today it has been re-calibrated to give a glamorous halo to the precarious conditions of the freelancer and portfolio worker. In contrast the grid of career offers a much more utilitarian, though no less individualistic reading of the life cycle. Here life is unfolded as so many steps up a ladder of progress, marked at each stage by increments of skill or status, or some other measurable index of personal achievement. The young person is pitted competitively against peers and is made the subject of more or less ruthless monitoring and evaluation. At the limit the contingencies of a life history are reduced to the predictabilities of a business plan, which is made to unfold according to a rigid timetable of developmental norms. Developmental psychologies have helped to make career the authorised version of the life course in western societies. Although a career remains the referential model to which we are all supposed to aspire, in reality its performativity is confined to the children of a diminishing elite, often privately educated, who enter the liberal professions. Careers are not quite what they used to be. They now subsume internships, portfolio working and other forms of pseudo apprenticeship. The orderly incremental progression has been replaced by intermittent and erratic forms of self-promotion. Career is once more approximating to its original sense of 'careering about'.

The four codes make use of different kinds of time to give a sense of duration and endurance to the lives whose histories they help shape. Within the apprenticeship/inheritance frame the cyclical time of generation and the seasons can be used to rework the irreversible time of biological aging to punctuate family time into sequential phases or transitions. Within the vocation/career couplet the reversible time of biography and popular memory can be used to plunder historical events for special leitmotifs of meaning (e.g. the shared biographies of the 60s generation). In its strongest form, each code throws a normative grid of periodisation and predicament over the life cycle, mapping out key moments and rituals of transition, establishing gender specific markers of im/maturity, and editing the syntax of experience accordingly. The grammars, when totalised, not only define certain developmental ideals, but the dispositions that have to be acquired to realise them. But as their normative strength weakens so their forms of articulation becomes ever more variegated and difficult to decode. Retro-modernity flourishes under the sign of inheritance regained or the quest for lost vocation, while apprenticeship marries up with career to re-invent the notion of modernity-as-progress. However, there are many sources of tension between the life historical messages conveyed by these codes. Once sons could no longer follow fathers and girls, mothers, into the same occupational culture and community, other life journeys became imaginable. Many of these tensions came to a head during youth and much of the emotional labour of traditional adolescence in fact consisted in learning to decode, differentiate and if possible reconcile competing life story lines. One reason for the current popularity of 'triumph over adversity' life stories is that they articulate elements from all four codes into a single aspirational mash up. Contemporary memoirs specialise in the assertion that that all forms of adversity, whether inherited or acquired, all obstacles to the achievement of a calling or set backs to a career, whether externally imposed or self-willed, are to be welcomed as spurs to the ultimate achievement of personal success.

Conclusion

I have argued that the Youth Question has come of age because it is no longer a question about what a particular cohort of young people think, feel or believe about themselves or the world in which they live. It is about what youth and subcultures are made to represent by what is projected onto them by virtue of the position that 'youth' occupies as a contradictory site of hyper-valorisation and disqualification in different forms of late capitalist modernity. As such it has become a potential space for C. Wright Mills' sociological imagination to gain some purchase, especially, but not only, among 'Generation Rent'; but equally, I have insisted, this space is continually at risk of being foreclosed by its more or less spectacular recuperation. Against this background we need to argue for a new life course politics, not to return to one-size-fits-all cradle to grave welfarism, but to re-assert the value of apprenticeship and career as biographical trajectories embedded in structures of *collective* aspiration open to all. But this is only half of the story. We also need to re-align the codes of inheritance and vocation within a moral economy that is no longer beholden to notions of race or gender, or the espousal of a superior, interiorised authenticity.

Further reading

Ainley, P. and Rainbird, H. (1999) *Apprenticeship: Towards a New Paradigm of Learning*, London: Kogan Page.

Back, L. (2009) 'Global attentiveness and the sociological ear', *Sociological Research Online* 14(4): 14 (http://www.socresonline.org.uk/14/4/14.html accessed 1 August 2015).

Bauman, Z. (2000) *Liquid Modernity*, Cambridge: Polity Press.

Benjamin, W. (1968/1999) *Illuminations*, London: Pimlico.

Berlant, L. (2011) *Cruel Optimism*, Durham: Duke University Press.

Berman, M. (1982) *All That is Solid Melts into Air: The Experience of Modernity*, London: Simon and Schuster.

Best, A. (2007) (ed.) *Representing Youth: Methodological Issues in Critical Youth Studies*, New York: New York University Press.

Blackman, S. (2014) 'Subculture Theory', *Deviant Behavior* 35(6): 496–512.

Boltanski, L. and Chiapello, E. (2005) *The New Spirit of Capitalism*, London: Verso.

Cohen, P. (1987) 'Against the New Vocationalism', in Bates, I., Clarke, J., Cohen, P., Finn, D., Moore, R. and Willis, P. (eds) *Schooling for the Dole*, London: Macmillan, 64–82.

Cohen, P. (1989) 'The Perversions of Inheritance', in Cohen, P. and Bains, H. (eds) *Multi-Racist Britain*, London: Macmillan, 18–50.

Cohen, P. (1998) *Rethinking the Youth Question: Education, Labour and Cultural Studies*, London: Palgrave, 42–56.

Cohen, P. and Ainley, P. (2000) 'In the Country of the Blind', *Journal of Youth Studies* 3(1): 79–85.

Cohen, P. (2003) 'Mods and Shockers', in Bennett, A., Cieslik, M. and Miles, S. (eds) *Researching Youth*, London: Macmillan, 29–54.

Cohen, P. (2015) 'The Centre will not hold', *Soundings*, August.

Cohen, P. (in press) *Material Dreams: Maps and Territories in the Un/Making of Modernity*, London: Palgrave Macmillan.

Dunkley, C. (2013) *The Precariat*, London: Oberon Books.

Esty, J. (2012) *Unseasonable Youth: Modernism, Colonialism and the Fiction of Development*, Oxford: Oxford University Press.

Fisher, M. and Gilbert, J. (2015) *Reclaim Modernity: Beyond Markets and Machines*, compassonline.org.uk/publications/reclaiming-modernity-beyond-markets-beyond-machines/.

Fornas, J. and Bolin, G. (1995) *Youth Culture in Late Modernity*, London: Sage.

Frank, T. (1997) *The Conquest of the Cool: Business Culture, Counter Culture and the Rise of Hip Consumerism*, Chicago, IL: University of Chicago Press.

Freud, S. (1929/2010) *Civilisation and Its Discontents*, Eastford, CT: Martino Fine Books.

Gramsci, A. (1994) *Letters from Prison*, Vols. 1 and 2 (Rosengarten, F., ed.), New York: Columbia University Press.

Gulli, B. (2015) *Labour of Fire: The Ontology of Labour Between Economy and Culture*, Philadelphia, PA: Temple University Press.

Halpern, R. (2009) *The Means to Grow Up: Reinventing Apprenticeship as a Developmental Support in Adolescence*, London: Routledge.

Hareven, T. (1978) *Transitions: The Family and Life Course in Historical Perspective*, Waltham: Academic Press.

Hebdige, D. (1987) *Hiding in the Light: On Images and Thing*, London: Routledge.

Jones, O. (2011) *Chavs: The Demonization of the Working Class*, London: Verso.

Latour, B. (2005) *Re-assembling the Social*, Oxford: Oxford University Press.

Lave, J. (2011) *Apprenticeship in Critical Ethnographic Practice*, Chicago, IL: University of Chicago Press.

McRobbie, A. (1991) *Feminism and Youth Culture*, London: Macmillan.

Marshall, P. (1996) *A Kind of Life Imposed on Man: Vocation and Social Order*, Toronto: University of Toronto Press.

Marx, K. (1926/1985) *The 18th Brumaire of Louis Napoleon*, London: Allen and Unwin.

Marx, K. (1845/1970) *The German Ideology*, London: Lawrence and Wishart.

Mills, C. W. (1959) The *Sociological Imagination*, Oxford: Oxford University Press.

Mitterauer, M. (1992) *A History of Youth*, Oxford: Blackwell.

Moretti, F. (1987) *The Way of the World: The Bildungsroman in European Culture*, London: Verso.

Pountain, P. and Robins, D. (2000) *Cool Rules: Anatomy of an Attitude*, London: Reaktion.

Reader, W. (1966) *Professional Men: The Rise of the Professional Classes in 19th Century England*, London: Weidenfeld and Nicholson.

Scott, J. and Nilsen, A. (2013) *C Wright Mills and the Sociological Imagination: Contemporary Perspectives*, Cheltenham: Edward Elgar.

Sennett, R. (2006) *The Culture of the New Capitalism*, New Haven, CT: Yale University Press.

Silva, J, M. (2013) *Coming Up Short: Working-Class Adulthood in an Age of Uncertainty*, Oxford: Oxford University Press.

Standing, G. (2010) *The Precariat: A New Dangerous Class*, London: Bloomsbury Academic.

Thompson, E. P. (1979) 'The Grid of Inheritance', in Goody, J. (ed.) *The Family and Inheritance*, Cambridge: Cambridge University Press, 328–359.

Tuck, E. and Yang, K. W. (2014) *Youth Resistance Research and Theories of Change*, London: Taylor and Francis.

Wacquant, L. (2008) *Urban Outcasts: A Comparative Sociology of Advanced Marginality*, Cambridge: Polity.

Walker, C. (2009) 'From Inheritance to Individuation: disembedding working class youth transitions in post Soviet Russia', *Journal of Youth studies* 12(5): 531–545.

Weber, M. (2004) *The Vocation Lectures*, Indianapolis, IN: Hackett Press.

2 Subcultural and post-subcultural compatibility

The case of Cuban underground rap

Eleni Dimou

Introduction

Starting with Mills's (2000 [1959]) key idea that the nature of sociological imagination is to take into consideration the interplay between biography and history, this chapter will examine contemporary debates in cultural studies on the interpretation of youth subcultures. Specifically it will address the ongoing "polemic" between the Birmingham School of Cultural Studies and post-subculture theory. Arguably the CCCS's "subcultural imagination" was closer to Mills' ideas, as it aimed to show the interconnectedness of the everyday life experiences of youth subcultures to the socio-historical context in which they found themselves (Clarke et al., 1976; Hall & Jefferson, 2006). Hence what was, and still is, valuable with the concept of subculture is that it is able to grasp and depict this interrelation between micro and macro aspects of life. With the post-subcultural turn in the early 1990s however, due to the explicit aim to move away from the CCCS's Marxist interpretation of subcultures, as well as a dismissal of the term subculture itself, the focus has shifted towards the biography side of the relationship.

Particularly, post-subculture theory tends to examine issues of individualisation, fragmentation of identities, consumerism and apolitical sentiments of contemporary youth cultures (Redhead, 1990, 1993; Bennett, 1999; Muggleton, 2000). Post-subculture theory has been very valuable in illuminating late-modern cultural trends in the construction of contemporary youth identities, such as media proliferation, consumerism, local and global interactions and affects, which are important to be considered when unfolding young people's lives. At the same time though, its focus on consumerism and individualism tends to ignore structural inequalities that continue to pose severe constraints to young people's lives (Blackman, 2005; Shildrick & MacDonald, 2006; Hall & Jefferson, 2006). In other words, it misses a critical examination of the complexities of young people's structural and cultural realities (ibid.). Thus we need to bring back the history–biography dynamic and the context-intuitive approach encouraged by Mills. While maintaining the concept of subcultures, a better understanding of the history–biography nexus can be achieved through a "double sidedness" (Hall & Jefferson, 2006: xii) perspective. This involves combining the useful elements of both theories. By "acknowledging the new without losing what may be serviceable in the old" (Hall & Jefferson, 2006: xii) the "double sidedness" approach, argues that by incorporating the valuable insights of both theories we can gain a better understanding of young people's practices and affiliations in relation to wider structural and cultural changes. Hence, through the "double sidedness" perspective a reworked notion of subcultures, adjusted to contemporary times, can be achieved.

In the first part of the chapter I will outline the useful aspects of both theories in relation to C. Wright Mills' idea on the importance of understanding the history–biography relationship in young people's lives. Through this discussion I aim to show that despite their perceived opposition, due to the different focus of the two perspectives they are actually compatible. Following Mills' insistence that we should understand notions and concepts in relation to the historical context within which they gain popularity, it will be also argued that the terms scenes, neo-tribes, lifestyle and club-culture that have been suggested to substitute the term subculture "obscure rather than illuminate the history–biography dynamic" (Nilsen & Brannen, 2013: 88). It will be demonstrated that the concept of subculture is still the most effective in understanding and depicting the relationship between biography and history in young people's lives.

After an exploration of Cuba's socio-historical context from the 1990s onwards, the last part of the chapter focuses on empirical material gained from a five month ethnographic study, (during 2008–2012), with rappers in Havana, Cuba. Here an analysis of the notion of the "underground", as well as, the meanings that the rappers attribute to their music will be presented. It will be argued that heterogeneous tastes, individual choice, agency and diverse affiliations that post-subculture theory was focusing on, go hand in hand with CCCS's focus on historical conjunctures, formations of collective identities, experiences of marginalisation, politics, power and resistance. Hence it will be shown how the bridging of the CCCS with post-subcultural elements can actually enrich the notion of subcultures in an endeavour to comprehend the interplay between biography and history in young people's lives. Despite the fact that Cuba might represent a "unique" case, it arguably demonstrates the extent to which bridging the CCCS and post-subcultural theory is useful even in atypical circumstances in global terms.

Back to subcultures through a history–biography perspective

Over the last two decades there has been an ongoing debate over the theorisation of youth subcultures. The core focus of this debate is between the Birmingham School of Cultural Studies (CCCS) interpretation of youth subcultures and post-subculture theory. Extensive criticism has been produced on both sides, with academics aligning themselves either with the CCCS (Blackman, 2004, 2005, 2014; Shildrick & MacDonald, 2006; Griffin, 2011) or post-subculture theory (Thornton, 1995; Bennett, 1999, 2005; Muggleton, 2000; Redhead, 1993 and Redhead et al., 1997). Currently, post-subculturalists such as Muggleton (2005), Bennett (2011) and Redhead (2012) argue that their claims on the death of subcultures have been widely exaggerated; while CCCS advocates such as Hall

& Jefferson (2006) acknowledge the late-modern cultural features and leisure practices that post-subculture theory has illuminated. At the same time though, they call to maintain the critical insight of the CCCS regarding the importance of linking everyday lived experiences of youth to wider historical, structural and socio-political changes, which was depicted within the notion of subculture (ibid.). Arguably it was this acknowledgement that the notion of subcultures needs to be adjusted to contemporary cultural changes as well as, criticisms addressed to the CCCS that led to the proposal of reconciliation of the two theories through a "double sidedness" approach (Hall & Jefferson, 2006: xii). Following C. Wright Mills' key idea on understanding personal biographies in relation to historical-structural contexts, I want to demonstrate that the two approaches are compatible. It will be argued that by bridging the two perspectives an up-to-date notion of subcultures can be achieved, which will help make better sense of the dialectic between young people's lives and socio-historical shifts.

To begin with, according to Mills (2000 [1959]: 3–4):

> [M]en [sic] do not usually define the troubles they endure in terms of historical change and institutional contradiction. The well-being they enjoy, they do not usually impute to the big ups and downs of the societies in which they live. Seldom aware of the intricate connexion between the patterns of their own lives and the course of world history, ordinary men [sic] do not usually know what this connexion means for the kinds of men [sic] they are becoming and the kind of history-making in which they might take part.

Arguably this theoretical framework runs through the CCCS's interpretation of youth subcultures and especially the collective volume of *Resistance Through Rituals* (*RTR*) (Clarke et al., 1976). Particularly the key aspiration of *RTR* was to explore the relationship between "lived experience and structural realities" (Hall & Jefferson, 2006: xiv). They insisted on the importance of interpreting and linking subcultures in relation to the historical conjuncture (socio-cultural, economic and political changes of the specific historical context) within which they found themselves (Hall & Jefferson, 2006). Inner life experience of subcultures was interpreted through the notions of bricolage (Clarke et al., 1976; Hebdige, 1979) and homology (Willis, 1978). The former aimed to show aspects of agency, autonomy and independence, as subcultural members through their styles and rituals gave different meaning and values to cultural commodities from the way that they were being used by the hegemonic culture. Homology, on the other hand, was used to demonstrate how rituals, practices and values of subcultural members forged collective identities and a "whole way of life" for individual members (Hebdige, 1979: 113).

Specifically, subcultures were seen as a working-class phenomena, which stemmed out of the "personal troubles" (Mills, 2000 [1959]) of collective feelings of subordination (Blackman, 2005). Similar to Mills's (2000 [1959]) idea that it is difficult for people to understand their private troubles in relation to social issues and hence change them, youth subcultures were not fully aware of their oppression and subordination stemming from their class position (Clarke et al., 1976; Blackman, 2005). As a result their resistance through style and rituals, although very important in terms of offering momentarily autonomy, freedom and independence (a "magical" (symbolic) solution to structural and cultural experiences of marginalisation), did not change or improve "their marginal position in society" (Williams, 2011: 29). Consequently, their resistance reproduced existing power structures (Clarke et al., 1976). Simultaneously, the notion of "hegemony" (Gramsci, 1971) as power was used in order to analyse how subcultural styles were either labelled as a threat creating moral panics or were appropriated and commodified for profit by the hegemonic culture (Clarke et al., 1976; Hebdige, 1979; Williams, 2011). In other words, the CCCS endeavoured to understand everyday life experiences and practices of subcultures and to link their potential micro-level (unconscious, symbolic) forms of resistance to hegemonic power structures (Dimou, 2014).

With the post-subcultural turn in the early 1990s, it was perceived that this period was fundamentally different to the 1960s and 1970s from which the CCCS emerged (Redhead, 1997). With an explicit aim to depart from the CCCS's Marxist interpretation of subcultures it was argued that "the 1990s were better characterized through the lens of postmodernism" (Williams, 2011: 31). In this perspective social class, gender, religion and ethnicity no longer had the same structuring role to people's lives as they used to (Hodkinson, 2007). Rather, in postmodernity biographies are increasingly unpredictable and subject to individuals' freedom to choose, shape and create their own destinies (Nilsen & Brannen, 2013; Hodkinson, 2007). In other words the "standard" biographies of modernity have been replaced by "choice" biographies (Nilsen & Brannen, 2013). As a result, according to post-subculture theory, contemporary subcultures are no longer centred either on previously restraining factors such as class, gender and ethnicity or on the formation of collective identities through style and rituals (Muggleton, 2000). Rather, heterogeneity, hybridity of style, media saturation, consumerism, individualism, commerciality, transient and fluid memberships, hedonism and apolitical sentiments prevail (Thornton, 1995; Redhead, 1993; Polhemus, 1997; Bennett, 1999; Muggleton, 2000).

In this perspective, resistance is perceived as the "'new' politics of pleasure: a pleasure for its own sake" (Redhead, 1993: 21, 7). This emphasis on the politics of pleasure, "'surface qualities' and diverse affiliation is suggested to give priority to subjective meaning allowing individuals' agency" (Blackman, 2005: 11). By emphasising agency, youth practices are not seen any more as "magical solutions" to material or ideological strains faced by working class youth (Clarke et al., 1976). Subsequently post-subculture theory by highlighting individualism and agency interprets youth cultures as active and positive (Williams, 2011), without however engaging in exploring conflicts, inequalities and power in society. Thus it does not question whether contemporary youths reproduce or change their situation in life (Williams, 2011). It seems therefore, that in an effort to move away from the CCCS's interpretation, history is interpreted in epochal terms rather than through the lens of socio-economic and political changes in a specific historical context (Nilsen & Brannen, 2013). Following C. Wright Mills (2000 [1959]) it could be argued hence, that post-subculture theory centres more on the agency/biographical side of the history–biography dynamic.

Stemming from the above, in the post-subcultural framework there has been a dismissal of the term subculture, with the notions of neo-tribes (Bennett, 1999), club-cultures (Thornton, 1995; Redhead et al., 1997), scenes (Straw, 2001) and lifestyle (Bennett, 1999) proposed as the best alternative notions to describe the ephemerality and hybridity of contemporary youth identities. However, as C. Wright Mills insisted we need to relate notions and theoretical perspectives in the historical context within which they emerge (Nilsen & Brannen, 2013). As Blackman (2004, 2005), Hall & Jefferson (2006), Griffin (2011) and Williams (2011) – among others – have argued, the celebration of individualisation, consumerism, ephemerality, hybridity and apolitical sentiments of contemporary youth cultures go hand in hand with the neoliberal ideology of "consuming yourself into being" (Griffin, 2011: 255). As implied earlier, the taken for granted aspects of affluent and equal societies, as well as the celebration of consumerism and market choices in post-subculture theory, largely tend to ignore and obscure structures of inequalities that create significant constraints to young people's choices (Nilsen and Brannen, 2013). In other words, the dominant focus in post-subculture theory on individualisation overshadows the concern of the "interplay between history and biography" (Nilsen & Brannen, 2013: 100). Consequently we need to bring back the history–biography dynamic by placing individualisation and power of agency into context.

With this framework in mind the concept of subcultures is arguably the best at capturing and interpreting individual choice and the shaping of collective identities through style and rituals, alongside the issues of inequality, marginalisation, power and resistance that play out in youth's everyday lives. Also subcultures in the CCCS were conceptualised as taking various forms, with some being more clear, distinctive and tightly bounded, while others were more loosely-defined and diffused (see Clarke et al., 1976: 35). The latter seems to have escaped post-subculture theory's attention. Most importantly, as Williams (2011) argues the CCCS tended to focus more on the former, while post-subculture theory centres more on the latter. Therefore the notion of subcultures used by the Birmingham School, is not as rigid as post-subculture theory interpreted it to be, and hence, it remains the most adequate to explore youth cultural formations with the qualifications stated above.

Due to the fact that the two perspectives were focusing on different forms and shapes of subcultures it can be argued, despite the alleged rifts, that they are actually compatible. As demonstrated at the beginning of this section, advocates from both approaches seem to acknowledge mistakes and benefits and to propose reconciliation between the two. Post-subculture theory has been very useful in illuminating late modern, media saturated, individualistic and consumerist ethos in the formation of youth identities (Blackman, 2014). By not intending to link, however, these characteristics to wider cultural and social processes that are taking place, it remains highly descriptive rather than critical and analytical of young people's everyday realities (Hall & Jefferson, 2006). By combining though, the descriptive elements of post-subculture theory with the critical analysis of the CCCS, a reworked and advanced notion of subcultures can be achieved. Building on ethnographic material and interviews with underground rap producers in Havana, Cuba, the rest of the chapter aims to provide an example on what the notion of subcultures through a "double sidedness" perspective might look like. Following C. Wright Mills and the Birmingham School on the importance of understanding subcultures within specific historical conjunctures, I will first provide the context within which Cuban underground rap emerged and developed.

Cuban context: socio-economic and cultural aspects

> Rap has given meaning to my life and to those that are following us. It is a way to see, interpret and re-interpret life, our society and the historical moment that we are living in [...] we are discovering and openly discussing our everyday experiences and problems in Cuba, in order to resolve them.
>
> (rapper Tafari,[1] interview 20 August 2010)

Cuban underground rap emerged in Alamar (a suburb of Havana) in the early 1990s during the midst of an economic crisis that hit the island after the collapse of the Soviet Union. As Kirk and Padura Fuentes (2001) argue, life in Cuba has changed more within the last two decades than in the previous 30 years of the post-revolutionary experience. Specifically, the severely austere conditions that followed the collapse of the Soviet Union led Fidel Castro to declare that Cuba was entering into a "Special Period in times of Peace" (Brenner et al., 2008: 1). Job insecurity, a tightening of the U.S. embargo, scarcity and rationing of food, lack of medicine and basic domestic supplies, power-cuts, problems with the transportation system, the rise of racism and marginalization of urban Afro-Cubans among others were some of the characteristics of the Special Period (Pérez-Sarduy & Stubbs, 2000; De la Fuente, 2001). At that time the government introduced one of the most crucial economic reforms, which was the inauguration of a double currency (Cuban pesos and convertible pesos-CUC)[2] (Eckstein, 2008). The consequences of this economic reform have been severe in terms of social equality and the rise of class divisions, as since its implementation, Cuban citizens tend to be divided along the lines of those who have or have not access to CUC (De la Fuente, 2001; Jimenez, 2008). Another implication of the economic reforms and austerity conditions was the proliferation of what is called "double morality" (Wirtz, 2004: 414). This term is used to describe the contradictory stances in private and public realms (ibid.) – namely, "espousing revolutionary values while discretely subverting those values in the name of economic survival" (Wirtz, 2004: 414). The result of the expansion of "double morality" has been for the majority of Cubans to live outside the boundaries of the law (Henken, 2008).

In addition, despite the fact the Cuban government continues to advocate defending socialism to "death", Cuba is slowly embracing a capitalist or socio-capitalist economic system (Fernandez, 2000; Moore, 2006). Particularly the introduction of the double currency was a means to adjust to the hard currency-based global economy (Eckstein, 2008). Furthermore, in an attempt to seek foreign investments, the government has opened up its doors to tourism and joint ventures with foreign tourist companies (Sharpley & Knight, 2009). This resulted in tourism being one of the principal resources of hard currency for the Cuban economy, since the 1990s (ibid.). A consequence of the promotion of tourism has been for average Cubans to be rendered as "second class" citizens (tourists can enjoy all the beauties of Cuba whereas the majority of Cubans, due to their economic condition and state restrictions, cannot) (Jimenez, 2008). Another implication has been the re-emergence of prostitution and sex-tourism, while increased levels of corruption and the spread of consumer values and materialism have been also among the effects of this socio-economic crisis (Fernandez, 2000; Kapcia, 2008).

Last but not least, the approximate five decade U.S. embargo forced on Cuba and the constant threat of a U.S. military invasion (combined with a condition of permanent crisis especially after the collapse of the Soviet Union) has led to what Kapcia (2000: 12) terms as "siege mentality". This siege mentality could be described at a governmental level as the persistent fear of being attacked by the U.S. (ibid.). It exists furthermore at the level of everyday life where it manifests in constant feelings of distrust and fear: that individuals might be serving the interests of U.S. counterintelligence on the island, or that the economy might implode at any moment (Kapcia, 2000). Consequently, personal feelings of fear and distrust as well as structural conditions are of paramount importance in Cuba's politics in general and cultural politics in particular. As the quote at the beginning of the section denotes, Cuban underground rap gradually developed into a critical discourse that describes and critiques the aforementioned problems.[3] Historical conjunctures are central hence to understand Cuban underground rap emergence and development. Frustrated by a lack of opportunity, highly disillusioned by the state's inability to fulfil its promises, its restraint on self-expression and experiences of deprivation, poverty, marginality, race discrimination and diverse forms of exclusion; Cuban youths found in rap a means of liberation and self-expression (Manolo, interview, 1 August 2010). In what follows it will be illustrated that the reworked notion of subculture through a "double sidedness" perspective can provide a better means of understanding of the relationship between history and biography in Cuban youth's everyday experiences and choices.

Double sidedness: the case of Cuban underground rap

At the time of the research (2008–2012) there were approximately 20 rap groups and individual artists in Havana. The most popular and radical ones at the time were Los Aldeanos, Silvito el Libre, Mano Armada and Escuadron Patriota. Cuban underground rap is a highly masculine subculture both in terms of its music producers and fans and is composed of individuals between the ages of 20 and 34. The subculture is also quite heterogeneous in terms of race encompassing "mulattos" (mixed race), blacks and whites, while (despite the fact that they are all dedicated to the production of rap) there is a wide heterogeneity in terms of music tastes within the group, ranging from reggae and rock to punk and electronic music. The diversity in music tastes but also in affiliations arguably stems from one of the principal spaces that young people in Havana tend to hang around during the night time:

> It was approximately 10 pm and I had just arrived at Park G for the first time in order to meet with Ernesto, Antonio and Alejandro (three of the rappers). Park G is about 2 kilometres long, with benches wide pavement and tall green bushes, in between the main avenue of Vedado in Havana. As soon as I arrived the mixing of subcultural youths amazed me. Rappers, reggae artists and fans, young trovadores, frikies (this name is used in Cuba to describe the punk, metal and rock fans and artists and arguably it denotes their dressing style) and miquies (mainly used for electronic dance music fans and middle-higher class youth) were all sitting next to one another, sharing bottles of rum, chatting and enjoying their night out. At the same time, police units of approximately 20 officers were in some of the corners of the Park watching the youths
>
> (Field-notes, Havana, July 2010)

As becomes apparent from the vignette heterogeneity and fluidity of boundaries describe the leisure practices of subcultural youths in the specific space. This fluidity and heterogeneity was also translated in collaborations between rappers, punk, and reggae music producers during the time of the research. At first glance it could be argued that Park G represents a neo-tribal setting of widespread and mobile tastes in music and style, in which youths "lose" their selves in the politics of pleasure through experiences of alcohol intoxication, laughter and fun, above existing power structures (Bennett, 1999; Redhead, 1993). At the same time this loose network of subcultures cannot be differentiated from issues of social exclusion and marginalisation. Principally, the majority of these youths are excluded (due to their economic condition) from the night-time economy of Havana that is mainly focused on tourist consumerism. As Malcolm, a Cuban cultural official (interview 19 August 2011) states: "In Cuba there does not exist a night-time economy for the average Cuban. For Cubans right? Because for tourists it surely exists." Thus, Park G is one of the few options available. In addition, as depicted in the vignette, Park G is a cause for alarm for the authorities and it tends to be highly policed. Hence, the diverse subcultural affiliations and the politics of pleasure encountered at Park G, reflect a contestation over public space and attempts to win relative autonomy and self-fulfilment that would be familiar to CCCS researchers (see Clarke et al., 1976). Most importantly they do represent a "magical" solution to shared experiences of marginalization by the tourist driven economy of Havana (ibid.). Thus while not changing the actual conditions of social exclusion and marginalisation, the formation of these subcultural networks provides them with momentary independence, autonomy and freedom. Therefore, Cuban subcultures illuminate post-subcultural elements such as politics of pleasure, heterogeneity and non-fixity in boundaries together with CCCS aspects of shared experiences of marginalisation and "symbolic" resistance to these experiences.

Furthermore, post-subculture theory dismisses binary distinctions such as underground/authentic versus mainstream/commercial that were embedded in the notion of subcultures by the CCCS (Redhead, 1990; Thornton, 1995; Muggleton, 2000). I would argue that we should neither dismiss them nor take them for granted. Rather, following C. Wright Mills we should critically examine what the specific notions mean within specific contexts and the meanings that they carry in particular subcultural biographies. Specifically, the term "underground" or "underground movement" that was used by the rappers denotes the heterogeneity in terms of affiliations but also issues of collective identities, forms of solidarity, marginalization and oppression. As Szemere (2001:16) argues on the meaning of underground rock subculture in Hungary, underground culture:

> emphasised recalcitrance toward the dominant (official) culture. The metaphor "underground", widely used by the musicians as a self-reference, suggested a position underneath a more powerful and more visible entity. The political connotation of the term was obvious [… a] force or compulsion [was] connoted by "underground" […] The local underground of the 1980s formed a close-knit and cohesive social world, an art world with solid boundaries.

Particularly, Cuban underground rap is highly revolutionary in its ideals and discourse and since the late 1990s has been officially supported by government's discourses and by two official cultural institutions (The Brothers Saiz Association and the Cuban Rap Agency). However, in everyday life it is censored, labelled as counter-revolutionary and criminalised by Cuban authorities (see Dimou, 2014), since it is characterised as a U.S. sound and because it manifests as protest and critique against the regime.[4] "Cuban rap is the black sheep of Cuban music right now," says José, one of the most prominent rappers; Alejandro (one of the youngest rappers) adds:

> This is partly because the sound is not Cuban but mainly because of its message. We do not use metaphors as they did in the past. Rap's message is crude, profound, strong, direct and honest about Cuban reality and this is not convenient for the government.

Juan, a rapper since the mid-1990s, explicitly states:

> So we have this problem, to be labelled as counter-revolutionaries, because we push for positive change, for dialogue and we talk about the lived everyday reality of the Cuban. But we are not counter-revolutionaries. We are more revolutionary than the revolutionaries!

Cuban underground rap expresses in a profound way the gap between official discourses on socialism and social equality and everyday reality in Cuba[5] (Dimou, 2014). However it is not counter-hegemonic or counter-revolutionary. Rather it is hyper-revolutionary (Baker, 2011: 51) in its discourse and values, while its critique is always done in a constructive way, in order for the revolutionary project to be realized in practice (Dimou, 2014). Hence, the term underground as defined by Szemere (2001) is pivotal in order to understand not only the diverse affiliations of the rappers with other subcultural groups but also issues of politics and power. It becomes apparent then that by maintaining the notion of subcultures and the critical analysis of the CCCS (while enriching it with descriptive post-subcultural elements), micro and macro aspects are revealed and particularly manifestations of power and resistance. An approach and understanding which, as stated earlier, would have been obscured were we to use the alternative terms proposed by post-subculture theorists to substitute subcultures.

Furthermore, the meaning that the rappers attribute to rap demonstrates elements of both the CCCS and post-subculture theory; hence highlighting the importance of reworking the term subculture through a "double sidedness" perspective. "Rap means everything to me," says rapper Ernesto (interview 21 August 2010):

> It is my life-partner. When I first listened to it, rap expressed what I was feeling and it gave me the means to express my feelings and release my frustration. When I am feeling sad, when I feel empty and I have something to say and I do not know how to express it, rap helps me to move forward. It is like a weapon. When I am writing I am expressing everything that I am feeling inside. It helped me discover myself and discover my values. It is the mean that gives me the power to say to the world what I am thinking, what I am feeling and what I desire.

While Juan (interview, 19 August 2010) corroborates:

> Underground rap is a way of life. I have changed and many rappers that were taking a bad route in their lives before have changed. Many people in Cuba that were connected to delinquency have changed their way of life due to listening to or singing rap. Because they are focusing on how to deal with their everyday problems and openly discuss them. Rap gives an alternative of how to deal with your problems in a more positive way. This, I believe is what rap is achieving; to make people express their opinions without fear. Because it's not the same to be in a state-reunion where someone says that things are "red" for everyone and everyone has to agree. No! Things are not only red! They are also blue, yellow, orange and green! So rap advocates being able to express your opinion freely.

It becomes clear in Ernesto's words that despite the state's restrictions and labelling practices, the power of agency, emotions and desire that post-subculture theory has stressed were essential in his individual choice of embracing rap as a means of expression. At the same time Juan's words reveal issues, which were reiterated by all the rappers, that common shared experiences of marginalisation, everyday realities, problems and common shared values and ideals (rap as a way of life) of liberty, equality, freedom of expression and love for their country and its people, play a very important role in constructing collective identities within the subculture.

Arguably then, exploring the meanings of the term underground in particular contexts as well as the meaning that subcultural music producers attribute to their choice of music can reveal elements from both the CCCS and post-subculture theory. As demonstrated post-subcultural elements such as the heterogeneity and diffusion of Cuban rap's boundaries, individual choice, agency, politics of pleasure, affects and desire go hand in hand with the formation of collective identities, historical conjunctures, power, politics and resistance in the specific subculture. If elements of both theoretical perspectives can be found in a highly conscious and political subculture such as Cuban rap then arguably, if we look closer at contemporary subcultures around the globe, we can reconcile the two approaches at a more general level. In other words a reworked notion of subcultures through a "double sidedness" perspective should be followed in our interpretation of contemporary youth cultures.

Conclusion

The notion of subcultures as interpreted by the CCCS largely depicted C. Wright Mills' (2000 [1959]) ideas on the dynamic relationship between history and biography. The "double sidedness" approach proposed in this chapter provides a reworked notion of subcultures, which is arguably the best strategy to be followed in order to make sense of subcultural biographies in relation to specific historical contexts. Hence, the notion of subcultures should be maintained, as it is the most effective concept to reveal the history–biography dynamic, but at the same time it should be adjusted to contemporary times (Hodkinson, 2002). As demonstrated in the discussion of Cuban underground rap both the descriptive elements of post-subcultural theory and the critical analysis of the CCCS need to be employed in order to interpret the specific subculture. Therefore, by adopting the "double sidedness" perspective the interconnectedness of the "personal troubles" and biographies to macro-structural features are brought to light. By maintaining the notion of subcultures, it is aspired that sociologists, criminologists and cultural studies scholars will draw equal attention to structural features and individual lives in the research and interpretation of subcultures that is to come.

Notes

1 The names of my participants in the interviews and field-notes have been altered in order to protect their confidentiality and ensure their well-being.
2 Currently 23 Cuban pesos approximately equal one CUC (1,10 U.S.$). The average Cuban salary, which is paid in Cuban pesos ranges from 15–20 CUC per month and does not cover even basic needs.
3 See Dimou (2014) for further details.
4 For details on the complexities of Cuba's cultural policies in relation to underground rap see Dimou (2014).
5 See previous section.

References

Baker, G. (2011) *Buena Vista in the Club: Rap, Reggaeton, and Revolution in Cuba*, Durham and London: Duke University Press.

Bennett, A. (1999) "Subcultures or Neo-tribes? Rethinking the Relationships between Youth, Style and Musical Taste", *Sociology*, 33 (3): 599–617.

Bennett, A. (2005) "In Defence of Neo-tribes: A Response to Blackman and Hesmondhalgh", *Journal of Youth Studies*, Vol. 8 (2): 255–259.

Bennett, A. (2011) "The Post-subcultural Turn: Some Reflections 10 Years On", *Journal of Youth Studies*, Vol. 14 (5): 493–506.

Blackman, S. (2004) *Chilling Out: The Cultural Politics of Substance Consumption, Youth and Drug Policy*, Maidenhead: McGraw-Hill Education.

Blackman, S. (2005) "Youth Subcultural Theory: A Critical Engagement with the Concept, its Origins and Politics, from the Chicago School to Postmodernism", *Journal of Youth Studies*, Vol. 8 (1): 1–20.

Blackman, S. (2014) "Subculture Theory: An Historical and Contemporary Assessment of the Concept for Understanding Deviance", *Deviant Behavior*, Vol. 35 (6): 496–512.

Brenner, P., Jiménez, M. R., Kirk, J. M. & Leogrande, W. M. (2008) *A Contemporary Cuba Reader: Reinventing the Revolution*, Plymouth: Rowman & Littlefield Publishers, Inc.

Clarke, J., Hall, S., Jefferson, T. & Roberts, B. (1976) "Subcultures, Cultures and Class", in Hall, S. & Jefferson, T. (eds), *Resistance Through Rituals: Youth Sub-cultures in Post-War Britain*, London: Routledge, 5–74.

De La Fuente, A. (2001) *A Nation for All: Race, Inequality, and Politics in Twentieth- Century Cuba*, Chapel Hill, NC & London: The University of North Carolina Press.

Dimou, E. (2014) "Deviance, Power and Resistance in Contemporary Cuba: The Case of Cuban Underground Rap", in *Subcultures, Popular Music and Social Change*, The Subcultural Network, Cambridge: Cambridge Scholars Publishing, 251–266.

Eckstein, S. (2008) "Dollarization and Its Discontents in the Post-Soviet Era", in Brenner, P., Jimenez, M. R., Kirk, J. M. & LeoGrande, W. M. (eds), *A Contemporary Cuba Reader: Reinventing the Revolution*, Plymouth: Rowman & Littlefield Publishers, Inc, 179–192.

Fernandez, D. J. (2000) *Cuba and the Politics of Passion*, Austin, TX: University of Texas Press.

Gramsci, A. (1971) *Selection from the Prison Notebooks.* Translated and edited by Hoare, Q. and Nowell Smith, G. London: Lawrence and Wishart.

Griffin, C.E. (2011) "The Trouble with Class: Researching Youth, Class and Culture Beyond the 'Birmingham School'", *Journal of Youth Studies*, Vol. 14 (3): 245–259.

Hall, S. & Jefferson, T. (2006) "Once More around Resistance Through Rituals", in Hall, S. & Jefferson, T. (eds), *Resistance Through Rituals: Youth Subcultures in Post-War Britain*, *2nd Edition*, Abingdon: Routledge, vii–xxxiii.

Hebdige, D. (1979) *Sub-culture: The Meaning of Style*, London: Methuen.

Henken, T. (2008) "Vale Todo: In Cuba's Paladares, Everything is prohibited but Everything Goes", in Brenner, P., Jimenez, M. R., Kirk, J. M., LeoGrande, W. M. (eds), *A Contemporary Cuba Reader: Reinventing the Revolution*, Plymouth: Rowman & Littlefield Publishers, Inc, 168–178.

Hodkinson, P. (2002) *Goth: Identity, Style and Subculture*, Oxford: Berg.

Hodkinson, P. (2007) "Youth Cultures: a Critical Outline of Key Debates" in Hodkinson, P. & Deicke, W. (eds) *Youth Cultures: Scenes, Subcultures and Tribes*. London: Routledge, 1–23.

Jiménez, M. R. (2008) 'The Political Economy of Leisure', in Brenner, P., Jimenez, M. R., Kirk, J. M. & LeoGrande, W. M. (eds), *A Contemporary Cuba Reader: Reinventing the Revolution*, Plymouth: Rowman & Littlefield Publishers, Inc, 146–155.

Kapcia, A. (2000) *Cuba: The Island of Dreams*, Oxford: Berg.

Kapcia, A. (2008) *Cuba in Revolution: A History since the Fifties*, London: Reaktion Books Ltd.

Kirk, J. & Padura Fuentes, L. (2001) *Culture and Cuban Resolution: Conversations in Havana*, Gainesville, FL: University Press Florida.

Mills, C. W. (2000 [1959]) *The Sociological Imagination: Fortieth Anniversary Edition*, Oxford: Oxford University Press.

Moore, R.D. (2006) *Music and Revolution: Cultural Change in Socialist Cuba*, London: University of California Press, Ltd.

Muggleton, D. (2000) *Inside Subculture: The Postmodern meaning of Style*, Oxford: Berg.

Muggleton, D. (2005) 'From Classlessness to Clubculture: A Geneology of Post-war British Youth Cultural Analysis'. *Young: Nordic Journal of Youth Research*, 13 (2): 205–219.

Nilsen, A. & Brannen, J. (2013) 'Contextualising Lives: The History Biography Dynamic Revisited', in *C. Wright Mills The Sociological Imagination: Contemporary Perspectives*, Scott, J. and Nilsen, A. (eds), Cheltenham: Edward Elgar Publishing Limited, 88–104.

Pérez Sarduy, P. & Stubbs, J. (2000) *Afro-Cuban Voices: On Race and Identity in Contemporary Cuba*, Gainesville, FL: University Press Florida.

Polhemus, T. (1997) 'In the Supermarket of Style', in Redhead, S., Wynne, D. & O'Connor, J. (eds), *The Clubcultures Reader: Readings in Popular Cultural Studies*, Oxford: Blackwell, 130–133.

Redhead, S. (1990) *The End of the Century Party: Youth and Pop Towards 2000*, Manchester: University of Manchester Press.

Redhead, S. (1993) *Rave Off: Politics and Deviance in Contemporary Youth Culture*, Aldershot: Avebury Press.

Redhead, S. (1997) 'Introduction: Reading Pop(ular) Cult(ural) Stud(ie)s' in Redhead, S., Wynne, D. and O'Connor, J. (eds), *The Clubcultures Reader: Readings in Popular Cultural Studies*, Oxford: Blackwell, 1–3.

Redhead, S. (2012) 'Soccer Casuals: A Slight Return of Youth Culture', *International Journal of Child, Youth and Family Studies*, 3(1): 65–82.

Redhead S., Wynne, D. & O'Connor, J. (eds) (1997) *The Clubcultures Reader: Readings in Popular Cultural Studies*, Oxford: Blackwell.

Sharpley, R. and Knight, M. (2009) 'Tourism and the State in Cuba: From the Past to the Future', *International Journal of Tourism Research*, 11: 241–254.

Shildrick, T. and MacDonald, R. (2006) 'In Defence of Subculture: Young People, Leisure and Social Divisions', *Journal of Youth Studies*, 9 (2): 125–140.

Straw, W. (1991) "Systems of Articulation, Logics of Change: Communities and Scenes in popular Music", *Cultural Studies*, Vol. 5 (3): 368–388.

Straw, W. (2001) 'Scenes and Sensibilities', *Public*, 22/23: 245–257.

Szemere, A. (2001) *Up from the Underground: The Culture of Rock Music in Postsocialist Hungary*, University Park, PA: Penn State University Press.

Thornton, S. (1995) *Club Cultures: Music, Media and Sub-cultural Capital*, Cambridge: Polity.

Williams J. P. (2011) *Subculture Theory: Traditions and Concepts*, Cambridge: Polity Press.

Willis, P. E. (1978) *Profane Culture*, London: Routledge & Kegan Paul.

Wirtz, K. (2004) Santeria in Cuban National Consciousness: A Religious Case of the Doble Moral, *The Journal of Latin American Anthropology*, 9(2): 409–438.

3 From bad to worse?

Marginalised youth and 'Road life' (mis)representations and realities

Anthony Gunter

Introduction

The August 2011 riots provided the pivotal moment when the changing nature of British urban youth cultures – specifically 'the proliferation of violent youth gangs and the culture they ferment' (Pitts, 2008:4) – was shown to the world via this spontaneous carnival of violence and criminality. Three months after the summer riots the coalition government launched its wide ranging 'Ending Gang and Youth Violence' (HM Government, 2011) initiative; at the close of 2011 the UK was officially in the grip of a gangs crisis. At the centre of this latest youth crisis was 'gangsta rap culture' which eulogised violent crime and the acquisition of wealth by any means necessary. This viewpoint was put forward by politicians and commentators such as the historian David Starkey – whom after the 2011 riots argued that white youths were becoming black by adopting the violent criminal values of 'gangsta rap' (Hastings, 2011). Indeed, the debates about dangerous urban youth cultures have largely been undertaken in the news-media, with stories drawing upon police statistics detailing the avalanche of violent crimes being committed on a daily basis by inner city youth gangs (Alderson, 2010; Bentham, 2014).

Considering the rich history of academic research examining working class youth subcultures in post War Britain, it is interesting to note that contemporary youth cultural studies and in particular 'post modern subcultural theory' (Blackman, 2005) has largely moved away from studying deviant and/or resistant cultures of poor and marginalised youth. Instead the field has been left to a small but growing number of youth gang criminologists who are largely detached from the ongoing debates about youth subcultures, transitions, identities, race/ethnicity, hybridity, and agency (see for example Alexander, 2000; Cohen and Ainley, 2000; McDonald et al., 2001; Bose, 2003; Nayak, 2003; Sanders, 2005; Gidley, 2007; Gunter, 2010). Consequently, rather than challenging police-media driven discourses that portray contemporary urban youth cultures as inherently violent and criminogenic, gang academics have similarly tended to fixate solely on the negative aspects of the 'Road based' subcultures and lifestyles of marginalised urban youth.

This chapter will firstly revisit the concept of 'Road culture' (Gunter, 2008) as a means to understand the role and significance of subculture, in the lives of young people growing up in two East London neighbourhoods. The term 'On Road' is consistently referred to by the young respondents to capture and describe the social and cultural worlds that they both create and inhabit, indicating where (on the streets) and how they spend the majority of their leisure time, it also informs their musical preferences, dress wear/styles and speech patterns (also Gunter 2008, 2010). Drawing on the voices and direct experiences of young people, this chapter – in stark contrast to the dominant problem centred perspectives that focus on gangs and violent crime – will demonstrate that contemporary Road based subculture plays a largely positive and creative role in young people's lives. This chapter will attempt to further contextualise the role of Road culture by examining the interconnectedness of 'the personal troubles of the milieu' and 'the public issues of social structure' (Mills, 1959:14); particularly with regard to how structural changes have impacted upon the lives of the young respondents.

Road culture revisited and biography

The empirical data derives from an ethnographic study of young people's cultures and transitions in two adjoining East London neighbourhoods, comprising in-depth biographical interviews with 66 young adults aged 14–24. The study attempts to give voice – filtered via the reflexive lens of the ethnographer – to its young participants with regard their experiences growing up in two poor and super-diverse neighbourhoods. I will revisit and update this ethnographic study 'Growing Up Bad' (2010), and will provide a locally situated counterweight to prevailing police-media and gang criminologist (mis)representations, that portray the Road based cultures and lifestyles of marginalised urban youth as being intrinsically criminogenic.

Before moving on to discuss the substantive findings of this study, it is incumbent that I firstly share my own brief biographical history with, and attachment to the research sites and informants. I have worked (and lived) in East London now for nearly 20 years, most notably as a detached (or street-based) community and youth worker. Consequently, I have been able to draw extensively on this knowledge and experience for both studies; particularly with regards to accessing the young research participants. Many of the participants featured in this study, were young people I had previously worked with:

> prior to the commencement of the field work. Field work methods entailed observing and interacting with my informants within a variety of settings – youth club, on the streets, in pubs and clubs, home environment ...
>
> (Gunter, 2010:38)

As the 'art and science of describing a group or culture' (Fetterman, 1998:1) ethnography, notwithstanding its limitations, has been central to my explorations of youth Road subcultures and transitions in East London. Researcher biases and 'meaning-making' judgements of this study incorporates both the stories of the young people featured and my particular way of telling them (McCarthy-Brown,

2001:xi). In so doing, it allows for a more nuanced and 'reflexive' (Bourdieu, 1992) understanding and examination of the connections between the personal problems of the social actors and the changes in the global political economy that inform their everyday lived experiences (Mills, 1959).

Ethnicity, youth and urban marginality

According to the 2011 Census, 64 per cent of the residents of Gulley and Dungle[1] neighbourhoods are from a Black, Asian and Minority Ethnic (BAME) background (ONS, 2012). In this study, approximately 10 per cent of the young respondents 'self identified' themselves as White British, 50 per cent as Black British or mixed (black/white) heritage, with the remainder describing themselves as White Other, Pakistani, Bangladeshi, Moroccan, Iranian, Mauritian or Somalian. As well as being characterised by super-diversity (Vertovec, 2007) the research sites are also amongst the 20 per cent of most deprived neighbourhoods in England (HM Government, 2010). The neighbourhoods of Gulley and Dungle are part of Manton Estate – built in the early 1970s, comprised of high rise tower blocks and 8-storey flats, interspersed with owner-occupied Victorian terraced houses. Within the early part of the 2000s, Manton had been regenerated by the local Housing Action Trust into a low-rise housing estate.

Neo-liberal government social policies and local authority housing decisions had combined, by the late 1990s, to create pockets of socio-economic disadvantage in particular localities of the UK 'and on social housing estates in particular'(Coles et al., 2000:1). Correspondingly, some estates – or more precisely those 'low status urban areas' (Hope, 1996) such as Dungle and Gulley – are characterised by: above-average concentrations of children, young people and lone-parent households; and high rates of unemployment, worklessness, educational disengagement, and crime. Over the past 20 years or so there has been a never ending loop of news-media headlines and comment pieces chronicling 'broken Britain' (BBC, 2010) lamenting the anti social and criminal activities of feral youth living on social housing estates in poor urban neighbourhoods. *Panorama*'s 'Trouble on the Estate!' (BBC, 2012) managed to distil all of these concerns into a one hour BBC television documentary about life on a housing estate in Blackburn. The documentary unsurprisingly uncovered a 'troubled estate' with high incidences of poverty, worklessness, lone-parent households and over-run with drugs and by gangs of young people engaging in criminal and anti-social behaviour.

Contemporary media-driven discourses about the anti-social and criminal subcultures of marginalised urban youth are part of a long history of moral panics (Cohen, 1972) and respectable fears (Pearson, 1983) concerning poor and working class youth in Britain. However, they have been updated to take in the additional public anxieties about race/immigration and problem housing estates. The perennial problematisation of poor youth centres upon their unsupervised use of decaying urban (public) spaces and resultant creation of deviant subcultures (Mays, 1954; Downes, 1966; Parker, 1974). Indeed, Bob Coles et al.'s study (2000) of young people's experiences growing up on 10 deprived social housing estates in

England and Wales, found that the biggest issue – according to 'key adult players' including residents, housing managers, police and youth workers – 'related to groups of children and young people "hanging around"'(Ibid.:24). Whilst there was a consensus amongst the key adult players about the problem of young people 'hanging around', there was less agreement on the causes and solutions for this. The study's authors noted that young people did congregate in public spaces, sometimes in large groups and sometimes being boisterous and noisy. 'Hanging around' in public spaces is a historic and key feature of working class community life which has become increasingly criminalised (Blackman and Wilson 2014).

Road life realities 1: leisure and pleasure

In contrast to contemporary media-driven portrayals and discourses that criminalise and misinterpret the 'urban music'[2] based Road subcultures of marginalised young people, my earlier research findings found that Road culture largely played a 'seductive yet humdrum and functional role'. Indeed, as opposed to the 'spectacular' Road culture served as a means by which the young people 'derive camaraderie, entertainment as well as a strong sense of identity' (Gunter, 2010:93) and attachment neighbourhood life. At the heart of neighbourhood life is the public setting of the open space or 'Road':

> Road culture in Manor (and the surrounding neighbourhoods) is played out predominantly within the public sphere, with young people choosing to spend the majority of their leisure time on the streets or within those open spaces to be found around the various local housing estates.
>
> (Ibid.:103)

Research evidence also points to the fact that street life is a central component of working class youth subcultural identities, leisure activities and neighbourhood attachment (Coles et al., 2000; McCulloch et al., 2006; Shildrick, 2006; MacDonald and Shildrick, 2007; Landolt, 2012; Neary et al., 2012). Furthermore, the public setting of the street/Road has significant historical cultural resonance throughout the black Atlantic (Liebow, 1967; Lieber, 1976; Anderson, 1990; Stolzoff, 2000; Sansone, 2003).

Recent criminological studies have made reference to 'on Road' subcultures of black and urban youth (Hallsworth and Silverstone, 2009; Earle, 2011; Ilan, 2012; Young et al., 2013; Glynn, 2014) but solely in relation to gangs and violent crime. However, this over emphasis upon deviance largely misinterprets and ignores the larger and more significant role that Road culture plays in the lives of poor and BAME urban youth:

> The young participants in this study noted their own subtle but significant distinction between 'being on road' as opposed to 'living on road'. Whilst many of the young people spoke about 'being on road' and 'catching joke'

with their friends, it was only those young people involved in 'badness'[3] who were referred to as 'living on road'

(Gunter, 2010:103)

The latter observation is still pertinent to Road life in Gulley and Dungle as it was a constant theme that recurred in group discussions and interviews with the young participants:

AG: Where do you spend most of leisure time?
Ramone: If I ain't at college or at football then I'm on the endz with these lot
Jamal: On road … with the fam ennit.
Skitz: Yeah … yeah OTF.
All: [laughing]
AG: What happens on Road?
Ramone: Nothing really, jus out doing whatever ennit. Kotch see whose about and that.
Skitz: Bus joke.
Jamal: Link some Yats …
Skitz: Definitely on that.
Jamal: Go over Memorials.
Skitz: Pass through the youth club … bare tings really. Yeah just out on Road.
AG: Just out doing whatever?
Jamal: Yeah, with the man dem, the girls. More time in summer there's nuff bodies around. Everything is lively like, always something happening when we're On Road. The youngers are usually trying a ting [being playfully rude].
Skitz: [laughing] You know them ones.
Jamal: They try it with you all the time to get a reaction. But man's ain't on that running around getting all sweaty and shit.
Skitz: Yeah but you have to ennit, its all jokes though still.
Jamal: Something's always going down on Road, definitely.

The majority of young people are involved in some way in the public settings of Road cultural life in their neighbourhoods, and this cuts across ethnicity and gender. Road life is particularly vibrant during the spring and summer months when the public spaces are full of young people on BMX bikes, skateboards, 'kicking ball', 'spitting bars' (rapping) over beats that are playing on their phones or just sitting on benches or play apparatus chatting and whiling away their time doing nothing (Corrigan, 1979). During the winter months neighbourhood life is quieter but there are still pockets of activity and movement on the streets. There is seemingly no particular pattern as to why the youth club is the place to be, for whatever reason, whilst at other times – and for relatively long periods of time – hardly anybody will 'go club'. Activities within 'club' are largely an extension of those activities undertaken in the other 'public spaces' of Road culture, so some young people will play computer game consoles, 'deejay' and 'spitting' using clubs decks and microphone, or make their own beats on portable studios in club or just 'kotch' and 'bus joke'. Also there is always one young person whose home serves as the unofficial youth club/indoor hang out spot where young people can congregate and 'spit', play computer games or 'jus chill' and 'bus joke'. Additionally, Road life for some young people – particularly young women – also extended to meeting friends in shopping malls outside of the neighbourhood and going to the cinema or ice skating:

Julie: [S]ometimes go cinema. We been going to the mall quite a bit actually as well, since it opened. A load of us from the endz used to all go up there and just walk around and that, looking around all the shops. Its nice.

AG: Does everyone go, I mean boys as well?

Julie: Yeah, well at first anyway. But like the security started getting stupid and that, stopping and hassling some of the boys like on a regular, so now they ain't bothered as much. But we still like going up there and just walking around.

Road life realities II: risk and danger

From the ethnography Road life is central to the young people's neighbourhood identity and their leisure activities, it also represented a place of risk and danger – particularly to the young males (see also Evans et al., 1996; Taylor et al., 1996; Watt and Stenson, 1998; Reay and Lucey, 2000; Gunter, 2008; Kintrea et al., 2008; Parkes and Conolly, 2011). When walking about or hanging around the neighbourhood the young men tended to adopt a confident street persona or 'swagger', that indicated they could handle themselves physically if they had to and that they also had 'back up' if needed. In order to successfully pull off the 'swagger' the young males had to be dressed in the right 'garms' including designer clothes and sportswear, and tended to also adopt a slow and rhythmical walking style or 'bowling'. This swagger was a visual signal that was deliberately given out by young males warning off potential foes indicating that they were not weak individuals or easy targets for bullying and robbery.

Many of the young people felt most safe when 'hanging about' within their own neighbourhoods, whilst at the same time being acutely aware of the dangers and risks posed outside their local area.

AG: Where do you feel most safe?

Kaydee: In my area because I know where to go, where I can go and basically I know who I can contact. If you go somewhere you don't know, it can be a safer place.

AG: Yeah.

Kaydee: But there's always idiots on the road and always people out there to rob someone so. You just got to mind your back.

AG: But generally you feel most safe in Gulley [name of neighbourhood].

Kaydee: Yeah, I feel more safe in Gully because I know what the threat is and where the safest spots are.

AG: And where would you say you feel least safe?

Kaydee: Probably in Haverhill, yeah, I'm not too bothered about it, I'd walk the Streets there, I couldn't give a f***k if someone tried to rob me, I wouldn't give them my phone, I'd rather get stabbed than f******g give my stuff to them.

Hamid: Definitely not Manley. I go to Manley. I used to go there on a regular, near enough every Tuesday because my Nan lives down there, but when I go down there on a bike ride, I've had people come to me, trying to stab me, one says he was going to shoot me. It didn't happen.

All of the young males talked about the threat of physical violence and robbery when travelling to and through different neighbourhoods:

Milton: Like we would look at the school gates and then we'd see a bunch of people running. And like why they running?

AG: Yeah.

Milton: And then someone will call me and they'll say yeah, blah, blah, blah these guys are here.

AG: Yeah.

Milton: And they're here for this one [some young person] and that's the way it is, and sometimes at my school people will come, for boys and if they're not there, they'll just come for whoever's around. I've had people getting stabbed in the head with a screwdriver, that's at my school.

AG: Is that when you went to school in Manley [neighbouring borough]?

Milton: No, no, I didn't go to school in Manley, I went to school in Riplets Bow [another neighbouring borough].

Apart from school the socio-spatial worlds of the young males was narrow and limited to the imagined boundaries of the neighbourhood estate. The young males only left the confines of their estate by themselves when they had to attend school, college, football training or visit family, otherwise they would deliberately visit other neighbourhoods mob-handed. This was done either for 'back up' and protection in numbers and this in itself is perceived by youth in other neighbourhoods as a provocative act, or to 'bring it' by engaging in retaliatory acts of violence in response to a previous incident or new threat of violence by young males from opposing neighbourhoods. Although it was the young males who were more at risk from getting drawn into Road life 'beefs' [petty disputes that quickly escalated into violence with use of knives or even guns] and robberies, young women in the neighbourhood were not immune to these risks and dangers:

AG: OK so what are the types of crime that happen in your area

Jamila: Mugging people, people getting their phones nicked or something like that.

Saraya: Yeah. My friend in the school, she was going home one day after a school club at school and she got loads of boys following her and they attacked her and took her phone and stuff.

AG: Really?

Saraya: Yeah, it was like this time of year where it gets dark earlier so she was like on the way home from school.

AG: And how old is she?

Saraya: She's now in Year 10 but it was when she was in Year 9.

AG: Have you ever been a victim of any of these crimes.

Jamila: No but I've been chased by two people on bikes.

AG: And what did they want?

Jamila: I don't know, I don't know because my aunty lives in a place where there's an alleyway and I was walking down and they just started calling some random names and started running after me with their bikes and I just went into a shop.

Saraya: On the way to school in the morning me and my friend were walking and we got this boy come up to us with a pen, but he kind of pretended it was a knife or something. He was threatening us and saying he wanted to talk to someone else that we knew that's in the school and we basically said we don't know where they are. He followed my friend the day before as well to where she was going, so the next morning when he came up to us he was asking us questions and trying to threaten us.

Official risk discourses and youth perspectives

The local authority, police and other justice sector agencies had labelled both of the neighbourhoods in this study as 'gang affected areas' and this was reflected with regards policing practice, and youth work provision. As was found in Hannah Smithson et al.'s (2013) study of a gang affected multi-ethnic neighbourhood in north west England, none of the young participants in this study identified with or validated the official risk discourses around 'gangs'. Most felt that the gang problem was a media invention that didn't speak about the daily realities of East London Road life.

AG: Are any of your friends, or do you know anyone in a gang?

Uddin: No.

AG: You don't know anyone in a gang.

Mo: No. What do you mean by a gang?

AG: I don't know, you tell me. When people talk to me, they always talk about gangs.

Uddin: Gangs as in they mean a group of friends.

AG: Okay.

Uddin: If you think a group of friends is a gang, then we can say then we know a lot of friends or group of friends, but I don't call them a gang as such. That's a strong word to say.

Mo: It's the media.
AG: So if there's violence between gangs it's just groups of friends who are fighting you think, it's not necessarily gangs.
Mo: I wouldn't call them gangs.
Uddin: It's one group of friends from one area and another group of friends from another area fighting.
AG: So gang violence doesn't really exist you don't think?
Uddin: No.
Mo: No, not really. It might exist but not that I know of.

This is clarified by the young people who did use the term gang when discussing violence and crime – sometimes its use was pejorative reflecting the influence of news-media and official agencies' youth risk discourses (see also Parkes and Connelly, 2013).

Debra: I do feel safe in my area, but there are a lot of gangs round here.
AG: Do the gangs fight each other?
Debra: No, they don't fight each other. They all friends and hang around together.
AG: Do they fight gangs from other areas?
Debra: Some of them might, but mostly they just hang around area together doing stupidness.

During the ethnography I met with a 16 year-old male, Marlon, who sat on the youth advisory panel of the local authority's borough-wide gang project and was officially described as an ex-gang member. I asked him about his experiences of gangs:

Marlon: Really when I talk about being in a gang, mostly I'm just talking about me and my boys on the estate … chillin' and doing whatever [badness].
AG: So the way you use the word gang is different to say how the gang project and police use it.
Marlon: Yeah, I sit down with them [managers in gang project] all the time and try explain to them that this gang stuff ain't real on Road.

All of the young respondents depicted the nuanced complexities and dangers of Road life beyond simplistic gang narratives and 'post code war' territorial disputes:

AG: Do you think that there is a gang problem in East London?
Michael: There is a gang problem but that's only because if you go to someone else's area. They just want to rob you.
AG: And is this in relation to young people representing their postcodes in areas?
Howie: Yeah but I wouldn't really call it a postcode war, it's all about money.
Michael: It's just their way of getting through isn't it.

Howie: If you see another kid and honestly if they're not from like your own neighbourhood.

AG: Yeah.

Howie: You can rob them because you know the next day you're not going to see him walking down your road or at your front door.

AG: Okay but you wouldn't define these young people as gangs, you'd define them as friends, yeah, like you said, friends from certain areas?

Mike: Yeah.

Howie: Mates like in a group you know what I mean, if f***king, if they're all living in the same area they're going to be mates.

Michael: Because it's not really a postcode war it's basically more like. Mates in groups.

Howie: If you come to my area then basically you just rob someone.

AG: And there is no comeback.

Howie: Exactly. More times they don't know who robbed them.

Whilst official youth risk discourses view gangs as inherently pathological, drawing on my biographical experiences and perspectives of its research subjects this author maintains that Road life and gangs are normal and largely positive developments in young people's lives. As such this study is greatly sympathetic to Thrasher's (1927) understanding of gangs and more generally the Chicago School approach that emphasises the normality of 'deviance' by explaining it in 'its cultural and community context in opposition to seeing it as a pathological condition'. (Blackman, 2014:498).

Understanding urban youth violence

In attempting to examine both the causes and preventative solutions to urban youth violence criminologists and sociologists have been attracted to subcultural theories and identities linked to street gangs (Klein, 1995; Decker and Weerman, 2005; Pitts, 2008; Densley, 2013) territoriality (Kintrea et al., 2008) or retaliation/'code of the street' (see Anderson, 1999; Gunter, 2008; Brookman et al., 2011; Parkes and Conolly, 2012). This is not surprising given that 'one of the attractions of the concept of subculture is its power to define and describe deviant behaviour in society' (Blackman, 2014:507). Within this study discourses around territoriality and the code of the street in conjunction with other neighbourhood factors – linked to poverty, worklessness, poor educational attainment, homelessness and overcrowding – provide better analyses for youth violence than do those that fixate on the escalation of youth gangs and their associated hyper violent youth cultures (Pitts, 2008).

Responses from the young people about the causes of crime and youth violence included bad parenting, lack of youth centres, poverty, the media, status and peer pressure – trying to emulate the badness (and the neighbourhood respect that comes with it) and reputations of older siblings and peers:

AG: So you think more youth clubs would help reduce crime in the area?

Rafi: It'll be good for the little kids, because little kids are getting influenced by the older kids … because for the little one's basically there's nothing happening in Dungle. I remember when there was youth clubs.

Karl: Even I used to go to a youth club, and when the youth club stopped everyone needed somewhere to hang out.

AG: Yeah.

Rafi: Yeah, so basically for younger kids, because younger kids have nowhere to go they go with their older brother and go out. Basically just his being with him and his friends, that's it and then I know my other cousin he was 12 and he used to carry a gun.

AG: Yeah.

Rafi: And when I found out I just slapped him up got it off him and threw it in the bin.

AG: So you think peer pressure is a big factor?

Santi: Yeah cos its like, all this badness and robbery ting that they're on, I think it's because like the young ones they're looking to the elders isn't it, like and they see what the elders do, so like they just following the footsteps, some of them don't need to do this ting because like they do have houses and things like that but I think they just do it because of the peer pressure really you know what I mean.

Whilst some young people felt that peer pressure was a key factor with regards youth violence and crime in the neighbourhood, many participants talked about the need to have 'back up' or the protection that comes from 'moving' in a big group of friends:

Jamila: I think that some people don't know what the meaning of gangs are. Like, because gangs might mean a little group of friends.

AG: Do you know anyone that's been part of gangs at all?

Jamila: I think my brother has probably been involved but I don't really know. Like he's older now but like when he was younger he always used to get in trouble and stuff like that. And like when I was younger I used to get bullied by this girl at primary school and he [brother] kind of ended up having an argument with her older brother and so it kind of didn't help him. And then he would be telling his friends and stuff moved on from there. So yes.

Saraya: Three of my cousins, they are involved in gangs but not like the sort of gangs where the police think they are going to do crime, like just a gang, but like a big group of friends hanging around.

Jamila: Yes, if someone says they are involved in a gang it's like they just want to be involved just so they know that if something goes wrong they have their back and they are going to help them.

The viewpoints of these young participants echo the arguments of Waller (1932:180) who in his discussion of Thrasher's classic study which asserts that 'the gang makes an indispensable contribution to personality, and a contribution which adults sometimes overlook' (Blackman, 2014:498).

Conclusion

Contemporary media-driven discourses about urban youth tend to be focussed upon crime and anti-social behaviour, with their subcultures seen as the driving force behind gang related violence and crime. According to the popular media (and police) and some gang academics, the negative influence of Black Atlantic popular musical forms such as 'gangsta rap' have negatively impacted upon the Road based subcultures of young people growing up in 'low status urban areas' (Hope, 1996) stigmatised by crime, poverty and immigration. Rather than focussing upon the acute social and economic disadvantage faced by young people (and their families), media and gang academic discourses instead are fixated with gangs, guns and knives and the continuing racialisation and criminalisation of urban youth subcultures.

This chapter maintains that in spite of those broader problems associated with stigmatised poor urban neighbourhoods, Road based subculture plays a largely positive role in their lives. There are real risks and dangers associated with Road life in the neighbourhood linked to violence and robbery. This chapter opposes John Pitts' (2008:4) argument that youth subcultures in Britain have changed irrevocably for the worst and created a 'proliferation of violent youth gangs'. Within the research sites featured in this study at least, robbery and associated youth violence – a genuine risk, although not the dominating feature, of Road life – was caused by a complex combination of factors including poverty, media reporting, peer pressure and the glorification of 'badness' within the urban music based styles, aesthetics and attitudes of contemporary Road youth culture (see Gunter, 2010). Lastly, it is important to remember that whilst contemporary debates about violent urban youth crime seem new, they in fact should be viewed as a continuation of longstanding populist crises about feral/delinquent/hooligan/ undisciplined/unsupervised poor, working class and black youth (Mays, 1954; Cohen, 1972; Pearson, 1983; Hall et al., 1978; Keith, 1993).

Glossary

Back up: where a young person can call on the physical support of friends, neighbourhood peers or family members where there is/has been threat of violence.

Badness: refers to a social world characterised by 'spectacular' hyper aggressive/ hypermasculine modes of behaviour, usually centring around violent/ petty crime and low level drug-dealing.

Beats: instrumental music tracks produced by young people themselves or taken from an already existing piece of recorded music.

Beef: where a young person (or group of young people) has a dispute or argument with another young person or group.

Bowling: a slow rhythmic and confident style of walking adopted by young males.

'Bring it' or 'Move to': where a group of young men violently assault a smaller group of young men (or an individual).

'Bus joke' or 'Catching joke': where young people relay humorous stories and situations back to each other, talk about girls or boys and generally 'diss' (name calling/mickey taking) each other.

Garms: refers to clothes/dress wear.

'Kicking ball': playing football .

'Kotch' or 'Chillin'': to sit down and relax/stay in one place as opposed to 'passing through'.

Linking Yats: sexual liaisons between young men and young women – more than just friends but less than girl/boyfriends. In this instance Yats refers to young women.

On the endz: where a young person is referring to being in their own neighbourhood.

OTF: refers to phrase 'only the fam' (family), fam/family here relates to a close group of neighbourhood peers/friends.

Pass through: visiting a place but not intending to stay for very long.

Swagger: confidence and style when 'kotching' or moving about the neighbourhood.

'Spitting' or MC ing: to rap song lyrics via use of rhythmic word flow and rhyming techniques.

Notes

1 All names referred to throughout this chapter, including participants and places are pseudonyms
2 UK Urban music might be referred to as the 'politically correct', and somewhat controversial , term for all contemporary music of black origin and incorporates black Atlantic (Gilroy, 1993a) forms such as Hip Hop, modern RnB, and Bashment as well as UK forms like Grime, Funky House and Dubstep.
3 Here, badness refers to a social world characterised by hyper-aggressive/hyper-masculine modes of behaviour, and might involve fraud, violent crime, and low-level drug dealing.

References

Alderson, A. (2010) Violent inner-city crime, the figures, and a question of race.The reality of violent inner-city crime is indicated today by statistics obtained by *The Sunday Telegraph*. *Sunday Telegraph*, 26 June 2010.

Alexander, C. (2000) *The Asian Gang: Ethnicity, Identity, Masculinity.* Oxford: Berg.

Anderson, E. (1990) *Street Wise: Race, Class, and Change in an Urban Community.* Chicago, IL and London: The University of Chicago Press.

Anderson, E. (1999) *Code of the Street: Decency, Violence, and the Moral Life of the Inner City.* New York and London: Norton.

BBC TV News (2010) David Cameron's plan to fix 'broken Britain'. Available at: http://news.bbc.co.uk/1/hi/uk_politics/8596877.stm.

BBC *Panorama* (2012) Trouble on the Estate! http://www.youtube.com/watch?v=0Sm5VSo43JM, 21 November 2014. [Accessed 15/1/12.]

Bentham, M. (2014) London gang members committ 6600 crimes including 24 murders in three years. *London Evening Standard*, 12 March 2014.

Blackman, S. (2005) Youth Subcultural Theory: a critical engagement with the concept, its origins and politics, from the Chicago School to postmodernism. *Journal of Youth Studies* 8: 1–20.

Blackman, S. (2014) Subculture Theory: an historical and contemporary assessment of the concept for understanding deviance. *Deviant Behavior* 35: 496–512.

Blackman, S. and Wilson, A. (2014) Psychotic (e)states: where anti-social behaviour is merged with recreational drug use to signify the social problem group. In: S. Pickard (ed.) *Anti-social Behaviour in Britain: Victorian and Contemporary Perspectives.* London: Palgrave, 285–295.

Bose, M. (2003) 'Race' and class in the 'post-subcultural' economy. In: D. M. a. R. Weinzierl (ed.) *The Post-Subcultures Reader.* Oxford: Berg, 167–180.

Bourdieu, P. (1992) The practice of reflexive sociology (the Paris Workshop). In: P. Bourdieu and L. J. D. Wacquant *An Invitation to Reflexive Sociology.* London: University of Chicago Press, 217–260.

Brookman, F., Bennett, T., Hochstetler, A. and Copes, H. (2011) The 'code of the street' and the generation of street violence in the UK. *European Journal of Criminology* 8: 17–31.

Cohen, S. (1972) *Folk Devils and Moral Panics: The Creation of Mods and Rockers.* London: MacGibbon & Kee.

Cohen, P. and Ainley, P. (2000) In the Country of the Blind?: Youth studies and cultural studies in Britain. *Journal of Youth Studies* 3 (1): 79–95.

Coles, B., England, J. and Rugg, J. (2000) Spaced out? Young people on social housing estates: social exclusion and multi-agency work. *Journal of Youth Studies* 3: 21–33.

Corrigan, P. (1979) *Schooling the Smash Street Kids.* London: Macmillan.

Decker, S. H. and Weerman, F. M. (2005) *European Street Gangs and Troublesome Youth Groups.* London: AltaMira Press.

Densley, J. (2013) *How Gangs Work: An Ethnography of Youth Violence.* London: Palgrave Macmillan.

Downes, D. (1966) *The Delinquent Solution: A Study in Sub-cultural Theory.* London: Routledge and Kegan Paul.

Earle, R. (2011) Boys' zone stories: perspectives from a young men's prison. *Criminology & Criminal Justice* 11: 129–143.

Evans, K., Fraser, P. and Watlake, S. (1996) Whom can you trust? The politics of 'grassing' on an inner city housing estate. *The Sociological Review* 44(3): 361–380.

Fetterman, D. (1998) *Ethnography: Step by Step.* London: Sage Publications.

Gidley, B. (2007) Youth culture and ethnicity: emerging youth interculture in South London. In: P. Hodkinson and W. Deicke (eds) *Youth Cultures: Scenes, Subcultures and Tribes.* Abimgdon: Routledge, 145–160.

Glynn, M. (2014) *Black Men, Invisibility, and Desistance from Crime: Towards a Critical Race Theory from Crime.* London: Routledge.

Gunter, A. (2008) Growing up bad: black youth, road culture and badness in an East London neighbourhood. *Crime Media Culture* 4: 349–365.

Gunter, A. (2010) *Growing Up Bad: Black Youth, Road Culture and Badness in an East London Neighbourhood.* London: The Tufnell Press.

Hall, S., Crichter, C., Jefferson, T., Clarke, J. and Roberts, B. (1978) *Policing the Crisis: Mugging, the State and Law and Order.* London: Macmillan.

Hallsworth, S. and Silverstone, D. (2009) 'That's life innit': a British perspective on guns, crime and social order. *Criminology & Criminal Justice: An International Journal* 9: 359–377.

Hastings, C. (2011) 'White chavs have become black': David Starkey TV outburst provokes race row as he claims Enoch Powell was right. *Daily Mail* [14/8/11].

HM Government Department for Communities and Local Government (2010) English Indices of Deprivation 2010. Available at: http://data.gov.uk/dataset/index-of-multiple-deprivation. [Accessed 2/10/2013.]

HM Government (2011) Ending Gang and Youth Violence: A Cross-Government Report including further evidence and good practice case studies. Available at: https://www.gov.uk/government/uploads/system/uploads/attachment_data/file/97862/gang-violence-detailreport.pdf. [Accessed 5/12/2012.]

Hope, T. (1996) Communities, crime and inequality in England and Wales. In: T. Bennett (ed) *Preventing Crime and Disorder: Targeting Strategies and Responsibilities.* Cambridge: University of Cambridge Press, 215–235

Ilan, J. (2012) The industry's the new road: crime, commodification and street cultural tropes in UK urban music. *Crime Media Culture* 8: 39–55.

Keith, M. (1993) *Race, Riots and Policing.* London: UCL Press.

Kintrea, K., Bannister, J., Pickering, J., Reid, M. and Suzuki, N. (2008) *Young People and Territoriality in British Cities.* London: Joseph Rowntree Foundation.

Klein, W. (1995) *The American Street Gang: Its Nature, Prevalence, and Control.* Oxford: Oxford University Press

Landolt, S. (2012) Co-productions of neighbourhood and social identity by young men living in an urban area with delinquent youth cliques. *Journal of Youth Studies* 16: 628–645.

Lieber, M. (1976) 'Liming' and other concerns: the style of street embedments in Port-Of-Spain, Trinidad. *Urban Anthropology* 5: 319–333.

Liebow, E. (1967) *Tally's Corner: A Study of Negro Street-Corner Men.* Boston, MA: Little Brown & Co.

MacDonald, R. and Shildrick, T. (2007) Street corner society: leisure careers, youth (sub) culture and social exclusion. *Leisure Studies* 26: 339–355.

Mays, J. B. (1954) *Growing Up in the City: A Study of Juvenile Delinquency in an Urban Neighbourhood.* Liverpool: Liverpool University Press.

McCarthy-Brown, K. (2001) *Mama Lola: A Vodou Priestess in Brooklyn.* London: University of California Press.

McCulloch, K., Stewart, A. and Lovegreen, N. (2006) 'We just hang out together': youth cultures and social class. *Journal of Youth Studies* 9: 539–556.

Mills, C. W. (1959) *The Sociological Imagination.* New York: Oxford University Press.

Nayak, A. (2003) *Race, Place and Globalization: Youth Cultures in a Changing World.* Oxford: Berg.

Neary, J., Egan, M., Keenan, P. J., Lawson, L. and Bond, L. (2012) Damned if they do, damned if they don't: negotiating the tricky context of anti-social behaviour and keeping safe in disadvantaged urban neighbourhoods. *Journal of Youth Studies* 16: 118–134.

Office for National Statistics (2012) Ethnicity and National Identity in England and Wales in 2011. Available at: http://www.ons.gov.uk/ons/rel/census/2011-census/key-statistics-for-local-authorities-in-england-and-wales/rpt-ethnicity.html. [Accessed 14/11/2014.]

Parker, H. (1974) *View From The Boys.* London: David and Charles.

Parkes, J. and Conolly, A. (2011) Risky positions? Shifting representations of urban youth in the talk of professionals and young people. *Children's Geographies* 9: 411–423.

Parkes, J. and Conolly, A. (2012) Dangerous encounters? Boys' peer dynamics and neighbourhood risk. *Discourse: Studies in the Cultural Politics of Education* 34: 94–106.

Pearson, G. (1983) *Hooligan: A History of Respectable Fears.* London: Macmillan.

Pitts, J. (2008) *Reluctant Gangsters: The Changing Face of Youth Crime.* Cullompton: Willan Publishing.

Reay, D. and Lucey, H. (2000) I don't really like it here but I don't wan't to be anywhere else: children and inner city council estates *Antipode*, 32: 410–428.

Sanders, B. (2005) *Youth Crime and Youth Culture in the Inner City.* London Routledge.

Sansone, L. (2003) *Blackness without Ethnicity: Constructing Race in Brazil.* Basingstoke: Palgrave MacMillan.

Shildrick, T. (2006) Youth culture, subculture and the importance of neighbourhood. *YOUNG: Nordic Journal of Youth Research* 14: 61–74.

Smithson, H., Ralphs, R. and Williams, P. (2013) Used and abused: the problematic usage of gang terminology in the United Kingdom and its implications for ethnic minority youth. *British Journal of Criminology* 53: 113–128.

Stolzoff, N. (2000) *Wake the Town and Tell the People: Dancehall Culture in Jamaica.* Durham and London: Duke University Press.

Taylor, I., Evans, K. and Fraser, P. (1996) *A Tale of Two Cities: A Study in Manchester and Sheffield.* London: Routledge.

Thrasher, F. (1927/2013) *The Gang: A Study of 1313 Gangs in Chicago.* Chicago, IL: University of Chicago Press.

Vertovec, S. (2007) New Complexities of Cohesion in Britain: Super-Diversity, Transnationalism an Civil Integration. Commision on Integration and Cohesion. Available at: http://www.compas.ox.ac.uk/fileadmin/files/Publications/Reports/Vertovec-new_complexities_of_cohesion_in_britain.pdf. [Accessed 21/10/2014].

Watt, P. and Stenson, K. (1998) The street: it's a bit dodgy around there: safety, danger, ethnicity and young people's use of public space. In: T. S. a. G. Valentine (ed.) *Cool Places: Geographies of Youth Cultures.* London: Routledge, 249–265.

Young, T., Fitzgibbon, W. and Silverstone, D. (2013) The role of the family in facilitating gang membership, criminality and exit. A report prepared for Catch22-Dawes Unit. London: London Metropolitan University. Available at: http://www.catch-22.org.uk/wp-content/uploads/2013/11/Catch22-Dawes-Unit-The-role-of-the-family-summary-June-2013.pdf. [Accessed 02/11/2013.]

Part II
Practising reflexivity in the field

4 The emotional imagination

Exploring critical ventriloquy and emotional edgework in reflexive sociological ethnography with young people

Shane Blackman

Introduction: setting out the emotional imagination

The aim of this chapter is to introduce the concept of the emotional imagination and to explore C. Wright Mills' notion that the craft of the discipline and biographical experience are connected in the construction of sociological theory. At the centre of the emotional imagination is the researcher's feeling and response to achieve Geertz's (1973: 14) objective of a 'thick description'. The researcher's emotional imagination is shaped through participatory research and the demands of immediate fieldwork action, informed by biography, experience, literature and researcher training. Through four ethnographic examples from different studies of young people in subcultures, this chapter seeks to explore the ideas of critical ventriloquy and emotional edgework to support the development of the emotional imagination in sociology. It takes up C. Wright Mills' (1959: 216) argument that life experience is intimately connected to the methodological craft and 'is the centre of yourself' as you move between 'two contexts' (244) fieldwork and writing, to discover 'the combination of ideas that no one expected were combinable' (233). I use data drawn from a range of published ethnographic studies on young people in subcultures across different research sites (Blackman 1997, 1998, 2007, Blackman and Commane 2012). Marcus (1998) and Abu-Lughod (2000: 264) advance the case of the 'multi-sited research imaginary' in ethnography – i.e. looking across a number of studies – not just to generate new knowledge, but, as Hine (2007: 656) argues, to craft 'a research object specifically designed to engage in a particular argument'. The emotional imagination can be seen as part of the new reflexivity where the researcher locates themselves in the research context, and offers an account of the feeling and play of interaction that explains how data was generated, selected and theorised.

Participant observation, craft, reflexivity and researcher positionality

What has sustained C. Wright Mills' methodological contribution to the craft of sociology is the way he lived out his biographical practice through his professional critiques of contemporary sociologists of the day. As a result, Brewer (2004: 330) notes *The Sociological Imagination* has benefited from 'being seen as a methodological framework for critique'. The combination of craft and critique releases the imagination to develop sociological theory, and the generation of this theory is to be situated in biography, history and social structure. What C. Wright Mills (1959: 216) describes as the importance of learning to use 'life experience' alongside academic work is based on 'the sociologist's need for systematic reflection'. He talks about the craft capturing your experience and grasping biography. The data in this chapter explores Mills' tension between the researchers' personal relationships with their participants and the demands of sociological objectivity in qualitative fieldwork. From its beginning, participant observation has been focused on 'live sociology', as C. Wright Mills (1959: 14) put it, for the purpose of 'astonishment'. The formal methodological practice of participant observation began, according to I. C. Jarvie (1969: 505), 'in May 1915 when Bronislaw Malinowski pitched his tent at Omarakana in the Trobriand Islands and set about learning the local language'. At the same time, Robert Park (1915) outlined the Chicago School's naturalistic urban research manifesto to observe the city (Hart 2010). Abbott (1999: 15) argues that Park was 'a descendent of the Malionwskian fieldwork tradition' who also championed biographical and reportage methods, for example Thomas and Znaniecki's (1918–21) *The Polish Peasant* and Shaw's (1930) *The Jack-Roller*. The Chicago School produced some classic ethnography, from Anderson's (1923) study of hobohemia to Becker's (1951, 1953) focus on jazz musicians and marijuana, which brought 'real life' to methodology through subjective and cultural proximity (Hodkinson 2005: 131). These studies attained canonical status within sociology through their popular concern with 'lived experience', yet in the process of writing biographic and subjective narratives their authors tended to render themselves largely invisible (Bennett 2002: 464).

The call for an increased personal stance in research has enabled the development of a responsive sociology (Bourdieu and Wacquant 1992). The emphasis on reflexivity has created new opportunities for ethnography to focus on locality, multiple voices, participation and exchange, dialogue, emotion, involvement and biography. Denzin and Lincoln (1998) confirm that the reflexive turn and its consequent challenge to the notion of objectivity has created the chance for ethnographers to write the self into the text. One consequence of the reflexive turn is increased preoccupation with the researcher. Coffey (1999: 115) notes that this approach is always personal, because the 'ethnographer serves as a biographer of others'. Hammersley and Atkinson (2007: 205) are advocates for increased reflexivity but they caution us not to 'put the ethnographer's self ahead of the others about whom she or he writes'. Pillow (2010: 272) notes: 'When objectivity became open to question, the researcher's subjectivity also became open to scrutiny.' The reflexive turn can provide increased validity and enable the researcher to place themselves within the text to avoid accusations of 'hidden ethnography' to show the ethical responsibility of their own subjectivity (Blackman 2007).

In sociology, reflexivity has brought new challenges. Clough (1992: 13) argues that 'the struggle for identity is complicated by the desire to correct history, to correct already authorised representations of empirical reality, that is, the desire to authorise another reality'. Previously, the canon had claimed authority over other people's culture and experience on the basis of privileged access, yet the voice of the colonised was absent. Coffey (1999:129) describes this corrective action as 'restoring a voice' now the new reflexivity demands openness and awareness of stance so that the researcher specifies their positionality (Savin-Baden and Howell Major 2013: 68–69). Trying to capture the researcher's commitment and influence is what C. Wright Mills saw as the promise of sociology to explain the craft, to understand how a text is constructed in relation to the subjectivity of the researcher (Letherby 2003: 8). William Foote Whyte (1943/55: 359) was one of the first sociologists to break the academic imposed 'conspiracy of silence regarding the personal experiences of field workers'. He notes further: 'It was impossible to find realistic accounts that revealed the error and confusions and the personal involvements.' Whyte participated in a range of different illegal activities and yet has been given the 'status of a sociological classic'. Laud Humphrey's (1970) *Tearoom Trade*, won the prestigious *C. Wright Mills Award of the Society for the Study of Social Problems* and yet it has been denounced frequently for its unethical invasion of privacy (O'Reilly (2005: 19–21). The different reception of both Whyte and Humphrey's work demonstrate that participant observation studies create what Polsky (1967: 138) calls, 'guilty knowledge', where the ethnographer participates in what is described by Hobbs (2001: 211) as a 'thin facade of normality'.

In order to gain reflexivity it is sometimes assumed that the observer has to become part of the group. Miller and Tewksbury (2010: 493) argue: 'Edge ethnographers share the ideological viewpoints of subject groups and justify their activities, including criminal behaviour, as part of the risk of going native.' Pearson (2009: 249) claims in his study of football hooligans 'I was accepted' within the group as a result of committing 'minor offences' (246) earning the label 'a bit of a nutter'. Yet for Hunter S. Thompson (1966: 283) researcher positionality focused on desperation: 'The heavy boots were punching into my ribs and jolting my head.' That in turn brought fieldwork to its conclusion, via his admission to the Santa Rosa hospital. Jackson (2004: 41) in his study of sex parties states: 'Hands wander up skirts and into waistbands. A lascivious mambo of desiring bodies getting off on themselves and the presence of others. I'm getting my cock sucked: it's hot, giggly fun and I relax into it.' Here positionality may enhance the researcher's self-image, promotes an exotic myth and reveal the danger and excitement of fieldwork, which blend together the researcher's self and the participant's narrative. These examples support Taylor's (2011: 9) assertion that ethnographic research 'involves a degree of, or may even be called a type of, autoethnography'. She emphasises there are limitations to reflexivity and it is not without its critics. Amanda Coffey (1999: 125) argues that the issue is 'whether these personalised accounts constitute ethnographic writing' or whether they are 'self-indulgent writings published under the guise of social research and ethnography' (155). Gray (2008: 948) warns, we have to guard against the way that researcher positionality can 'turn research itself and the knowledge of informants into a possession of the researcher self, thus appropriating epistemological authority to the researcher'. Meanwhile, Letherby, Scott and Williams (2013: 91) assert that reflexivity is not 'a substitute for objectivity'. For sociology the key to advancing researcher positionality and reflexivity is to guard against becoming what we have already criticised (Karakayali 2004: 361). Furthermore, Bourdieu and his co-authors (1999) warned of the necessity to not collapse into subjectivism. Positionality is about how researchers locate themselves in relation to participants, and how relationships are formed that demonstrate honesty and openness. The emotional imagination highlights the individual response of the researcher to show an awareness of feeling at multiple levels.

Critical ventriloquy: theory

In sociology ventriloquism is often negatively defined, as a form of voice throwing generally understood as speaking on behalf of people on the basis that they have been metaphorically captured (Connor 2000). Within ethnography, ventriloquism has been critically addressed by Geertz (1988: 145) as 'the claim to speak not just about another form of life but to speak from within it; to represent'. Spivak's (1999: 28) concern is about the misrepresentation of marginalised people, specifically the subaltern, and how theorists claim that they are speaking for oppressed groups, which amounts to a form of ventriloquism. Bridges (2001: 381) understands ventriloquism as a form of 'temptation' 'using the voice of the participant to give expression to the things, which the researcher wants to say or to have said'. Thus, ventriloquism could be described as an illusion of listening because the data collected affirms the theory already upheld by the social researcher. For Back (2009: 5) ventriloquism is an act of violation that prevents critical dialogue, which fetishizes the power of the ethnographer resulting in Haraway's (1992: 301) concern that participants' voices are 'permanently speechless. Forever requiring the services of a ventriloquist.' Fine (1994a: 17) argues that ventriloquism is an act that 'transmits' data and interpretation as neutral in an effort to remove a political or rhetorical stance. Here the researcher has removed themselves from the text; as Fine (1992: 214) notes, the researcher's 'interests are camouflaged'. Making oneself visible in fieldwork and the writing process is part of the reflexive challenge of sociological ethnography.

The theorists above focus on the problem of ventriloquism; in the following section I want to put forward critical ventriloquy as a mechanism to show the influence of the researcher and how the researcher may craft the ethnographic product. Griffiths (1998: 128) considers that ventriloquism is useful to address how the 'researcher chooses extracts from data which make her respondents appear to speak for themselves, but which are actually chosen to underpin her own perspectives. No one is suggesting that this can be avoided completely, of course. The point is how far the perspectives of the researcher are open to change and dissension in the voices she has collected.' Thus, when undertaking interpretation there is an active engagement with the different types of data, including observation, documents, interviews, participatory experiences, the field diary, gifts, story telling, meta data and commentary. Gwyn (2000: 317) understands this process of creating meaning through data as 'a collage of many voices, ventriloquized through the voice of the speaker'. Critical ventriloquy focuses on how selectivity within fieldwork data and interpretation occurs as the text is crafted by the researcher on the basis of a collage to represent the ethnographer's interpretation of the research participants' culture. It allows us to view the process of textual construction by the researcher and to raise questions about the dominant authority of the researcher. Thus, the starting point for critical ventriloquy is Geertz's (1988) idea of the 'ethnographer as author'. Critical ventriloquy addresses the degree of collaboration between the researcher and the researched. Ardoin, Gontarski and Mattison (2014: 5) suggest that there exists a 'creative ventriloquism' where the researcher has to be responsive. Camilla Damkjær (2005: 8) states that Gilles Deleuze's work on ventriloquy as having 'nothing to do with imitation or even reproduction'. She goes on to argue that: 'He does not deform the material, but he forms his own material by making the material speak in his own way. This happens both on the level of the content in his way of explaining the arguments, but also stylistically through a very subtle kind of style indirect libre. He becomes one with the material and yet transforms himself and the material into something else.' Sharlene Swartz suggests there is a possibility to speak for research participants, but it has to be achieved through dialogue, commitment and on the basis of building relationships during fieldwork. Swartz (20011: 49) argues that ethnography has to practise an 'intentional ethics of reciprocation … to give back ownership of knowledge and material benefits to those participating in research.' Through critical ventriloquy, the researcher explains how meaning is crafted in the text and overall. For D. Soyini Madison (2005: 7) ethnographers have to 'acknowledge our own power, privilege and biases just as we are denouncing the power structures that surround our research subjects'. In the next section I will explore two moments of critical ventriloquy – first letter writing with the youth 'underclass' and second the staging of an ethnographic play about homeless youth.

'Aggressive Beggars': ethnographic description of writing the letter

During my ethnographic study on young homeless and unemployed people in Brighton, I joined a group of twenty-two individuals who had been given the subcultural label 'youth underclass' by many residents in the town. I spent a year with them at the soup run, on street corners, playing football, on the beach, in cafes and pubs, at the park and at the 108 Arch on Brighton sea front. During the fieldwork, a letter appeared in the *Brighton Evening Argus* newspaper from a resident and former business person entitled: 'Aggressive Beggars'. The letter states: 'We need to rid the streets of Brighton of these dropouts' who are 'pestering the public', 'littering the pavement and hassling people for money and cigarettes'.

It concludes: 'They can be seen running after people until they get what they want ... for goodness sake will Brighton Council social services and the police give us a chance and clean the streets of these aggressive beggars.'

Reading the letter, the young homeless people were aggrieved. Their response was to write a letter in reply to send to the editor of the *Evening Argus*. Collectively, they argued that I should write the letter for them, stating: 'As Shane's from university he could write a good letter that would be published.' Alcoff (1992: 24) makes it clear that 'the practice of speaking for others remains the best (political) possibility in some existing situations'. In this circumstance the potential for ventriloquy was at its zenith, as I could be the spokesperson for the labelled youth 'underclass' and structure my words as their experience. However, after some considerable thought I declined the invitation to write the letter, and this hurt them. Initially, they felt hostile, even let down by my decision. However, I managed to convince them that if I wrote the letter the local paper would know the young homeless people did not produce it. Finally, they agreed and were pleased that I would check spellings and phrases. On this basis I did play a role in writing the letter but it was through facilitating the process and getting everyone to talk about the issues. The letter of reply galvanised all the young people to express views, assert themselves and to be vocal in a political sense, which was not the type of response that was familiar to them. The letter of reply focused on their limited resources, and the difficulty of finding accommodation. It concluded: 'If you see anyone of us on the street please do not turn your nose up at us. Have a heart and talk to us. We're not "layabouts" we are HUMAN BEINGS without a home.'

During the ethnography I arranged discussions. It became evident that the young homeless had the motivation to 'put something together' as a result of becoming aware of how others labelled them. The act of writing the letter brought my personal feelings close to the surface and at a micro level, as C. Wright Mills (1959: 205) notes, research became a political matter: where there was a sharing of 'personal troubles' which became understood as 'public issues' within their everyday milieu. Within the 108 Arch arguments were weighed up as individuals engaged in shouting and reflection. Through participant observation I experienced cultural slippage in the sense described by Stan Cohen (1979) in *The Last Seminar*. Inside the arch, being in charge of a heated discussion with homeless and unemployed young people on the topic of the 'underclass', I keenly felt the dangers of ventriloquism and misrepresentation. Practicing reflexive fieldwork in sociology can lead to serious self-examination. As C. Wright Mills (1959: 216) saw, 'You must learn to use your life experience in your intellectual work.' I was not co-ordinating a university seminar on poverty; I was directly in the midst of inequality and personal hardship. The real impact of writing the letter was to give confidence to certain individuals in turn motivating them to gain employment, secure better housing or a place on a college course through the development of a non-deviant attitude. The key features here are craft and critique, which enabled the letter to be a mediating voice that was both individual and collective, and reached an external power. Through my intervention, participants were taking up C. Wright Mills (1959: 235) notion of 'thinking of the opposite': on the one hand the letter writing gave them temporary solidarity and confidence, but on the other hand they had experienced physical attacks and had been labelled as an 'underclass' subculture. During the fieldwork I was a mediator, where critical ventriloquy took the form of listening and challenging their attitudes, which to a limited extent encouraged their thinking to interrogate culture, authority and produce the letter.

Ethnographic play

The next example of critical ventriloquy comes from an ethnographic study of youth homelessness in Kent commissioned by Medway City Authority who organised a research forum to share information from the report with practitioners and policy makers. The guest speaker was John Bird, founder of *The Big Issue* newspaper. To start things off, unknown to me, the research Steering Committee decided to use the ethnographic conversations in the report to construct a play – acted out by young people from a local secondary school. Here critical ventriloquy was taken to a different level with theatrical performance, a stage, costumes and an audience. The words of the research participants via the ethnographer were given a new trajectory in terms of public presentation. Certain professionals from the local authority were negative about the theatrical event as 'something rather unusual' even superfluous, before the 'proper policy based discussion'. The audience watched intently as the young people spoke the ethnographic dialogue. At the end of the play the young people gained a standing ovation. Some council leaders, social service professionals and staff from charities were in tears, hugging each other or drying their eyes. Tim, a Housing Officer, said: 'What this brought home is how close it was for me when I was that age. It could have been my life they were performing up there.' Brenda, a senior social worker, commented:

> Shane's report said it like it really is – painted it real – and now with the play it has had a double impact and I have to look at how I am responding to my own teenage daughter and son, not just the young people I have responsibility for in my professional life.

The surprise act of presenting the ethnographic play meant I was not prepared. If this idea had been built into the research project, I would have been aware of the potential for the ventriloquist act of directly putting words in to the mouths of mediators who acted out the characterisation of homeless young people. In another example, Mark Peel (2011: 4) has used social work case files of the 1920s and 1930s from different cities in the USA to create a dramatised script, refashioning real-life stories of people's experience of poverty from the perspective of clients and caseworkers. Although his approach is on a larger scale, the key idea is that through drama and dialogue a humanistic value can be attached to 'the voices, perspectives and knowledge of poor people themselves'.

Critical ventriloquy highlights the degree of mediation involved in the construction of the young homeless voice, which affirms Gilles Deleuze understanding of the material, and its transformations into something else. The play did not offer a complete picture of the research subjects' perspective but it did represent a partial moment in their lives, which had a positive impact on the practitioners and professional staff who were able to reflect on the implementation of policies. John Bird summed it up: 'It was harrowing – the real deal. Great idea.' Putting the words of the young homeless into a script was a difficult and emotional experience for me because during the fieldwork it was found that they did not consider that their voice and experience were of value. Therefore, the stage production of the play took ventriloquy to a different level. The example of the play highlights a critical issue raised by Michelle Fine (1994b: 70) who states: 'I want to hear your story. And then I will tell it back to you in a new way … I am still author, authority. I am still the colonizer.' In other words, we have to avoid the research participants being reduced to the puppets of the theorist. For Letherby, Scott and Williams (2013: 91) it is the researchers' story which can stand in opposition to, and as a criticism of, other stories. In this case the research led to a series of policy outcomes to tackle the question of youth homelessness within the region. By staging the play the Steering Committee of the project saw the attraction and potential impact of the ethnographic data to influence policy makers. The committee told me that the play was undertaken as 'praise for producing such a realistic account'. There was good intention here but ultimately the voices of the young homeless garnered through trust were now mediated within a different setting and context into 'something different'.

Emotional edgework: theory

Here I will explore my emotional imagination as a sociological researcher through developing the idea of emotional edgework. Bringing together emotion and edgework follows C. Wright Mills (1959: 23) notion of 'considering extremes – by thinking of opposites'. As a conceptual idea, 'edgework' was first developed by Stephen Lyng (1990) and (2005). He points out (1990: 4–5) that edgework theory emerged alongside the conceptualisation of risk taking experiences, where his aim was to use edgework to connect with 'social structures' and demonstrate how an individual can develop 'self-determination' and 'confidence'. Early on edgework theory was criticised not only for its masculine and middle class preoccupation with leisured risk but also for failing to recognise its gender bias. Batchelor (2007: 23) argues, edgework is 'a means to block out powerful emotions' where white males undertake extreme leisure based activities, and become in, Jennifer Lois' (2003: 181) words, 'emotional cool'. Sociology still remains suspicious of the emotions, but with the growth of reflexivity and research positionality it has become identified as offering illumination on the subjective experience (Flam and Kleres 2015: 23). C. Wright Mills (1959:69) grasped this early on to suggest, 'The creative process is so closely tied in with the emotional structure of an individual.' Being emotionally receptive in ethnographic fieldwork is desirable and emotional edgework can hold the opportunity to channel rather than suppress feelings. Burkitt (2012: 459) demands that we 'put emotions back into the context of social interactions and relationships'. The aim here is to build on Stanley and Wise's (1993: 10) understanding of emotion and subjectivity as something constructive and meaningful, to put forward a realistic account of the politics of fieldwork and interpretation. In this sense emotional edgework is one way to rethink, in Alison Jaggar's (1989: 157) words, where reason and emotion are 'mutually constitutive rather than oppositional'. I want to suggest that emotional edgework could operate within a feminist analysis, in situations of high emotion and intense feeling. The two different examples below explore the personal sensitivities of participants in challenging encounters for the researcher's emotional imagination.

Terry – the ethnographic challenge of love and hate

I have selected the case study of Terry from the ethnography of homeless young people because he was part of a subcultural group who engaged in violence. The fieldwork with Terry could be described as 'live sociology' because it supports Lyng's (1990: 858–9) idea whereby the ethnographer directly engages in, or is exposed to encounters where there is an 'observable threat to one's physical or mental well being'. During fieldwork I felt simultaneously depressed, scared and thrilled. Knowing Terry's previous subcultural activities from social workers did not lessen the strain and anxiety of establishing an empathetic relationship with a violent person. I felt worried, ashamed and confused because I was establishing rapport with an aggressor. Lyng (2005: 196) argues that each 'situation requires one to be engaged in a manner that enables one to "feel" the situation in contrast merely to cognitively knowing it'. My professional research training wanted to maintain distance; more immediately my feelings were geared towards my own safety. Two months after our first meetings I received an invitation to go and see Terry, in his new flat. He welcomed me and we spent 20 minutes talking about the new place and the neighbourhood with his girlfriend Holly, but then she left to go shopping with her mother. Terry stated: 'Now! I've had some problems':

> Beating people up is an effective way of stopping things. You put your point across by smashing a bloke's jaw in. This Kevin, he was coming round here, it was really getting on me wick, his comments and such. It had to stop. So I hit him in the face with the end of the snooker cue, you can see where the blood went, all – there [pointing out the location of the blood] still a little bit on the wall and splatters on lid of the blanket box. Blood everywhere. That calmed him down. It stopped the problem. It was pucka!

Terry was becoming animated and then he showed me his secret armoury of knives. I began to feel ill at ease when he demonstrated their proficiency by slashing at the table. Thankfully, as quickly as it had started, it stopped. He began to talk about problems in his family. He felt that people never listened to him. Terry's action corroborated Fenwick and Hayward's (2000: 49) finding that through transgressive acts young deviants 'come alive', and through telling their stories young people generate an original excitement, which the ethnographer can understand and channel. The setting enabled the participant to gain control, to create a sense of self through reflection. This can be unsettling for the ethnographer and unpalatable for those involved in the original act (Peterson 2000:190). After a light lunch of a couple of rounds of toast, Terry brought out a crushed box that held some of his drawings and paintings; he also read some of the poems on love, tragedy, confusion and life without his mother. The artwork was accomplished and I encouraged him to think of Art School to develop his talent. Terry was a little surprised at my suggestion, which he received with a smile. He said: 'Come on, you know I hate the idea of going to school!' He was also sceptical because nobody else had encouraged him before. We spent all day together and he felt sad when it was early evening and I had to leave, but he concluded: 'This has really been fun Shane, all the stuff we've talked about.' We parted on a positive note.

Ethnography can make a difference in people's lives, due to its highly personal tone, yet failure to see its limitations can bring about false expectations. Winlow, Hobbs, Lister and Hadfield (2001: 537) caution against 'losing oneself in edgework'. They affirm that ethnography is not to be undertaken in terms of thrill seeking. I had built a strong emotional relationship with Terry. He was prepared to be open and discuss his vulnerabilities and creative ideas but access to this came with a heavy emotional investment. Here emotional edgework as a fieldwork strategy crossed-over with 'situated ethics' which was unsettling for myself in terms of posing physical danger and being upsetting. Our relationship demonstrated that the researcher and the participant can share moments but at the same time experience very different feelings or understandings within the same research encounter.

Virginity note

Here emotional edgework is applied in a different context where a male ethnographer and a female research participant engaged in discussion on personal intimate sexual experiences. Here the researcher's ethnographic imagination is influenced by the potential of embarrassment. The questions and issues Sally put to me were a reflection of the intimacy that I had shared with this female subcultural group. In my ethnographic study of the new wave girls they were aged 15–16 and I was 22. Quite often I found that the subcultural and the academic could be shared – for example, the subcultural imagination between myself and the girls was interactive when together we saw The Cure live. Also, I went to jumble sales, pubs, gigs, all girl gatherings and parties with the girls (Blackman 2007). At one all-night party at a boyfriend's house, the new wave girls decided to demonstrate their emotional feelings. It had been an intense party in the company of ex-girl friends and ex-boy friends; some bitter words and looks spread throughout participants. A note from the field diary states: 'During the night sleeping arrangements changed on a number of occasions and at half past four in the morning the girls gathered in the sitting room.'

The girls began questioning each other in mock voices, asking each other, 'Have you had it yet?' They were screaming with laughter and making derogatory remarks about sexual behaviour in the spirit of fun. They were talking about oral sex, the stains on the sheets, 'being on' and farting, while laughing and acting crazy. The boy friends remained in the bedrooms. Tension mounted as the boys increased the volume of their guitars and music. The atmosphere was degenerating and then the girls decided it was time to leave on mass. One of the girls, Sally, wanted to leave but she lived the furthest away, so she asked me to walk her home. On reflection, I was aware as a male researcher there was a blurring of boundaries between friendships and being a researcher (Cotterill's (1992: 599) but due to the immediacy of the situation I was more focused on her safety. I had become accustomed to the girls' use of personal and collective space: we arrived together and we left together. A couple of the boys asked me to stay, but it came as no surprise that I left with the girls. The boyfriend's positive response towards me made me feel like a subcultural subject together with the new wave girls. The girls' invocation became a collective representation; here their reflexivity, as Holmes (2010:148) argues, 'can change participants' relations with others and change how they feel'. I had participated in, and observed, the girls in many intimate and challenging situations. Ethnography with the new wave girls was exciting and fun, but also challenging in terms of my own gender identity. I was often called upon to imagine myself as a girl! It was quite common for the different girls to ask 'What would you do?' How would you react?

The ethnographic diary reads: 'It was nearly six o'clock in the morning, with frost on the grass, coldness in the air, and as I walked along the coast road with Sally, she spelled out why it was good to leave just then.' She stated: 'Loudness, people half asleep, everyone shouting, it was all bad taste, nobody willing to be conversant, I'm really pissed off with it. Pissed off with them [her boyfriend.]' Sally gave me a note as we strolled; she said her boyfriend (Richard) had given her this piece of paper in the early morning, after they had slept together. I did not look at it straightaway because Sally was beginning to cry as she was telling me about her virginity, love, desire and Richard. She said:

> I feel it is important whom you give it to, whether they respect you. Perhaps in a few years' time, I might think, my virginity, I was really silly and stupid but at the moment it feels really important.

The message given to her had been cut out from a magazine, and read: 'The beauty and love of sleeping next to a woman without making love with her'. She began to smile and said further: 'I would have let him do it last night but the stupid sod did not have one [a condom], did he.' She concluded the message was 'really nice'.

In this the setting Sally felt in control to express her feelings, and I sought to reassure her. Fieldwork friendship between male researchers and young females can cause confusion in terms of sexual roles (Kulick and Willson 1995). As we walked, we chatted and we exchanged positions to talk about my virginity. She was not ashamed nor did she feel self-conscious talking about her virginity and sexual desire at that time when we were alone. For me as a young male researcher I had to be not embarrassed by the intimacy, and neither turn the situation to my advantage. I deliberately blended the researcher's sense of self with Sally's narrative, where emotional edgework framed our intimate talks, both amusing and serious, making reflexivity part of the emotional fun. Being allowed in to the girls' lives, I was in the middle of the blur between researcher friendship and friendship. She realised that my concern for her was because I cared as both researcher and friend. Simpson, Bloor and Fincham (2008: 925) insist we need to be aware of the 'associated emotional costs when researchers' internalise such values'. Through offering me the 'pocket ethnography' of the 'virginity note' Sally demonstrated how a male ethnographer could gain access to a female voice. Stuhmiller (2001: 78) states: 'Narrative research methods can exert a therapeutic effect because they have the strength, power and generative capacity to uncover and foster growth, possibility, and relatedness.' Here emotional edgework was used to gain personal intimacy without embarrassment. The researcher's emotional imagination could only be successful through shared trust with the research participants.

Conclusion

Doing ethnography is about working together. Today the emotional imagination of the sociologist is shaped by the aspiration of reflexivity that you write yourself into the text on the basis of intimate dialogue, sharing your life with the research participant, demonstrating your personal stance. At the same time I have suggested the ideas of critical ventriloquy and emotional edgework can explore C. Wright Mills' concern to explain how the research participants are interpreted, theorised and represented within sociological research. This should also allow us to see how the researched gauge the responsibility and commitment of the researcher. Fieldwork on young people in subcultures can be unsettling in terms of physical danger, but at the same time I have sought to show that sociological research, while emotionally troubling, can also be exhilarating. The different fieldwork studies on youth demonstrate how the researcher's personal, social class or gender identities are central to the exchange relations with participants, which shape fieldwork, interpretation, theory and publication.

References

Abbott, A. (1999) *Department and Discipline: Chicago Sociology at One Hundred.* Chicago: University of Chicago Press.

Abu-Lughod, L. (2000) Locating ethnography, *Ethnography* 1(1): 261–267.

Alcoff, L. (1992) The problem of speaking for others, *Cultural Critique* 20: 5–32.

Anderson, N. (1923/1967) *The Hobo.* Chicago, IL: University of Chicago Press.

Back, L. (2007) *The Art of Listening.* Oxford: Berg.

Back, L. (2009) Global attentiveness and the sociological ear, *Sociological Research online* 14(4)14 (socresonline.org.uk/14/4/14 [accessed 1/8/2015]).

Batchelor, S. (2007) Getting mad wi'it: risk-seeking by young women. In *Gendered Risks*, Hannah-Moffat, K. and O'Malley, P. (eds) Abingdon: Routledge-Cavendish, 205–228.

Becker, H. S. (1951) The professional dance musician and his audience, *American Journal of Sociology* LVII: 136–144.

Becker, H. S. (1953) Becoming a marihuana user, *American Journal of Sociology* LIX: 235–242.

Bennett, A. (2002) Researching youth culture and poplar music: a methodological critique, *British Journal of Sociology* 55(3): 451–466.

Blackman, S. (1997) 'Destructing a giro': a critical and ethnographic study of the youth 'underclass'. In *Youth, the 'Underclass' and Social Exclusion*, MacDonald, R. (ed.) London: Routledge, 113–129.

Blackman, S. (1998) 'Poxy cupid': an ethnographic and feminist account of a resistant female youth culture – the New Wave Girls. In *Cool Places: Geographies of Youth Cultures*, Skelton, T. and Valentine, G. (eds) London: Routledge, 207–228.

Blackman, S. (2007) 'Hidden ethnography': crossing emotional borders in qualitative accounts of young people's lives, *Sociology* 41(4): 699–716.

Blackman, S. and Commane, G. (2012) Double reflexivity. In *Innovations in Researching Youth*, Heath, S. and Walker, C. (eds) London: Palgrave, 229–247.

Bourdieu, P. and Wacquant, L. (1992) *An Invitation to Reflexive Sociology*. Cambridge: Polity Press.

Bourdieu et al. (1999) *The Weight of the World: Social Suffering in Contemporary Society*. Translated by P. P. Ferguson. Palo Alto, CA: Stanford University Press.

Brewer, J. (2000) *Ethnography*. London: Sage.

Brewer, J. (2004) Imagining The Sociological Imagination: the biographical context of a sociological classic, *British Journal of Sociology* 55(3): 317–333.

Bridges, D. (2001) The Ethics of Outsider Research, *Journal of Philosophy of Education* 35(3): 371–386.

Burkitt, I. (2012) Emotional reflexivity: feeling, emotion and imagination in reflexive dialogues, *Sociology* 46(3): 458–472.

Clifford, J. and Marcus, G. (1986) (eds) *Writing Cultures*. Berkeley, CA: University of California Press.

Clough, P. T. (1992) *The End(s) of Ethnography*. London: Sage.

Coffey, A. (1999) *The Ethnographic Self*. London: Sage.

Cohen, S. (1979) The Last Seminar, *The Sociological Review* 27(1): 5–20.

Cohen, S. (1988) *Against Criminology*. New York: Transaction.

Connor, S. (2000) *Dumbstruck: A Cultural History of Ventriloquism*. Oxford: Oxford University Press.

Cotterill, P. (1992) Interviewing women, *Women's Studies International Forum* 15(5/6): 593–606.

Damkjær, C. (2005) The aesthetics of movement variations on Gilles Deleuze and Merce Cunningham. Doctoral dissertation, Performance Studies University of Stockholm.

Denzin, N. and Lincoln, Y. (1998) (eds) *The Landscape of Qualitative Research*. Thousand Oaks, CA: Sage.

Fenwick, M. and Hayward, K. (2000) Youth crime, excitement and consumer culture, the reconstruction of aetiology in contemporary criminology. In *Youth Justice*, Pickford, J. (ed.) London: Cavendish, 31–50.

Fine, M. (1992) *Disruptive Voices: The Possibilities of Feminist Research*. Ann Arbor: University of Michigan Press.

Fine, M. (1994a) Dis-stance and stances: negotiations of power inside feminist research, in *Power and Methods*, Gitlin, A. (ed.) New York. Routledge: 13–55.

Fine, M. (1994b) Working the hyphens. In Denzin, N. and Lincoln, Y. (eds) *Handbook of Qualitative Research*, Thousand Oaks, CA: Sage, 65–84.

Flam, H. and Kleres, J. (2015) *Methods of Exploring Emotions*. London: Routledge.

Geertz, C. (1973) *The Interpretation of Culture*. London: Hutchinson.

Geertz, C. (1988) *Works and Lives*. Polity Press: Cambridge.

Gray, B. (2008) Putting emotion and reflexivity to work in researching migration, *Sociology* 42(5): 935–952.

Griffiths, M. (1998) *Educational Research for Social Justice*. Buckingham: Open University Press.

Gwyn, R. (2000) Really Unreal: narrative evaluation and the objectification of experience, *Narrative Inquiry* 10(2): 313–340.

Hammersley, M. and Atkinson, P. (1995/2007) *Ethnography: Principles in Practice*. London: Routledge.

Haraway, D. (1992) Promises of monsters. In *Cultural Studies*, Grossberg, L. Nelson, C. and Treichler, P. (eds) New York: Routledge, 295–337.

Hart, C. (2010) (ed.) *The Legacy of the Chicago School of Sociology*. Kingswinsford: Midrash Publishing.

Hine, C. (2007) Multi-sited ethnography as a middle range methodology for contemporary STS, *Science, Technology & Human Values* 6: 652–671.

Hobbs, D. (2001) Ethnography and the study of deviance. In *Handbook of Ethnography*, Atkinson, P., Coffey, A., Delamont, S., Lofland, J. and Lofland L. (eds) London: Sage, 204–219.

Hodkinson, P. (2005) Insider research in the study of youth culture, *Journal of Youth Studies* 8(2): 131–150.

Holmes, M. (2010) The emotionalisation of reflexivity, *Sociology* 44(1): 139–154.

Humphreys, L. (1970) *Tearoom Trade*. New York: Aldine de Gruyter.

Jackson, P. (2004) *Inside Clubbing*. London: Berg.

Jaggar, A. (1989) Love and knowledge: emotion in feminist epistemology. In *Gender/Body? Knowledge: Feminist Reconstructions of Being and Knowing*, Bordo, S. and Jaggar, A. (eds) New Brunswick, NJ: Rutgers University Press, 145–171.

Jarvie, I. C. (1969) The problem of ethical integrity in participant observation, *Current Anthropology* 10(5): 505–508.

Karakayali, N. (2004) Reading Bourdieu with Adorno: the limits of critical theory and reflexive sociology, *Sociology* 38(2): 351–368.

Kulick, D. and Willson, M. (1995) (eds) *Taboo*. London: Routledge.

Letherby, G. (2003) *Feminist Research in Theory and Practice*. Buckingham: Open University Press.

Letherby, G., Scott, J. and Williams, M. (2013) *Objectivity and Subjectivity in Social Research*. London: Sage.

Lois, J. (2003) *Heroic Efforts*. New York: New York University Press.

Lyng, S. (1990) Edgework a social psychological analysis of voluntary risk taking, *American Journal of Sociology* 95: 851–886.

Lyng, S. (2005) *Edgework*. Routledge: London.

Madison, S. (2005) *Critical Ethnography*. London: Sage.

Marcus, G. (1998) *Ethnography Through Thick and Thin*. Ithaca, NY: Cornell University Press.

Miller, M. and Tewksbury, R. (2010) The case for edge ethnography, *Journal of Criminal Justice Education* 21(4): 488–502.

O'Reilly, K. (2005) *Ethnographic Methods*. London: Routledge.

Palmer, V. (1928) *Field Studies in Sociology: A Student's Manual*. Chicago, IL: University of Chicago Press.

Park, R. (1915) The city: suggestions for the investigation of human behavior in the city environment, *American Journal of Sociology* 20(5): 577–612.

Pearson, G. (2009) The researcher as hooligan: where 'participant' observation means breaking the law, *International Journal of Social Research Methodology* 12(3): 243–255.

Peel, M. (2011) *Miss Cutler and the Case of the Resurrected Horse*. Chicago, IL: University of Chicago Press.

Peterson, J. D. (2000) Sheer foolishness. In *Danger in the Field. Risk and Ethics in Social Research*, Lee-Treweek, G. and Linkogle, S. (eds) London and New York: Routledge, 181–196.

Pillow, W. S. (2010) Dangerous reflexivity. In *The Routledge Doctoral Students' Companion*, Thompson, P. and Walker, M. (eds) Routledge: London, 270–282.

Polsky, N. (1967) *Hustlers, Beats and Others*. London: Penguin.

Savin-Baden, M. and Howell Major, C. (2013) *Qualitative Research*. Routledge: London.

Simpson, H., Bloor, M. and Fincham, B. (2008) A price worth paying? Considering the cost of reflexive research methods and the influence of the feminist ways of doing, *Sociology* 42(5): 919–934.

Shaw, C. (1930/1966) *The Jack-Roller: A Delinquent Boy's Own Story*. Chicago, IL: University of Chicago Press.

Spivak, G. (1999) *A Critique of Postcolonial Reason: Toward a History of the Vanishing Present*. Cambridge, MA: Harvard University Press.

Stanley, L. and Wise, S. (1993) *Breaking Out Again*. London: Routledge.

Stuhmiller, C. (2001) Narrative methods in qualitative research. In *Emotional Nature of Qualitative Research*, Gilbert, K. (ed.) Boca Raton, FL: CRC Press, 63–80.

Swartz, S. (2011) Going deep and giving back, *Qualitative Research* 11(1): 47–68.

Taylor, J. (2011) The intimate insider: negotiating the ethics of friendship when doing insider research, *Qualitative Research* 11(1): 3–22.

Thomas, W. I. and Znaniecki, F. (1918–20) *The Polish Peasant in Europe and America, 5 vols*. Chicago, IL: University of Chicago Press.

Thompson, H. S. (1966) *Hell's Angels*. Harmondsworth: Penguin.

Whyte, W. (1943/55) *Street Corner Society*. Chicago, IL: University of Chicago Press.

Winlow, S., Hobbs, D., Lister, S. and Hadfield, P. (2001) Get ready to duck: bouncers and the realities of ethnographic research on violent groups, *British Journal of Criminology* 41(3): 536–548.

Wright Mills, C. (1959) *The Sociological Imagination*. New York: Oxford University Press.

5 Rachela through the looking glass

Researching the occupational subculture of lap-dancers

Rachela Colosi

Introduction

This chapter draws upon my own autoethnographic research, where I used my own experiences, knowledge and understanding as a lap-dancer, to explore the subculture of lap-dancers in a club named 'Starlets'.[1] I was able to relate my own experiences as a member of the subculture to understand and analyse the subcultural lives of the other lap-dancers, situating this within a Chicagoan model of subculture (see Colosi, 2010b). In doing so I have taken an analytic approach to authoethnographic research, yet continued to have emotional and personal connections with the culture under study, to ensure I maintained empathy with participants.

(Auto)ethnography, empathy and analysis

In presenting his idea of the 'sociological imagination', C. Wright Mills argues that the ability to empathise with others allows us to gain a deeper understanding of different social phenomena (1959). Therefore, we must be able to see the social world from different perspectives, in particular, from the point of view of those we seek to understand; attempting to set aside our own biases. As a researcher, it is not always easy to empathise with participants; this is often the case when there are distinct cultural, social and sometimes political differences between the researcher and the participant(s) (Labaree, 2002). It requires a set of unique social skills, which allow us to disconnect from our own perspective(s) and engage with those of others. Researchers have acknowledged the difficulties of empathising with participants; Blee (2007) discusses this in relation to his work on the far-right movement, in which there were clear ideological differences between the researcher and the participants.

The *ways* in which researchers explore the social world can be significant in terms of how they are able to relate to their participants, and for encouraging an empathetic approach, as advocated by Mills (1959). The methodology adopted by the researcher can determine how the relationship between the researcher and participants develops. For example, it is argued that ethnographic research, which, through the use of participant observation, immerses the researcher in the field of study, thus bringing about an intimacy with participants that other approaches are perhaps less likely to do (Whyte, 1984). Such closeness in the field makes it easier for the researcher to understand social phenomena from the perspectives of the participants. However, despite this, mastering the craft of social understanding, through empathy (Mills, 1959), can still be difficult for the ethnographer, particularly if they are positioned as 'outsiders' in the field of study. The difficulties of being an 'outsider' have been widely discussed amongst ethnographers. From such discussions, a consensus has emerged that having some sort of 'insider' status is advantageous (See Hobbs, 1993). These debates highlight the importance of researcher positionality during the research process (Colosi, 2015) – sharing biography with your research participants allows for the social empathy that Mills (1959) calls for. Autoethnographic research, unlike 'ethnographic' research, grants automatic 'insider' status. There are a number of definitions of autoethnography, but there is agreement that through personal narrative 'the self [the researcher]' is situated 'within a social context' (Reed-Danahay, 1997: 9). This tradition is rooted in the Chicagoan ethnographic turn, during which Robert Park encouraged his students to research areas they had (auto)biographical connections with, athough they did not always situate their narratives within the research (Anderson, 2006). Autoethnography is now an approach that is embraced by many qualitative researchers, who strive to reflect the realities of social phenomena as part of their social inquiries, by drawing upon their own narratives. Examples of this approach, which are diverse and in abundance, include: the autoethnographic explorations of the body (Cook, 2014; Drummond, 2010); lap-dancers' cultural experiences (Colosi, 2010a; Manaster, 2006); 'rude-boy' subcultures (Williams and Jauhari bin Zaini, 2014); gymnastics (Baker-Ruchti, 2007); and the experience of chronic physical pain (White and Siebold, 2008).

Despite, the usefulness of autoethnography, the ways in which it is drawn upon need to be considered carefully; there is a danger that it can become self-indulgent, whereby the researcher takes centre stage, rather than the underlying culture it seeks to explore and depict (Atkinson, 2006). In order for C. Wright Mills' 'sociological imagination' to be realised effectively, it is necessary for the autoethnographer to use their autobiographical experiences and relationships with participants to make sense of the social phenomenon under study, relating it to the cultural experiences of *all* the participants involved, and not, just, offer 'self-indulgent' accounts. Furthermore, in order for analysis to be viable Cook (2014) suggests that the autoethnographer must avoid simply describing their experiences, arguing that they must be analysed within a theoretical context. There have been criticisms directed at what has been described as the 'evocative' tradition of autoethnography, which serves as an 'emotional' exploration of social phenomena and the positionality of the autoethnographer (Anderson, 2006). However, our emotions, as researchers, are useful tools, which can lead to great insight to the field under study (Blackman, 2007). Other ethnographers, such as Blackman (2007), have suggested that we should not be afraid to embrace our natural emotional responses during conversational interviews with participants when working in the field, as they can elicit significant truth from those we study. In Anderson's critique of the 'emotional paradigm' of autoethnography, he argues for what he calls an 'analytic' ethnographic paradigm which is 'focussed on improving theoretical understandings of broader social phenomena' (2006: 375). Anderson's argument has merit, as autoethnographers must be able to think analytically about the data they generate; however, as Blackman suggests, we must maintain and demonstrate emotional connections with participants, in both autoethnographic and ethnographic fieldwork, not only to sustain their trust and encourage a sense of ease, but in order to generate 'truthful' and meaningful data. Therefore, the use of autoethnography is a valuable empathetic (and emotional) methodological approach, when applied in a critical and analytical way.

Researching lap-dancing club culture

There have been a number of studies which have explored women's engagement with erotic dancing, both here in the UK (Colosi, 2010a; Grandy and Marvin, 2012; Sanders and Hardy, 2014) and in the USA (Barton, 2005; Egan, 2006; Frank, 2003; Price, 2008; Rambo-Ronai and Ellis, 1989). Research considers the interactional strategies of erotic dancers and/or their relationships with customers (Egan, 2003; Frank, 2006; Rambo-Ronai and Ellis, 1989); or dancers' general experiences of working in the sex-industry (Colosi, 2010a; Grandy and Marvin, 2012; Price 2008; Sanders and Hardy, 2014). Overall, academic research has tended to explore erotic dance as a form of (physical and emotional) labour, with little emphasise placed on how these dancers' work practices can take on the role of 'leisure' in their work setting. This is perhaps because 'work' and 'leisure' are often seen as distinct, and disconnected from one another, with the engagement of 'fun' seen as non-work related (Colosi, 2010c). More widely, both subcultural and post-subcultural studies have mostly focused on the leisurely practices of (young) people (see Bennett, 1999; Hall and Jefferson, 1976; Hodkinson, 2005; Malbon, 2000; Thornton, 1997; Williams and Jauhari bin Zaini, 2014), not on their occupational (sub)cultural practices. This is with the exception of some of the early Chicago School ethnographers (Cressey (1932), for example, considered the leisure-based practices of taxi-dancers.[2]

The autoethnographic project I conducted aimed to explore the subculture of lap-dancers and the relationships they shared with one another. In doing so I was able to transgress traditional perceptions about the relationship between 'work' and 'leisure' in an occupation and (sex)industry which is characterised as being the antithesis of 'fun' and 'pleasure'. My fieldwork for this project was conducted in a club, named as 'Starlets', in the North of England. The use of ethnography to explore the lives of erotic dancers is quite a common approach, with researchers entering the field to observe in the guise of customers (Barton, 2006; Brewster, 2003; Lewis, 1998); by becoming dancers; or by employing researchers to work in these spaces (Boles and Garbin, 1974; Enck and Preston, 1988; Egan, 2006; Frank, 2002; Holsopple, 1999; Manaster, 2006; Rambo-Ronai, 1992). Being able to develop trust and bonds between researcher and participant is an important perceived advantage, as discussed earlier. In relation to this, I had a close association with 'Starlets' prior to carrying out my research, as I had worked there as a lap-dancer for a number of years, and continued to do so during my field work. My decision to continue working during my observations was pragmatic – I felt that my continued participation in the culture of lap-dancers would help me generate meaningful data, whilst maintaining my insider status and ultimately my understanding of the social phenomena I was observing (Colosi, 2010a).

My observations took place over an 18-month period and were predominantly carried out during the shifts I worked in 'Starlets'. Some observations were made during social events with dancers, and observing the 'work' and 'play' of lap-dancers provided me with an in-depth understanding of their subculture. As this chapter will argue, I was able to use my position as an established lap-dancer to my advantage; if my positionality had been different, I would not have been able to capture the subculture of lap-dancers.

The subculture of lap-dancers

My autoethnographic exploration of the lap-dancing club subculture in 'Starlets' led me to identify a hierarchical subculture (see Colosi, 2010a and b) of lap-dancers.[3] The term subculture has been adopted to describe the group of lap-dancers studied, as it was evident that the work with which they engaged involved sets of distinct subcultural ritualistic practices and rules, as I will discuss in this chapter, that were unique to 'Starlets' and the lap-dancers who worked there. Furthermore, the dancers, saw their work as much more than a means of an income, but acknowledged that it was part of their *cultural* lives, to which these women shared a sense of membership, but also derived a sense of fun and pleasure (Colosi, 2010a).

To situate this subculture, I draw upon the Chicagoan model of subculture (Colosi, 2010b; Blackman, 2005), in which the dancers were part of their own distinctive 'subculture', presenting their own unique 'scheme of life' (Cressey, 1932). The Chicagoan notion of subculture is implicit in their work – for example, Cressey, 1932; Thrasher, 1927; Whyte, 1943 – except for Palmer 1928 (see Blackman, 2014), with researchers from the Chicago School, referring instead, to different and distinct 'social worlds' (Cressey, 1932) or 'gangs' (Thrasher, 1927; Whyte, 1943). Given the significant Chicagoan approach, which has no doubt played some role in shaping traditional concepts of subculture (see Gelder, 2007), it makes sense to draw upon these Chicagoan ideas in the contemporary study of subcultures (Colosi, 2010b). The Chicago School's model of subculture is embedded in the methodological approach taken in the study of youth cultures and relates to a more grounded approach (Colosi, 2010b). The use of ethnographic methods, such as participant observation, have been central to the work of some of the early key Chicago School scholars (such as Whyte (1943), Cressey (1932) and Thrasher (1927)). Though implicit, all were able to identify distinct '(sub)cultures' through engaging with this methodological approach (Colosi, 2010b). Cressey

(1932), in his ethnographic exploration of taxi-dancers, suggests that occupations are not just a necessary means of generating income, but that they exhibit cultural value and significance for their workers. In this sense then, subcultures are not just necessarily leisure-based, but can also be based on occupation (see Colosi, 2010b). The Chicagoan model of subculture differs from British subcultural theory (as developed by the CCCS – see Hall and Jefferson, 1976), American 'deviant' subcultural theory (see Cohen, 1955), and indeed post-subcultural theories (see Muggleton, 2000; Redhead, 1998). All of these approaches in some way or another have been theoretically prescriptive and/or reductionist in their analysis of cultural engagement (see Colosi, 2010b). Although the Chicagoan model drew loosely upon the idea of a 'human ecology' (see Park and Burgess, 1925), the analysis of subcultural engagement was open-minded and not grounded in any particular grand theories. Mills (1959) is critical of the overuse of grand theories in the exploration of social life, arguing that it potentially limits our understanding and influences our analysis, stifling the 'sociological imagination'. In this way it can prevent the researcher from being open-minded and may inhibit them from taking on alternative perspectives. As Mills (1959: 35) points out: 'Claiming to set forth 'a general sociological theory', the grand theorists in fact set forth a realm of concepts from which are excluded many structural features of human society'. The Chicagoan model of subculture provides a less 'grand' theoretical analysis, offering a more 'grounded' approach, enabling the analysis of youth cultural groups to be driven by the narratives of those from the subcultures under study.

The subculture identified in 'Starlets' fits closely with Chicago model of subculture, as this study of lap-dancing culture was embedded in ethnography, taking a more theoretically grounded approach in order to offer insight into a distinct 'subculture'. The subculture of lap-dancers shares important features with other Chicago School 'subcultures', relating to unique sets of rules and rituals, including 'tacit rules'; and 'social' and 'emotional' rituals, which were all evident in the group dynamics of the subculture. The 'tacit rules' of the subculture of lap-dancers, underpinned both the structure of the subculture and the (social and emotional) ritualistic practices with which the dancers engaged. Like other 'social worlds' (Cressey, 1932), the 'tacit rules', reflected the 'norms' and 'values' of the lap-dancers' subculture, working as discourse, maintaining and simultaneously producing the power-knowledge relationship (Foucault, 1980). In doing so, the 'tacit rules' were able to sustain the hierarchy of lap-dancers, reflected in three different status roles: 'new girl'; 'transition'; and 'old school'. 'New girl' dancers held the lowest status position in 'Starlets', which represents a period of acceptance and adaptation. Here, lap-dancers would not only learn how to do their job, but start to familiarise themselves with the 'tacit rules'. This was like a subcultural apprenticeship, in which women were initially socialised into the occupational and cultural role of lap-dancers (see Lewis, 1998). The next stage refers to one of 'transition', in which lap-dancers were learning to become established members of the subculture, having taken on the 'tacit rules' and adapted to the 'social world' of the lap-dancing club. This stage was one in which lap-dancers would be fully engaged in the occupational and cultural experience of 'Starlets'. The highest status of lap-dancer was 'old school', a stage during which the dancer had been fully accepted and was respected in the 'social world'. This lap-dancer's influence would be reflected in her role in the maintenance, and (re)construction of the 'tacit rules'.

The ritualistic practices provided the dancers with a medium through which they could develop and sustain their shared sense of subcultural membership, as well as keeping them in tune with the 'tacit rules'. Two sets of ritualistic practice were identified: 'social rituals' and 'emotional rituals'. The practice of 'social rituals' was encouraged, but controlled by the 'tacit rules', which shaped how and by whom they were practised. 'Social rituals' were practised before, during and after shifts and would include drinking alcohol and sometimes taking recreational drugs (Colosi, 2010a). The following extract taken from my field work highlights this:

> Karen came out of the toilet, with white powder still visible around the entrance of her nostrils; she was sniffing and looked uncomfortable as I observed her frantically playing with her purse. Karen smiled anxiously and looked up at me, snapping:
> 'What!?'
> 'Nothing,' I said, pointing at her nose and she quickly wiped away evidence of her cocaine consumption before heading on to the main floor.

'Social rituals' such as drug-taking often took place in the changing room, though not always in the toilet cubicle: I had observed some dancers snorting lines of cocaine off the dressing table (Colosi, 2010a). Observing drug use, was not unusual in 'Starlets', and inevitably brought about an ethical challenge, leading me to consider how I should proceed as a researcher when confronting such behaviour. Clive Norris (1993) talks about how ethnographers must take a 'situational' approach when dealing with sensitive or ethically questionable data; given the unpredictable and at times ethically challenging nature of ethnographic field work, each case must be dealt with individually, with the overall benefits of recording and using sensitive data carefully assessed. As Norris (1993) argues, there are times when we must observe, record, analyse and write about sensitive and/or ethically problematic encounters, as the overall benefit of revealing these behaviours provides important insight to a particular culture or way of life. In 'Starlets', for this very reason, I took this 'situational' approach, and given the prevalence and cultural significance of drug-taking, it was vitally important that I used this data.

'Emotional rituals', like 'social rituals', served to strengthen the bonds between dancers, but also, formed part of an informal support network amongst dancers, which, given that lap-dancing is emotional labour, enabled the dancers to manage the strain their work sometimes caused (Colosi, 2010a). These rituals would often take place away from the main floor where dancers would work; instead the changing room was the main space in which these practices took place – this is perhaps because the changing room was the 'home quarters' for the dancers

(Colosi, 2010a: 48), not used by either customers or other members of staff in the club. 'Emotional rituals' included the dancers airing their concerns about managers, customers, or other work colleagues, or discussing other personal relationship issues that were not necessarily connected with the lap-dancing club environment. In relation to this, I would often find myself playing 'counsellor' to the lap-dancers. I have written elsewhere about the relationship difficulties faced by dancers and how they would be discussed amongst dancers (including myself) as part of the emotional ritualistic behaviour (see Colosi, 2010a).

Situating myself within the subculture

As a lap-dancer, regardless of my researcher status, I continued to engage with the 'tacit rules' and 'social' and 'emotional' rituals as I had done before embarking on this project. As stated earlier, it was important for me to continue to fully participate in the subculture, taking on a 'dancer-researcher' identity; my membership of the subculture maintained my positionality as an insider (see Colosi, 2015). C. Wright Mills (1959) wanted social researchers to empathise, to use their own experiences to relate to others; therefore, in drawing upon our 'sociological imagination', we must consider and use our positionality to give us sociological insight into the social worlds we study. In order to identify my own postionality in the subculture, I have had to carefully consider my own engagement with and membership to the subculture. In doing so, I positioned myself as an 'old school' dancer.

During my fieldwork I made field notes which reflected upon my participation in ritualistic behaviour; the example below illustrates my engagement with 'social rituals':

> I was standing by the DJ booth with Danny (a bartender) watching the other dancers work the floor. It was a Saturday night and approaching midnight. On this particular evening I had pushed the 'researcher' part of me to the back of my mind and been seduced by the 'dancer' in me. I decided to have a few drinks (or at least, looking back, perhaps a few too many). Danny and I were drinking bottles of Corona, cautiously, as Gerard (manager) would not have been happy seeing one of the dancers glugging lager from a bottle! Another dancer, Davina, had been instrumental in my slip into 'dancer mode', and in my pursuit of inebriation which inevitably followed. She had been encouraging me all night, insisting: 'Just get pissed and enjoy yourself; you only live once!'[4]
>
> (Colosi, 2010c: 181)

Davina had 'old school' status; this is significant as it is clear from our conversation, outlined in the above extract, that she not only encouraged my participation in this 'social ritual', but in doing so consented to my behaviour. 'Old school' dancers, as I argued earlier, played a significant role in shaping the 'tacit rules', which not only underpinned general dancer conduct, but also guided the 'social rituals', defining how dancers of different statuses should engage with ritualistic practices. In relation to this, there were clearly different rules for different dancers. For example, in 'Starlets', with regard to the consumption of alcohol (as a 'social ritual'), 'old school' dancers were without restriction (as far as the other dancers were concerned), which meant they did not have to manage their use of alcohol in the same ways that 'new girl' or 'transition' dancers did. Although I did not consume alcohol during every shift – as a researcher I felt the need to control some of my 'social rituals' during my fieldwork – there were occasions when I immersed myself in heavy drinking, as outlined in the field note extract above. As an 'old school' dancer, I did not feel the need to closely control my use of alcohol (for me, self-imposed restrictions *only* related to my researcher status); I felt my drunken behaviour would not be challenged or frowned upon by the other dancers. This is reflected in my field note extract above, whereby, Davina, by encouraging and consenting to my action to drink to the point of inebriation (or beyond), was confirming my high status position in the subcultural hierarchy. Although the 'transition' dancers had more privileges in 'Starlets' than the 'new girls', they still had restrictions imposed upon them. Again, this was apparent with the consumption of alcohol during shifts, as suggested in the field diary extract below:

> I had been observing Elle during my shift, she was getting increasingly drunk as the night progressed – I was aware that some of the other dancers, Phoenix and Charlie in particular, had been watching her too. At one point, I followed Phoenix and Charlie as they approached Elle. There was an uncomfortable atmosphere, as Elle was told: 'You've had enough to drink' and 'You had better think about stopping'.

Elle was a 'transition' dancer and was therefore carefully monitored by the 'old school' dancers. Although, she was not quite restricted in the same ways as the 'new girls',[5] her use of 'social rituals' were nonetheless controlled.

As an 'old school' dancer, not only was my use of the rituals less restricted than those of lower status dancers, I was also immersed in ritualistic patterns of behaviour in such a way that they had become innate, automatic and natural – they were second nature to me – suggesting my status. For example, I would automatically offer 'new girls' emotional support, at times when it was not necessarily asked for, thereby inviting them to engage in 'emotional rituals' – also reflecting my role in the production and maintenance of the 'tacit rules'. During my field work, one of the other 'old school' dancers, Charlie, recalled how I offered her support when she first started, stating: 'You took me under your wing'; she suggested that I guided her in such a way that I was able to share my experiences with her and emotionally reassure her about working as a lap-dancer. Unlike the more established, 'old school' dancers, 'new girls' are still learning to engage with 'social' and 'emotional' rituals, they are not automatic responses, but carefully considered practices, as reflected in the extract from my field diary:

> Kate sat close to Charlie, Davina and Kitten as they chatted and gulped down glasses of the cheap white wine they'd purchased from the bar, on the two

for £5 offer. I could see Kate taking in everything they were saying, as if she was in awe of these old school dancers, waiting for her moment to join in on the conversation.

Kate was a 'new girl'; she had only worked in 'Starlets' for a very short space of time, but was clearly learning the practices through her observations. Similarly, 'transition' dancers, despite their more intense engagement with the subcultural ritualistic practices and the 'tacit rules', still sought guidance from 'old school' dancers. This was evident in some of the friendships which formed in 'Starlets', in which 'transition' dancers would closely associate themselves with the more established, 'old school' dancers, engaging in 'social rituals' with them, such as drinking alcohol and taking drugs. These ritualistic practices were often led, and guided, by the 'old school' dancers who would sometimes supply the drugs (in instances were drug use took place).

Understanding, and being able to distinguish between the different hierarchical positions through my own personal experiences was important as it helped me to empathise with the other dancers; therefore, I was able to use my 'sociological imagination' to make sense of phenomena in the subculture of the lap-dancers working in 'Starlets'. However, as I will also discuss, as an 'old school' dancer, empathising with 'new girls' and 'transition' dancers was not without its challenges.

Observing as an 'old school' dancer

The positionality of the researcher is significant in relation to the entire research process (Mullings, 1999); being reflexive about the time spent in (and out) of the field is therefore necessary (Madden, 2010) as it helps the researcher identify their own positionality and the impact it is likely to have on the participants and therefore the data generated. Like other ethnographers (see Labaree, 2002; Oriola and Hoggard, 2012), I have argued that researcher positionality is complex: it is fluid, continually changing and influencing *how* we observe, generate and analyse data (Colosi, 2015).

As an 'old school' dancer I had passed through the other stages of 'new girl' and 'transition' and had therefore shared, at some point, their experiences, which helped me to understand their (different) narratives. I was able to observe from a position of knowledge, and identify how each stage experienced the 'tacit rules', as well as the 'social' and 'emotional' rituals. Being able to recognise the different experiences in relation to the different status roles was important as it helped me to fully depict the lap-dancing subculture. For example, the subtle shifts in behaviour of dancers as they passed from 'new girl', to 'transition', and finally on to 'old school' status roles, were possible to identify because I was able to observe their journey from a position of knowledge, based on my personal experience. The nuances of behaviour included the use of 'social' and 'emotional' rituals, and 'tacit rules' – I was aware of how this changed throughout the hierarchy of lap-dancers (Colosi, 2010a). Furthermore, being able to identify the significant role of emotional labour (Hochschild, 1983) in lap-dancing, which caused, at times, emotional strains on the lap-dancers, was made easier by the significant level of empathy I had as a member of that subculture. I too had experienced the emotional labour lap-dancing involved and felt the emotional strains of working in that environment. The lap-dancers in 'Starlets' too, were aware of my experiences and saw me as a full member of their subculture; this meant that I was included in the day-to-day activities without question, despite their knowledge of the research I was conducting. They did not believe that I would betray them by using my findings to discredit them or portray them inaccurately or negatively.

However, regardless of the researcher's positionality as a member of the culture under study, there are always difficult relationships in the field. The researcher will, at times, have different views from some of the participants, which can result in difficult relationships (Colosi, 2015). Such problems can more closely be related to my own positionality as an 'old school' dancer during the time of my fieldwork. For example, although this position provided me with special insight into the different status roles, I was still mindful that my 'old school' status was different, and at times in conflict with 'transition' and 'new girl' status roles. Such differences in status were not just recognised by me but by other dancers whose perceptions of me were inevitably shaped by their *own* status role and their recognition of those differences between the hierarchical positions. Although this did not necessarily lead to hostility, it did sometimes mean that dancers altered their behaviour in my presence.

'Old school' dancers would sometimes monitor the behaviour of different lap-dancers in 'Starlets'; on behalf of management in exchange for different 'old school' privileges – this was to identify if any of the formal house rules[6] were being breached (see Colosi, 2010a; 2010c). Although not all 'old school' dancers would actively police the dancers, lower status dancers were nonetheless aware that it did take place. In response to this, some lower status dancers would appear secretive, hiding certain behaviours from 'old school' dancers. Any 'new girl' and 'transition' dancers who regularly breached the 'tacit rules' of the club were punished either through being ostracised by the other dancers, or, if management became involved (when formal rules were reported as being breached), would face more formal punishments, including, the use of fines, suspending dancers temporarily, or dismissing them from working in the club on a permanent basis. The awareness of this naturally made 'new girl' and 'transition' dancers cautious; some of my field notes reflect this, for example, during my conversation with Annie, a 'new girl', in which I was asking her about her shift:

> Annie was sitting on her own so I decided to go and see how she was getting on. It had been a fairly quiet night for the dancers, but I had noticed Annie had been sitting with, and dancing for, the same customer most of the night. I sat with her and made conversation, eventually asking her about the customer she had been with for most of her shift. Annie seemed uncomfortable and slightly defensive about me asking; she didn't seem to trust me enough to discuss the customer with me.

It was quite clear that Annie did not want to share her experiences with me. In relation to this, there were 'tacit rules', as well as formal house rules, which guided the interactions between dancers and customers; for instance, this could relate to physical contact between dancer and customer (see Colosi, 2010a). Annie's cautious behaviour does not necessarily indicate that she had breached any contact rules, but perhaps that she was concerned I might make that judgement.

Encountering the suspicions of participants is not uncommon for researchers observing erotic dancers; this is often documented as being a consequence of having outsider status (see Barton, 2006; Lewis, 1998). However, as suggested earlier researcher positionality is not fixed, as an ethnographer's status is nuanced, subtly shifting between 'insider' and 'outsider', depending upon the participants the researcher is engaging with. This is reflected in how my 'old school' status influenced the behaviour of the dancers from other status roles. Although I was not always able to reassure suspicious dancers about my intentions, their cautious behaviour was insightful; for example, the suspicion directed at me by some of the lower status dancers helped me analyse the relationships between dancers from the different status roles. Observing, and experiencing these relationships helped me to identify the nuanced behaviours of the different dancers, and, in particular, suggested the power dynamics of the different relationships between lap-dancers in 'Starlets'.

Conclusion

By taking an autoethnographic and theoretically grounded approach, I drew upon the Chicagoan model of subculture to identify a subculture of lap-dancers. Unlike other traditional theoretical approaches, the Chicago School's exploration of subcultures was implicit and did not rely on the use of grand theoretical approaches. Applying the Chicagoan notion of subculture enabled me to reflect upon the subcultural value of work and use my 'sociological imagination', through the practice of autoethnography, to explore the subculture of lap-dancers in 'Starlets', and identify a true sense of the participants' narratives. Having pre-existing relationships with the women who worked in 'Starlets' played a significant role in the research process, giving me important insight to their subculture. The relationships researchers share with participants is indicative of their position in the field and is also significant in relation to how data is generated. Having a biographical connection with participants, as reflected in autoethnographic research, provides opportunity for empathetic relationships. Being able to empathise with participants can help the researcher understand participant narratives their perspective. In my study of lap-dancers, as an insider, I was able to use my own experiences of working as and socialising with the other lap-dancers to guide my analysis. Rather than just offering 'evocative' accounts, I have produced an 'analytic' autoethnographic account, yet have still considered my emotional connections (with the dancers) and experiences; both approaches are important in order to produce critical, yet empathetic and 'human' accounts of social life. It is the analytical, yet emotionally connected and empathetic accounts of social phenomena that Mills' (1959) advocated, as this ensures we reflect the realities of human life. Sharing biography with the other lap-dancers helped me to empathise with them, but also provided me with unique insight to the ritualistic behaviours and 'tacit rules'. The lap-dancers in 'Starlets' were aware of the research I was conducting but they still viewed me as one of their fellow lap-dancers, not as a 'researcher'. Although this was to my advantage, it also meant that I experienced the same difficulties manifest in the relationships I was observing between different dancers in 'Starlets'. However, by experiencing this first hand I was able to gain a better understanding of the nuanced relationships between dancers, helping me to identify a hierarchical subculture. As a researcher, it is therefore important that we can relate to and empathise with our participants in such a way that they are not only open and honest with us, but so that we can identify the real cultural meanings of their behaviours.

Notes

1 All the names of participants, places and venues have been changed to protect the identity of the research participants.
2 For a discussion relating to the different approaches to understanding youth cultures see Blackman (2005; 2014).
3 The life cycle of lap-dancers, as they enter and leave the occupational subculture is explored in detail elsewhere (see Colosi, 2010a).
4 All observational and interview data presented in this chapter was recorded between November 2003 and February 2006; pseudonyms have been used to protect the identities of those involved.
5 For a more detailed discussion about the different status roles and the restrictions imposed upon them see Colosi (2010a).
6 Formal house rules were those created and maintained by management and were different from the tacit rules, which were created and maintained by the dancers.

References

Anderson, L. (2006) 'Analytic autoethnography', *Journal of Contemporary Ethnography*, 35(4): 373–395.
Atkinson, P. (2006) 'Rescuing autoethnography', *Journal of Contemporary Ethnography*, 35: 400–404.
Barton, B. (2006) *Stripped: Inside the Lives of Exotic Dancers*. London: New York University Press.
Becker, H. (1963) *Outsiders: Studies in the Sociology of Deviance*. New York: Free Press.
Blackman, S. (2005) 'Youth subcultural theory: a critical engagement with the concept, its origins and politics, from the Chicago School to post modernism', *Journal of Youth Studies*, 8(1): 1–20.
Blackman, S. (2007) '"Hidden ethnography": crossing emotional borders in qualitative accounts of young people's lives', *Sociology*, 41(4): 699–716.
Blackman, S. (2014) 'Subcultural theory: an historical and contemporary assessment of the concept for understanding deviance', *Deviant Behaviour*, 35(6): 496–512.
Blee, K. (2007) 'Ethnographies of the far right', *Journal of Contemporary Ethnography*, 36(2): 119–128.

Bradley, M. (2008) 'Selling sex in the new millennium: thinking about changes in adult entertainment and dancers' lives', *Sociology Compass*, 2(2): 503–518.

Brewster, Z. W. (2003) 'Behavioural and interactional patrons: tipping techniques and club attendance', *Deviant behaviour: An Interdisciplinary Journal*, 24(3): 221–243.

Brill, D. (2009). 'Gender, status and subcultural capital in the Goth scene'. In P. Hodkinson, and W. Deicke (eds) *Youth Cultures: Scenes, Subcultures and Tribes*. New York and Oxon: Routledge.

Cohen, A. (1955) *Delinquent Boys: The Culture of the Gang*. New York: Free Press.

Colosi, R. (2010a) *Dirty Dancing? An Ethnography of Lap-Dancing*. London: Routledge.

Colosi, R. (2010b) 'A return to the Chicago school? From the "subculture" of the taxi-dancer to the contemporary lap-dancer', *Journal of Youth Studies*, 13(1): 1–16.

Colosi, R. (2010c) '"Get pissed and enjoy yourself". Understanding lap-dancing as "anti" work'. In K. Hardy, S. Kingston and T. Sanders (eds) *New Sociologies of Sex Work*. London: Ashgate.

Colosi, R. (2015) 'Positioning the participant observer: an exploration of the shifting roles of the observer in a lap-dancing club setting.' In H. Bude, M. Dellwing and S. Grills (eds) *Kleine Geheimnisse: Alltagssoziologische Einsichten*. Germany: Springer.

Cook, P. (2014) '"To actually be sociological": autoethnography as an assessment learning tool', *The Journal of Sociology*, 50: 269.

Cressey, P. (1932) *The Taxi-Dance Hall*. Chicago: Chicago University Press.

Egan, D. (2003) 'I'll be your fantasy girl, if you'll be my money man: mapping desire, fantasy and power in two exotic dance clubs', *Journal of Psychoanalysis, Culture and Society*, 8(1): 109–120

Egan, D. (2006) *Dancing for Dollars and Paying for Love: The Relationships Between Exotic Dancers and Their Regulars*. Basingstoke: Palgrave Macmillan.

Enck, G. E. and Preston, J. (1988) 'Counterfeit intimacy: dramaturgical analysis of an erotic performance', *Deviant Behaviour*, 9: 369–381.

Foucault, M. (1980) *Power/Knowledge: Selected Interviews with Other Writings, 1972–1977*. London: Harvester.

Frank, K. (2002) *G-Strings and Sympathy: Strip Club Regulars and Male Desires*. London: Duke University Press.

Grandy, G. and Mavin, S. (2012) 'Doing gender dirty work: exotic dancers' construction of self-enhancing identities'. In R. Simpson, N. Slutskaya, P. Lewis and H. Nopfl (eds) *Dirty Work – Concepts and Identities*. Basingstoke: Palgrave Macmillan.

Hall, S. and Jefferson, T. (eds) (1976) *Resistance Through Rituals: Youth Subcultures in Post War Britain*. London: Hutchinson.

Hobbs, D. (1993) 'Peers, careers, and academic fears: writing as fieldwork'. In D. Hobbs and T. May (eds) *Interpreting the Field*. Oxford: Oxford University Press.

Hochschild, A. (1983) *The Managed Heart: Commercialization of Human Feeling*. London: University of California Press.

Holsopple, K. (1999) 'Stripclubs according to strippers: exposing workplace sexual violence'. In D. Hughes and C. Roche (eds) *Making the Harm Visible: Global Sexual Exploitation of Women and Girls, Speaking Out and Providing Services*. Kingston: Coalition Against Trafficking in Women.

Labaree, R. (2002) 'The risk of going "observationalist": negotiating the hidden dilemmas of being an insider participant observer', *Qualitative Research*, 22(1): 97–122.

Lewis, J. (1998) 'Learning to strip: the socialization experiences of exotic dancers', *Canadian Journal of Human Sexuality*, 7(1): 51–66.

McNamee, S. (1998) 'Youth, gender and video games: power and control in the home'. In T. Skelton and G. Valentine (eds) *Cool Places – Geographies of Youth Cultures*. London: Routledge.

McRobbie, A. and Garber, J. (1976) 'Girls and Subcultures: An Exploration'. In S. Hall and T. Jefferson (eds) *Resistance Through Rituals: Youth Subcultures in Post War Britain*. London: Routledge.

MacDonald, R. and Shildrick, T. (2006) 'In defence of subculture: young people, leisure and social divisions', *Journal of Youth Studies*, 9(2): 125–140.

Madden, R (2010) *Being Ethnographic. A Guide to the Theory and Practice of Ethnography*. London: Sage.

Malbon, B. (1999) *Clubbing: Dancing, Ecstasy and Vitality*. London: Routledge.

Manaster, S. (2006) 'Treading water: an autoethnographic account(ing) of the lap-dance'. In D. Egan, K. Frank and M. L. Johnson (eds) *Flesh for Fantasy: Producing and Consuming Exotic Dance*. New York: Thunder Mouth Press.

Muggleton, D. (1998) *Inside Subculture*. London: Berg.

Mullings, B. (1999) 'Insider or outsider: a chapter in the sociology of knowledge', *American Journal of Sociology*, Geoforum, 30: 337–350.

Mills, C. W. (1959) *The Sociological Imagination*. Oxford: Oxford University Press.

Oriola, T. and Hoggart, K. (2014) 'The ambivalent insider/outsider of academic "Homecomers": observations on identity and field research in the Nigerian Delta', *Sociology*, 46(3): 540–548.

Palmer, V. (1928) *Field Studies in Sociology: A Student's Manual*. Chicago, IL: University of Chicago Press.

Park, R. and Burgess, E. (eds) (1925) *The City*. Chicago, IL: Chicago University Press.

Philaretou, A. and Allen, K. (2007) 'Researching sensitive topics through autoethnographic means', *The Journal of Men's Studies*, 14(1): 65–78.

Price, K. (2008) 'Keeping the dancers in check: the gendered organization of stripping work in the lion's den', *Gender and Society*, 22: 367–389.

Reed-Danahay, D. E. (1997) 'Autobiography, intimacy and ethnography'. In P. Atkinson, A. Coffey, S. Delamont, J. Loftland and L. Loftland (eds), *The Handbook of Ethnography*. London: Sage, 407–425.

Rambo-Ronai, C. (1992) 'The Reflexive self through narrative: a night in the life of an erotic dancer/researcher'. In C. Ellis and G. Flaherty (eds) *Investigating Subjectivity: Research on Lived Experience*. London: Sage.

Sanders, T. and Hardy, T. (2014) *Flexible Workers: Labour, Regulation and Political Economy of the Stripping Industry*. London: Routledge.

Thornton, S. (1995) *Club Cultures: Music, Media and Subcultural Capital*. Cambridge: Polity Press.

Thrasher, F. (1927) *The Gang: A Study of 1,313 Gangs in Chicago*. Chicago, IL: University of Chicago Press.

White, S. and Siebold, C. (2008) 'Walk a mile in my shoes: an autoethnographic study', *Contemporary Nurse*, 30(1): 57–68.

Whyte, W. F. (1943) *Street Corner Society: The Social Structure of an Italian Slum*. Chicago, IL: University of Chicago Press.

Whyte, W. F. (1984) *Learning the Field*. London: Sage.

Williams, P. and Jauhari bin Zaini, M. K. (2014) 'Rude boy subculture, critical pedagogy, and the collaborative construction of an analytic and evocative autoethnography', *Journal of Contemporary Ethnography* (published online, available at: http://jce.sagepub.com/content/early/2014/09/21/0891241614549835, accessed November 2014).

6 'Biography in the laboratory'

Applying the Chicago School approach
to dual researcher positionality within
the night-time economy

Robert McPherson

Introduction

This chapter presents data from an ethnographic study of a city-centre pub from the dual perspective of bartender/researcher. The aim is to focus on the position of the bartender within the context of the pub, and how this immersive position initiated subjective data focused on the biography of participants, who were members of a hard-drinking/hard-grafting subculture of young adult men. Using Colosi (2010) and Cressey (1932) as the theoretical base, this chapter seeks to demonstrate the subjective strengths of research which focuses on the biographical background of participants. The notions of biography and autobiography are central to the research of C. Wright Mills (1959: 7) who argues that by use of the sociological imagination that people "now hope to grasp what is going on in the world, and to understand what is happening in themselves as minute points of the intersections of biography and history within society". A series of ethnographic data examples, centred upon the spontaneously occurring fieldwork moments of the self-titled "rock 'n' roll builders"; will be introduced in accordance with how the role of bartender impacted upon the role of the researcher within this research scenario.

Research context: the Chicago School, the night-time economy and subculture

This research was an ethnographic study into young adults' (18–34) alcohol consumption in a city-centre pub, known herewith as The Mitre, in Canterbury, south-east England. Chatterton and Hollands (2002: 95) describe cities as:

> sites of entertainment and pleasure seeking [where] a central focus of recent rebranding has been the promotion of the night-time economy, much of which is characterised by the ritual descent of young adults into city-centre bars, pubs and clubs especially during the weekend.

The Mitre was located within the city-walls, which encircle the centre; it operated weekly from Monday to Saturday with a late licence of 1 a.m. for the serving of alcohol. These hours of trade meant that it occupied a central position within the late-night pub drinking culture of the Canterbury night-time economy. The research correlates with Measham and Moore (2009: 438) who argue: "The expansion of the British night-time economy has led to a growing body of research focused on drinking, alcohol-related crime and broader cultural and criminological aspects of the alcohol-focused licensed leisure industry." Several subcultural drinking groups prevalent within the Canterbury night-time economy frequented the pub, with the research focusing upon students and workers from around the city. Blackman (2005: 2) states: "The concept of subculture at its base is concerned with agency and action belonging to a subset or social group that is distinct from but related to the dominant culture." Identification was made of a hard-drinking/hard-grafting subculture of young adult men drinking outside of the manual-workplace, who described themselves as the "rock 'n' roll builders".

The position of bartender at The Mitre was secured after a spell of fieldwork familiarisation was undertaken within Canterbury city-centre drinking spaces. Having spent time socialising with acquaintances in a range of pubs within the night-time economy, including licensees, bar staff and door staff, I was offered the position of bartender at The Mitre by its licensee Andrew (aged 52). The positioning of the researcher as bartender corresponded with the research into young adult's culture at the Chicago School as outlined by Park (1915) in *The City: Suggestions for the Study of Human Nature in the Urban Environment*. This research plan was subsequently undertaken by Thrasher in *The Gang* (1927), and Cressey in *Taxi-Dance Hall* (1932). Thrasher and Cressey each immersed themselves within fieldwork settings regarding previously unstudied urban groups within society; each also subsequently reflected upon their methodological practices and processes of immersion (Thrasher, 1928; Cressey, 1927/1983). The role of bartender allowed an extension of space and time within the research context to spend a pre-planned variety of hours and days immersed within the social institution of the pub, and to learn about the biographical lives of participants within the night-time economy through the access this role extended. This strategic immersion supported the researcher's intention to "set-up a scenario" with potentially willing participants, and the position of Merrill and West (2009: 107) who state: "One person who volunteers willingly to tell their life story can be preferable to any number who are reluctant."

Park (1915: 586) made explicit links between the role of bartender and other areas of social life relevant to sociological research within an urban context:

Among the types it would be interesting to study are: the shopgirl, the policeman, the peddler, the cab-man, the nightwatchman, the clairvoyant, the vaudeville performer, the quack doctor, the bartender, the ward boss, the strike-breaker, the labour agitator, the school teacher, the reporter, the stockbroker, the pawnbroker; all of these are the characteristic products of the conditions of city life; each, with its special experience, insight and point of view determines for each vocational group and for the city as a whole its individuality.

Use of one of Park's stated vocational groups from which to initiate research, inaugurated access across groups of young adults and drinking subcultures to study within the Canterbury night-time economy, for example: students and manual-workers. The compatibility of the occupation of the dual roles of bartender/researcher within the Chicago School tradition provided avenues of accessibility into multiple social and subcultural groups through ethnographic research practices. Blackman (2010: 195–196) supports this tradition: "Contemporary accounts of ethnography as a research method usually cite the Chicago School of Sociology under Robert Park and Ernest Burgess as the starting point for urban participant observation, the use of life history and the gathering of personal documents as valid sources of ethnographic data collection." Occupying dual roles gave access to a wide-range of participants within the night-time economy; using ethnography, the aim was to collect biographical data and use The Mitre as Park's idea of an urban "laboratory" (Park, 1915: 612).

Researcher positionality

Researcher positionality was central to the research context, and also the duality of roles presented by the bartender/researcher. This was related to the particular theme of "personal stance", which is reflected in the beliefs and understandings of the researcher in relation to their research participants and their *chosen* research context. Savin-Baden and Howell-Major (2013: 7) argue: "Positionality emanates from personal stance. Positionality, however, is more narrowly defined than researcher stance in that it reflects the position the researcher has chosen to adopt *within* a given research study." The intentional *choosing* of the research context of the Canterbury night-time economy meant that the position of bartender *chosen* by the researcher became integral to the research process. Consequently autobiographical background and personality became central to the research strategy and research practice. Moser (2008: 383) describes the impact of researcher postionality:

> I found that it was aspects of my personality, such as my social skills, my emotional responses to and interest in local events, how I conducted myself and the manner in which I navigated the personalities of others that were the main criteria by which I was judged. This is turn affected my access to certain people, the degree to which they opened up and their shared stories and views, and ultimately had an impact on the material gathered.

Similarly, by building upon my own personal youthful experiences within sites of intoxication and workplace background within manual-labour jobs as well as the world of academia, the flexibility conferred upon the dual roles of bartender/researcher was used to establish my autobiographical identity and personality as a key aspect of the research process. This flexibility led to intentional fieldwork experiences with students and workers from around the Canterbury night-time economy, which built upon aspects of my autobiography and personality as a form of access where "occupying certain positions and being aware of them may, for example, encourage researchers to take up projects that will place them at an advantage as an 'insider'" (Moser, 2008: 385). As Savin-Baden and Howell-Major argue "research necessarily will influence and be influenced by research context" (2013: 73); these autobiographical experiences exacted an inevitable influence upon the research process and the interaction with the "rock 'n' roll builders".

The process of immersion: adapting The Mitre to the urban "laboratory"

My research position of the role of bartender within *The Mitre* was a constantly recurring feature in the Canterbury night-time economy, where the patrons were a sporadic presence as governed by the transient nature of the licensed alcohol industry. Similarly, Colosi (2010: 5) argues that during the research of Cressey (1932) "the taxi dancers are a constant feature of this setting, unlike the patrons, whose presence is sporadic". Colosi's own research position correlates with the immersive research position of bartender, taking place in a "chain-operated, UK-based lap-dancing club […] while *continuing* to work as a lap dancer and engaging as a member of the culture being observed" (7: original emphasis). Her statement explains this: "[P]rior to this study, I had been an established lap dancer in the chosen setting for almost 2 years" (7). This meant that she "did not have to spend time developing rapport and empathy with the participants, as this was already in place, and I was able to maintain 'emotional' connection by continuing to participate in the 'culture' throughout the research process" (7). Cressey's (1932: 31) research within the unfamiliar context of the taxi-dance hall also outlines that a period of acclimatisation towards this research context was necessary:

> For those that attend the taxi-dance hall, even irregularly, it is a distinctive social world, with its own ways of acting, talking, and thinking. It has its own vocabulary, its own activities and interests, its own conception of what is significant in life, and – to a certain extent – its own scheme of life.

Cressey was aware of this distinct social world providing potential boundaries of access and immersion to his research. However, he subsequently described his strategic approach to overcoming this distinction through the use of language familiar to the research context: "In my dance hall study … a special study of vocabulary is frequently necessary. Conventional 'slang' and its proper use is very important" (Cressey, 1927/1983: 111).

Within my research, Cressey's (1927/1983: 111) approach to a "special study [which] is frequently necessary before entering upon a special study" to gather requisite skills was reflected within my own immersion into the role of bartender, and the acquisition of the skills which are demanded within a busy work environment such as The Mitre. For me, the position of researcher and the potential building of "rapport" (Thrasher, 1928) with participants from within the role of bartender was developed from an initial "blank canvas" of no previous experience of bar work. I initially spent three or four occasions at the pub observing how bar work was undertaken and obtaining a basic familiarity with the role. This included: how to pour pints of lager correctly; the process of cleaning and organisation behind the bar; learning pricing; obtaining brand knowledge. These early fieldwork experiences demonstrated for me an understanding of the interactive nature of the pub environment when spending extended periods within the space, and the specific knowledge, which was required to perform the role of bartender fluently. This is demonstrated in the following extract from the field diary:

> I arrive at the pub at around 7pm, and order a pint of lager. I chat with the bartender, Seb, when he is not serving customers or undertaking the various functions of cleaning and preparation, which are the bartender's duty. The pub is not busy and at times is empty other than Seb and I. Groups of drinkers arrive at various moments, ordering drinks for their party. Seb is busy in these moments, engaging with customers, preparing their drinks and asking and answering questions where necessary. These questions make the customers happily engaged with Seb, which forges an initial relationship between bartender and customer. Whilst Seb is not engaged in these moments, he spends time interacting with myself and the other drinkers in the pub around other topics of conversation.

Stretching and overlapping the role of bartender into researcher through the types of naturally-occurring interactions observed with Seb made the roles of Andrew, as licensee/gate-keeper, central to the research process and its success. My roles as bartender/researcher required adherence to the ethos of The Mitre as outlined by Andrew. Cressey (1927/1983: 110) positioned himself within the role of patron "centered [*sic*] largely in one type of public dance hall", approaching potential participants based upon the access granted by the freedom that this role presented:

> finally, noticing a rather flashily dressed man – apparently about thirty – who did not dance but sat alone, I strolled casually over in his direction and after due non-chalance [*sic*] I slumped down in the chair next to him. We sat in silence for a few moments and I then essayed some conversation. He responded, and in due time began revealing to me some of the business principles of petty bootlegging (111).

Andrew as licensee acted as both a visible and invisible gate-keeper within the fieldwork, through his agenda-setting towards his staff. Whether Andrew was present or not, there were workplace parameters by which I abided. This he achieved by: reminding me of my specific duties as bartender; how to approach these duties; the behavioural policy of The Mitre; the business philosophy of The Mitre. These parameters became central to the research process by contributing towards my own position and approach to bar work and research as bartender/ researcher. For example, at the outset of my first shift Andrew asserted in a half-joking/half-serious tone: "The worst thing you can do is make a mistake – just try not to do it twice." Andrew's emphasis upon being allowed to make "human error" provided a release from any prospect of being under the microscope and enabled my development of confidence and assurance towards the role of bartender. The nurturing attitude of Andrew towards his staff was central to my role of bartender within the research process; by maintaining a distance from members of staff when undertaking bar work, Andrew bred confidence within his staff to assess different situations as they occurred. Space was allowed to back personal instincts and judgement regarding spontaneously occurring scenarios within the pub as exemplified by this assertion from Andrew to me:

> We serve alcohol, so we expect to have to deal with different types of behaviour. But it's your call – if you think someone has had too much, don't serve them. If you want them to leave because you think that they'll upset other people, or are rude to you or anyone else, tell them to leave. I might ask afterwards why, but it's about your own judgement and we'll all back it.

Alongside the flexibility which the role of bartender provided, these clearly stated parameters assisted me in the navigation of potential opportunities of data collection. This was characterised by the identification of a subculture of hard-grafting/hard-drinking amongst young adult male manual-workers, where the requirements of the pub and the research process became simultaneous: to make customers/research participants as welcome and comfortable as possible, and to maintain an interactive atmosphere conducive to the overall atmosphere of The Mitre as a public drinking space and fieldwork location. Andrew states:

> Above all else, talk to the customers. Make them feel welcome and wanted. We're here to serve alcohol, but pubs also have a social function for people. If they want to talk to you, make that time. They might have another drink, they might not. But the chances that they'll want to come back are greater. And possibly they'll tell other people the The Mitre is a nice little boozer.

This request from Andrew further reinforced his position as a gate-keeper, and his centrality to the research setting. It was possible for me to combine the role of bartender and researcher within the same space behind the bar inside the same interaction. Andrew's business-minded philosophy towards the value of interaction with customers supported the strategic implementation of an ethnographic research process within The Mitre.

Encountering drinking subcultures: "The rock 'n' roll builders"

My occupation of the dual roles of bartender/researcher within the Canterbury night-time economy was inspired by Park's (1915: 586) suggestion that the occupation of bartender was one of the most "interesting to study". These dual roles were situated to enable me to take strategic advantage of opportunities created by my *chosen* position of bartender, and through my *chosen* research context of the night-time economy. My dual roles led to access to groups of young adults and members of drinking subcultures, for example: students, manual-workers, street musicians and pub workers. This initial access produced a series of spontaneously occurring ethnographic "set-up scenarios" with drinking subcultures, including one, which involved two young adult men known here, as: "the rock 'n' roll builders". This strategic positioning was followed by my establishment of "rapport" (Thrasher, 1928) between the "rock 'n' roll builders" and the bartender/researcher, which placed primacy upon the access granted to me as *bartender* and my ability to navigate the research process as *researcher*. My approach towards establishing rapport as researcher was also centred upon the strategic use of aspects of my autobiographical background, which corresponded with the interwoven academic life and personal life working practices of C. Wright Mills (1959: 195) who argues: "[T]o the individual social scientist ... social science is the practice of a craft."

Establishing rapport with the "rock 'n' roll builders"

My fieldwork strategy was to establish rapport with participants through use of the bartender role. Thrasher (1928: 244) also describes his approach towards the boys' gang as the establishment of rapport between the researcher and the research participants. He defines rapport as:

> that condition of mutual responsiveness which encourages free interchange of confidences and promotes sympathetic understanding without the interposition of formal explanations and qualifications. It involves a community of experience which provides a common universe of discourse and common sentiments and attitudes.

Within the "set-up scenario" of the "rock 'n' roll builders", I took the conscious decision within my role as researcher to establish rapport with the two young adult men. This was because upon their arrival at The Mitre, in correlation with Thrasher's (1928: 245) statement that: "Rapport may be established more quickly ... if the investigator is alert to take advantage of opportunities which may arise", it was apparent that this scenario held both potential ethnographic value to the research, and also economic value to the pub. These were both important considerations; establishing rapport with participants within my role of bartender involved my responding to Andrew's roles as licensee/gate-keeper, who requested that the economic requirements of The Mitre were central to my presence in the pub. Andrew had highlighted this to me upon my initial point of employment; outlining that every piece of business was economically valuable: "Make customers comfortable, keep them here, ask if they fancy another." Within this context, rapport was established as researcher with the "rock 'n' roll builders" using the role of bartender as a strategic method of access and interaction. Initially, both men were visibly keen to consume alcohol. They had finished their week's work as this extract from the field diary revealed:

> Two men, Simon and Darren, arrive in the pub around 5:30pm on a Friday evening. They are both still in their work clothes, smothered in dust and grime. The pub is empty other than the three of us. It is apparent that they are manual-workers due to the condition of their clothes. The men position themselves on the barstools at the front of the bar, facing directly towards me. I greet them: "Alright lads, how's it going. Looks like you've had a hard week." The older builder, Darren, replies: "Yeah, good mate. Glad the week's over, been on the building site all week. Need a drink. Two pints of Stella, and two shots of vodka to get started."

My impression that the presence of the "rock 'n' roll builders" was of ethnographic and economic value gained validity as the intentions of Darren and Simon were clear: they were out to get drunk after their working week. My initial greetings towards them were characterised by my *sympathy* towards the hard working week which they had obviously had, with which I was familiar from my autobiographical background. The following field diary extract reveals how I instinctively dropped into a less-formal style of address, which was more familiar within my previous workplaces, which reflected that used by Darren and Simon:

> I produce the drinks for them immediately, placing the drinks in front of them at the bar: "Twelve quid please mate." I take their money, which comes from a wad of notes that Darren produces from his pocket: "Fuck knows how much of this'll be left by the time I get home to the missus." I smile and say, "Well, you've earned it, aintcha. Fucking hard graft out on the site innit", which is greeted with a knowing nod and a smile from both men.

This interaction developed upon the theme of researcher positionality, and the statement of C. Wright Mills (1959: 196) that: "You [the researcher] must learn to use your life experience in your intellectual work." By using posture, language and accent with which Darren and Simon were familiar and comfortable, I was establishing rapport by presenting myself as an integral figure who they could 'act themselves' in front of. This contrasts with how Cressey (1932: 34) was viewed "differently" by a female taxi-hall dancer on first impression:

> The first time I saw you [Cressey] I knew right away that you didn't belong … You didn't act like the other white fellows who came up to the hall …

They wouldn't talk very much, but you did ... then you danced differently ... you talked differently, used different words.

Rather than reflecting a "difference" between the two men and myself by reacting negatively to their language or intention to become intoxicated, I made strategic use of aspects of my autobiographical background to present an image of "belonging" within a subculture of hard-drinking/hard-grafting young adult men. This established an initial sympathetic relationship, which is reflected in this extract from the field diary:

> Darren is looking towards me in amusement and laughing at his younger colleague Simon, who is already a little drunk. He says: "Comeon Simon, get the shot down you. Let's go. Weekend style." They drink their "shots" immediately, slamming their shot glasses down and pulling faces which denote a lack of pleasure at the taste. Simon now speaks to me loudly displaying pleasure at the effect of the "shot": "Woohoo, two more please barman. Line them up. Let's get them in Darren." Darren looks at me, and says: "Oh to be eighteen again mate, eh? Thinks he can take on the world."

C. Wright Mills (1959: 195) argues: "The most admirable thinkers within the scholarly community ... do not split their work from their lives." This view reciprocated with my conscious utilisation of the interactive position of bartender, and my outward demonstration of sympathy through my autobiographical background towards Darren and Simon's desire to consume alcohol, which established rapport "of a community of experience" (Thrasher, 1928: 244). Outward displays of reservation on my behalf as bartender towards Darren and Simon's status of intoxication could negate any rapport established as researcher. My autobiographical background within sites of intoxication and manual-labour jobs prevented this, as described in this passage from the field dairy:

> I do not feel uncomfortable in their presence as other members of staff often admit that they do, as I have ten years' experience in manual-labour workplaces to look back on ... I am also sympathetic towards the feeling of relief that Friday afternoon brings after a hard week's graft.

Cressey (1927/1983: 112) discusses this potential difficulty in terms of the researcher's own "moral standards":

> One's own moral inhibitions and pre-judgements [can] cause him involuntarily to erect a wall of social distance between himself and his subject. Apprehension and disgust makes it impossible for the subject to reveal himself, even should he be very much in the mood for it.

These "moral standards" I had experienced myself when drinking with colleagues when I worked as a manual-labourer. Often bar staff could allow the frenetic nature of such scenarios to overcome them; this could result in customers from a manual-labour background leaving an establishment and moving to another, as they felt unwelcome: "My money is as good as anyone else's" (Darren). My comfort within the scenario established a sense of sympathy between both parties, as the absence of any outward intimidation or reservations on my behalf towards their presence in the pub established the research process.

Ethnographic relationships of this embryonic state demanded the further "promoting [of] rapport ... by creating a body of common experience" (Thrasher, 1928: 250). I strategically utilised knowledge of terminology with which I had become familiarised within manual-labour workplaces and social circles, for example: "You lads look up for it today. Is it a POETS Day thing?" "POETS Day" is an acronym commonly used within hard-grafting manual-labour jobs translating as "Piss Off Early Tomorrow's Saturday". It is reflective of the attitude of "work hard – play hard" prevalent within hard-grafting manual-workplaces, as described by Hoggart (1957: 131) in his biographical account of working-class men in the 1950s and their predilection towards alcohol as relaxation outside the workplace: "On weekend nights he [the working man] is likely to drink more, and about these nights there is a pervading air of ''aving a good time'." This terminology was greeted with a laugh and agreement:

> You've got that spot-on mate. We finished at half two, had a couple of cans in the van, and were at the pub for four. Ready for the weekend (Darren).

By aligning myself with the two men in this way by saying "No worries, I know that feeling", the realisation within Darren and Simon grew that I had participated within similar workplaces to themselves and was familiar with the culture of leisure-time intoxication which often surrounds the manual-workplace. This minimised any potential "difference", as Darren and Simon responded towards my sympathetic approach and became at ease in my company. The manual-labour aspect of my own autobiographical experiences established rapport, enabling Darren and Simon to feel at ease to drink towards intoxication, and to be conversational towards me as bartender/researcher.

"The rock 'n' roll builders": a subculture of hard-drinking/ hard-grafting young adult men

Having established rapport with Darren and Simon through the use of "POETS Day", they continued purposively consuming alcohol. When invited to engage in conversation with Darren and Simon, I used biographical and contextually relevant statements, corresponding with C. Wright Mills (1959: 196) who argues that the researcher "will not be afraid to use your experience and relate it directly to various work". This maintained communication with Darren and Simon upon a level which was familiar to them; they engaged me in conversation throughout their stay in the pub, which Thrasher (1928: 247) defines as "what may be called a 'collective interview', although the participants themselves would not have recognised it as such". Conversation ranged between topics such as music, relationships, work and intoxication. Strategic methods of field note-taking were used; observations and conversation were committed to memory or scribbled on scrap paper and written down in full upon my return home from the shift. The use of "scratch" notes (O'Reilly, 2009: 102) placed less pressure upon either the role of bartender or researcher. This specific technique of note-taking also reflected the research of Cressey (1927/1983: 113) who stated: "[The researcher] must retain in his memory the substance of the conversation, along with a verbatim memory of the 'high-points' of the conversation." Due to the absence of any other parties in the pub, I was able to act as Darren and Simon's personal bartender, which allowed space for them to engage directly with me. Darren and Simon spoke freely within their relative state of intoxication; it soon emerged that they had been paid in cash for their labour on the building-site throughout the previous week. Darren was the building-site foreman; he had £800 in his pocket, which he brandished freely, saying: "Look at this wad mate, 800 quid." He was evidently comfortable within the social context of the pub environment: "Just a nice bit of time, spend my own money, no one watching me. I love the pub, I can be myself."

The scenario revealed data related to the balance of work-life/leisure-time within participants in the Canterbury night-time economy, with emphasis upon how alcohol consumption amongst young adult men was perceived both by themselves and others. The actions of Simon, when Darren briefly went outside The Mitre for a cigarette, suggested that young adult men were keen to drink, but also not to be seen to be drinking too much, as this extract from the field diary reveals:

Simon: Quick, give me a rum and coke while he's not about. He'll tell me to slow down if he sees me.
Rob: Are you sure mate, you don't want to piss your mate off. You've already got a pint.
Simon: Yeah, I know. But my girlfriend is waiting for me and I don't have much time. I'd just rather Darren didn't see that's all.
Rob: Well, no problem. I just wanted to be sure. Those shots are quite strong aren't they.

With this note of caution, I produce the rum and coke, and Simon pays before consuming the drink in two gulps, quickly returning the glass to me with a knowing wink. He begins to sip his pint again, looking round to see Darren finishing his cigarette: "You won't tell him, will you" he asks me. I reply: "Not if you don't want me to mate, it's your choice".

The hard-drinking style in which the men were consuming alcohol was especially embodied by the manner in which Simon consumed his secretive rum and coke. This was evidence of hard-drinking among young adult men, and there was now a firmly established rapport between Simon and me as we shared his 'secret'. When Darren returned, I jokily referred to the speed and volume of

Darren and Simon's alcohol consumption, saying, "Steady on boys, the night is long", to which Darren responded:

> It's Friday, I've grafted all week; it's time to live life on my own terms for a few hours. I just like to stay out of the house for a bit longer after a long week's work. Let the missus deal with the kids for a while longer while I just get a few drinks and my relaxation in.

The volume and speed of their consumption demonstrated that Darren and Simon were involved in what Measham and Brain (2005: 265) term "the new culture of intoxication", as after an hour-and-a-half of being in the pub they had consumed their fourth large "shot" of vodka each alongside three pints of lager. This was something which they associated with being away from their girlfriends and the home, and outside of the workplace: "My girlfriend ... if she knew I was here ... she'd kill me. She hates me drinking after work and spending my money" (Simon). Spending time in an all-male environment, where the drink flows freely, was akin to a level of freedom which is outside of the confines of the workplace and the home: "This is *my* free time, *my* leisure" (Darren). The impression given by Darren and Simon was that hard-earned cash wages were effectively *theirs* and were earned to enhance opportunities to get intoxicated at the weekend. While Darren had £800, and would evidently have plenty of money left over even after spending a considerable amount of it, stating, "Fuck it mate, I can spend what I want. We're rock 'n' roll builders", Simon was an apprentice builder and earned the lesser amount of £140 a week. However, at this moment he was treating his money with even more abandon than his far better earning colleague, telling us: "It's only money isn't it! I'll just earn more next week." Within the immediacy of the situation, and under the influence of intoxication, Simon was dominated by the thrill of reaching the climax of a working week and having his wages in his pocket. His sole intention was summed up in his dismissal of our friendly suggestions towards a little more self-control: "I'm out, work's over, I just want to drink ... come on Darren let's have more to drink ... it's the weekend!"

Simon and Darren's honest accounts of their lives and position within a hard-drinking/hard-grafting subculture of young adult men drinking outside of the workplace supported Hoggart's (1957) view of working-class men and increased weekend alcohol consumption. This developed upon the work of C. Wright Mills (1959: 6), who argues that the "sociological imagination enables us to grasp history and biography and the relations between the two in society".

Conclusion

This chapter highlights the notions of biography and autobiography in sociological research (Mills, 1959), also reflecting upon the aims of the Chicago School approach to urban studies (Park, 1915). My occupation of the dual roles of bartender/researcher within The Mitre was shown to enable the establishment of rapport (Thrasher, 1928) with "the rock 'n' roll builders" from this immersive position. This was achieved by strategic use of aspects of my autobiographical background, while considering the roles of Andrew as licensee/gate-keeper; developing into biographical insight into the lives of participants in a subculture of hard-drinking/hard-grafting young adult men. The approach was highlighted through reflection upon the notion of researcher positionality within the field, which developed upon the research of Cressey (1932) and Colosi (2010) by positioning the researcher's autobiographical background as central to the research process within the chosen research context. This autobiographical background allowed The Mitre, as an "urban laboratory", to become a strategic access point for biographical research with spontaneously occurring participants to be made; while discussing the processes of immersion which were undertaken before this research could occur (Thrasher, 1928; Cressey, 1927/1983). A series of ethnographic extracts from the field diary were used to highlight how rapport was established from the origins of initial immersion within the research context and my autobiographical background. These related towards the notion of "belonging" within the research context and towards the aim of gaining a "thick description" of ethnographic data (Geertz 1973: 28).

References

Blackman, S. (2005) 'Youth Subcultural Theory: A Critical Engagement with the Concept, its Origins and Politics, from the Chicago School to Postmodernism', *Journal of Youth Studies*, 8(5): 1–20.

Blackman, S. (2010) '"The Ethnographic Mosaic" of the Chicago School: Critically Locating Vivien Palmer, Clifford Shaw and Frederic Thrasher's Research Methods in Contemporary Reflexive Sociological Interpretation.' In Chris Hart (ed.), *The Legacy of the Chicago School of Sociology*. Kingswinsford: Midrash Publishing, 195–215.

Chatterton, P. and Hollands, R. (2002) 'Theorising Urban Playscapes: Producing, Regulating and Consuming Youthful Nightlife City Spaces', *Urban Studies*, 39(1): 95–116.

Colosi, R. (2010) 'A Return to the Chicago School? From the "Subculture" of Taxi Dancers to the Contemporary Lap Dancer', *Journal of Youth Studies*, 13(1): 1–16.

Cressey, P. G. (1927/1983) 'A Comparison of the Role of the Sociological Stranger and the Anonymous Stranger in Field Research', *Urban Life*, 12(1): 102–120.

Cressey, P. G. (1932) *The Taxi-Dance Hall*. Chicago, IL: University of Chicago Press.

Geertz, C. (1973) *The Interpretation of Culture*. London: Hutchinson.

Hoggart, R. (1957) *The Uses of Literacy: Aspects of Working Class Life*. London: Penguin.

Measham, F. and Brain, K. (2005) 'Binge' Drinking, British Alcohol Policy and the New Culture of Intoxication', *Crime, Media, Culture*, 1(3): 262–283.

Measham, F. and Moore, K. (2009) 'Repertoires of Distinction: Exploring Patterns of Weekend Polydrug Use Within Local Leisure Scenes Across the English Night Time Economy', *Criminology & Criminal Justice*, 9(4): 437–464.

Merrill, B. and West, L. (2009) *Using Biographical Methods in Social Research*. London: Sage.

Moser, S. (2008) 'Personality: A New Positionality?', *Area*, 40(3): 383–392.

O'Reilly, K. (2009) *Key Concepts in Ethnography*. London: Sage.

Park, R. E. (1915) 'The City: Suggestions for the Investigation of Human Behavior in the City Environment', *American Journal of Sociology*, 20(5): 577–612.

Savin-Baden, M. and Howell-Major, C. (2013) *Qualitative Research: The Essential Guide to Research and Practice.* London, New York: Routledge.

Thrasher, F. (1927) *The Gang.* Chicago, IL: University of Chicago Press.

Thrasher, F. (1928) 'How to Study the Boys' Gang in the Open', *Journal of Educational Sociology,* 1(5): 244–254.

Wright Mills, C. (1959) *The Sociological Imagination.* New York: Oxford University Press.

7 Temporary reflexive disempowerment

Working through fieldwork ethnography and its impact on a female researcher

Gemma Commane

Introduction

The chapter will explore the notion of temporary reflexive disempowerment after viewing a sexually explicit performance at a BDSM fetish club called Club X (pseudonym). I will assess what *temporary reflexive disempowerment* means for the ethnographic researcher. The dilemma I was faced with was representing what I had seen without pathologising or stigmatising those on stage or the research participants in the club. During the fieldwork I experienced C. Wright Mills' (1959: 215–216) dilemma of the 'split' between scholarship and biography where my personal involvement became estranged and I felt I did not know my research participants, who were part of this subculture. The chapter will explore the value of emotions in the process of becoming a 'reflexive' researcher, and what benefits might arise from reflecting upon negative fieldwork. These benefits may be especially the case when ethnographic research is focused on marginalised identities or non-normative social behaviours within subcultural contexts. It will be argued that the subcultural imagination became my route back to reflexivity: creating an opportunity to reflect on my sense of self as researcher and my relationships with research participants.

Social norms and complexity within subcultural settings

The fieldwork took place in a range of BDSM, fetish and performance art clubs in the UK, and methods used included participant observation, discussion styled interviews and case studies. Between 2008 and 2012 my doctoral research focused on femininity and female sexuality in burlesque striptease and BDSM, fetish and performance club spaces. The fieldwork in BDSM, fetish and performance club spaces quickly discovered social norms, which defined interactions. The research negotiated a range of clubs that allowed research participants to explore their sexuality, identity and sensuality in spaces where they felt safe (Commane 2012; Wilkins 2008; Williams and Storm 2012). The research spanned several clubs in various cities, which included London, Birmingham, Brighton and Manchester. Before exploring Club X – the case study of this chapter – it is important to acknowledge the complexity of BDSM clubbing contexts and how a range of social expectations shape how people interact and generate meaning with one another. Giving context to any space is important when understanding how meanings, expressions and values of any community are communicated and negotiated through complex relations in social, emotional and physical spheres (Cresswell 2004; Lefebvre 1991; Massey 2005). This enables a general sense of the happenings, allowing the researcher to have some subcultural knowledge to negotiate the scenes. Closeness with research participants develops a range of affective relationships, where the physical location of fieldwork connects also to thoughts, memories and emotions. This makes place and space complex and not easily reducible to one set definition (Cresswell 2004; Massey 2005). Seeing complexity is something that Mills (1959) maintains as essential in the sociological imagination, as the sociologist continually reflects, questions and examines social phenomena through many lenses. It is important for researchers to map out and note down how their understandings of the scenes they become part of, develop over time, and how this development can open space for deeper reflexivity.

The social spaces within the BDSM fetish club settings enabled participants to have agency without experiencing the impact of negative wider social norms on their individual, personal and private life. During fieldwork research participants expressed that they felt they belonged in the clubs. The numbers of research participants in club spaces were dependent on the type of club and its city location. Every club in the research booked their night at the venue, thus clubs were housed in buildings, which ran regular non-fetish nights. Club X was relatively small-scale with around 200 clubbers, all mainly white and aged between 18 and 65. Every club in the research had regulars who went to the clubs (as well as first-timers too) and, as some club nights were every month or few months, research participants would then save their money so they could plan their outfits, accommodation and transport. Many research participants expressed that they liked going to small-scale clubs than the larger popular clubs (such as Torture Garden or the Skin Two Rubber Ball), so they could enjoy variety and to also see their friends in their networks. Usually clubs would open around 9pm, but research participants recommended that going later (around 12pm) would be better as the club would be in full-swing and would enable you to stay out later (clubs would close between 4am and 6am depending on the city), with the possibility of an after-party at someone's house. Research participants conveyed that the clubs enabled them to openly socialise with like-minded people, where they felt they had a sense of value from friends made in the community, and where they could express without being threatened. Female research participants commented that the clubs did not put them at risk of sexual assault and that they felt they were not stigmatised or harassed by virtue of what they were wearing or whom they may be intimate with in the clubs, a point reiterated by Wilkins (2008) on Goth women's experiences in Goth clubs.

Subcultural etiquettes and rules

There was a range of norms and etiquettes within subcultural spaces during fieldwork relating to conduct, details of which can be found on club websites under club policy statements, frequently asked questions or rules and etiquettes. The clubs opened space for a range of sexualities and gender expressions, sexual practices and bodily experiences. The rules and etiquettes are made clear by clubs and people participating in the subcultures in the spaces; particularly due to sexual undertones to the events, the state of undress and dress, and the opening of specific rooms for BDSM/fetish play. Fieldwork encounters with participants and observations of activities enabled me to see etiquettes and norms in practice. Research had to negotiate certain etiquettes, codes and conducts within club spaces and rooms in order to respect research participants, to adhere to the door and club policies, and to experience what was actually happening in the space(s). Although behaviour is a product of social forces (Cresswell 2004; Foucault 1977; Lefebvre 1991; Massey 2005), your personal and emotional experiences also shape how the world appears to you. As meaning is made through exchanges and encounters with other people, then any social group acquires 'a definite and recognisable spatial order' (Hillier and Hanson 1984:26), which individuals need to negotiate to gain a sense of identity and to feel a sense of belonging. Subcultural spaces in the research also adhered to these spatial orderings, where research participants could express in a familiar environment in which they could relate to likeminded others. This 'relating' cannot be seen as fixed, but relative and allowing space for prefixes to be challenged by variability, which is important when exploring and sustaining the agency of participant's within subcultural groups. Mills (1959:196–197) argues that we must control, capture and examine this complex interplay of experiences, thus to shape ourselves as an intellectual crafts person. Understanding complexity and not reducing the field to personal experience only, is therefore achieved through applying self-reflexivity and not seeing the research setting and relationships as isolated and static. What this means is that the researcher sees how their experiences configure the research setting, but also how wider social responses, attitudes and beliefs 'outside' of the setting, interplay with interpretation too. What had to be appreciated and acknowledged, throughout the research process, was the interplay of attitudes and beliefs that governed the expected behaviours happening inside club spaces (Blackman and Commane 2011; Commane 2012).

Contrary to assumptions, BDSM, kinky and fetish clubs involved in my research were highly organised through written and unwritten values and rules generating a space that had 'structure' (Commane 2012). These rules – which research participants were supposed to respect – governed all of the clubbing space, which included the chill out areas, the bar, the dungeon, the couple's rooms (club permitting) and any of the dance and performance spaces. Rules for entry generally covered no street clothing, with an emphasis on rubber/latex (gimp, uniform, inflatables, couture), fantasy, burlesque, theatrical clothing, DIY and Goth. Upon entry to the clubs there were general rules concerning behaviour and personal conduct. These rules included safe, sane and consensual behaviour (Lindemann 2013; Williams and Storm 2012), respecting other clubbers, no means no, no photography, no uniforms that would cause offence (Nazi uniforms, etc.), no full frontal nudity, and to not interrupt play scenes in the dungeon. Enforcing dress codes made sure a certain crowd was attracted to the venue allowing a harmonious, safe and welcoming space for those within. The dress codes permitted a certain scope of individuals to enter the space who looked the part, with expectations that clubbers would respect the rules. Permitting individuals on the merit of how they look does not always mean that they will act respectfully, despite club websites, dungeon monitors, managers and research participants alike stressing that anyone found to be harassing other clubbers, touching without asking, joining a play scene without being invited, sitting on dungeon equipment and masturbating outside of a scene, would find themselves being ejected (Commane 2012). Thus, subcultural spaces and identities can therefore be reconceived as sites 'through which an alternative and possibly highly organised set of values are articulated' (Gelder 2005:22).

Female research participants felt they would be able to dress 'slutty' without being stigmatised or objectified by men as they perceived they would be in mainstream patriarchal spaces. The elevation of an alternative set of values, which were body-positive and sex-positive, were normalised making female research participants feel at ease with their bodies, sexuality and experiences at clubs. It was found that if there are rules and etiquettes, how punters negotiate and experience the club spaces during their night out, is often varied and changeable. Also, it is important to acknowledge that definitions are always relative, flexible and moving. This is essential when critiquing certain club spaces that are perceived to be environments where individuals are able to explore fantasies and their self-identity, without seemingly risking personal safety or experiencing emotional negativity. The presence of dominant readings concerning women's bodies and objectification even *within* subcultural settings, still shows that dominant discourses are not completely suspended and need to be considered when analysing the research setting. This can result in bodies, behaviours and identities producing problems that some research participants cannot always escape from, such as uninvited sexual comments. Mills (1959:206) maintains that 'the popular awareness of the problem – the problem as an issue and as a trouble – must be carefully taken into account: that is part of the problem'. This includes the researchers own response to the social setting of field research, and how their response can have an impact on how communities and research participants are reconceived in written accounts. As Coffey (1999:8) states, 'fieldwork itself is a "social setting" inhabited by embodied, emotional, physical selves,' and the researcher needs to carefully understand how 'fieldwork helps to shape, challenge, reproduce, maintain, reconstruct and represent ourselves and the selves of others'. The social setting I found myself in was a space where I felt at home, which can be problematic when interpretations can be overly celebratory or when feelings of 'homeliness' undermine the complexity of the research setting, and the varieties of research participants who converge in the spaces for a range of reasons, kinks and desires. This 'complexity' will now be explored through Club X and an ethnographic account of a performance, which resulted in the researcher being temporary reflexively disempowered.

Club X: belonging, fun and 'being at home'

Club X was a fetish BDSM performance art club located centrally in a busy city centre. Club X was included in research due to the diversity of research participants in the space. The club was located in a busy evening leisure area in a city centre, and the entry fee was £10, which was relatively cheaper than other clubs such as Torture Garden, where tickets were priced at £26. The types of styles worn by clubbers included Goth, rubber, burlesque/vintage, fantasy, uniform, punk and alternative wear. The types of clubbers in Club X included students, professionals, sex workers and artists. Research participants in the club were mainly white and aged between 18 and 65. The club marketed itself as a BDSM, fetish, Goth and performance art, so catered for a range of tastes and expectations. Club X had a room for dancing, where performances were held on a small stage, a chill out smoking area, another room with a bar for socialising, and a dungeon for BDSM play. A dress code was enforced for entry and those coming to the club included a mix of ages, genders and styles. The management wanted diversity and did not want to adhere to expectations of certain factions in the club, such as BDSMers. Clubbers were friendly, the management and dungeon monitors were welcoming, and the vibe of the club night itself was really positive. Over a year and a half spent at this club I always had a good time and developed several friendships with research participants who knew about the research. Club X was vibrant, fun, bizarre and exciting. I always felt at home. At Club X, the performances on stage were diverse and the management always wanted to entertain the crowd. The club strove to be different and always booked artists that tested the resolve, morals and stomachs of clubbers. Some of the performances were expected to be 'extreme' but they never did overstep the mark or shake the mutual moral foundations of safe, sane and consensual behaviour. This links to C. Wright Mills' (1959) questioning of our assumptions on the causal characteristics of deviant behaviour in sociology. Our relationship towards an object of study can change and develop depending on how we view and value it, thus research participants in the BDSM, fetish and kinky clubs were immersed in a social world that normalised their identities through a collective sense of respect. However at one of the nights I went to, the performance on stage made me detach from the clubbers and my friends around me, making me feel vulnerable, different and upset. The following performance challenged my research subjectivity and role(s) due to my emotional reaction towards the research setting.

An ethnographic journey of conflicting emotions: a military stage show

The performance at Club X involved three people (two women and one man), the performers were aged between 25 and 50, and they were all well known in the scene and to the club. The performance themes and outcomes felt different this time to the other styles and types of performances viewed and experienced during fieldwork. The club had always opened space for a variety of tastes and expectations of clubbers who wanted to be entertained. It is important to note that the happenings in the club – from drugs being consumed in toilets (cocaine and speed) and the chill out area (mainly spliffs being passed around), to intimacies on the dance floor and in the dungeon – are normal leisure time experiences connected to pleasure. Feeling at home and having a sense of belonging is, therefore, generated by and through encounters in the field, highlighting the experiential factors that shape the clubbing experience (Anderson 2004; Jackson 2004). The feelings of being at home and having a strong sense of belonging, within fieldwork locations, are not always present despite identifying with research participants. This is something I experienced whilst observing a sexually explicit performance on stage at Club X, where I felt my reflexivity disempowered. The performance activated a very uncomfortable space for me despite my initial excitement of being at Club X that night.

As the lights lowered, old gramophone music started to fill the club arena and the performance began. Mr. O and Ms. D came on stage wearing military uniforms with another women. As they sat down and he placed a suitcase on the floor, the candlelight took over and transported them and me back in time. The following scene was an enactment of sexual abuse, violence and humiliation, which was broken up with the song 'YMCA' and in the final part of the show the young woman was shot in the head by an imitation pistol. The performance ended, the performers took a bow and, as the audience clapped and cheered, dance music filled the room. Clubbers reconvened on the dance floor in front of the stage and started swaying and twisting to the music. The performance faded away and the rest of the night took over, but the performance had made me feel completely disconnected from those around me. The performance themes disgusted me and, in observing friends laughing, these 'friends' who were research participants all seemed alien to me. I felt disempowered, unable to critically engage with the thoughts and feelings generated by the performance, which was no fault of the performers or something that they intended. I chose to remove the experience from the fieldwork. I could not immediately engage with my emotional response to the fieldwork. Through fieldwork diaries, email exchanges with my supervisor, conversations in my head and maintenance of a file, I learned how to keep my 'inner world awake' (Mills 1959:197), developing a reflexive habit. The temporality of disempowerment meant that I was able to apply reflexivity after some critical distance, enabling me to understand why I had felt a range of emotions and what this, then, could mean when interpreting the field setting. The situation, feelings and initial ethnographic description of the performance can, therefore, be viewed through several interconnected stances. In committing myself to develop a sociological, reflexive and multidimensional perspective meant interrogating the meanings behind my emotions, and the possible implications of my positionality on my research participants in the study. As C. Wright Mills (1959:197) states:

Whenever you feel strongly about events or ideas you must try not to let them pass your mind, but instead formulate them for your files and in doing so draw out their implications, show yourself either how foolish these feeling or ideas are, or how they might be articulated into productive shape.

Emotional reverberations: the challenge of reflexivity

When the researcher is immersed in the field, it can be easy to feel comfortable, as the development of relationships with research participants and the familiarity with locations, make the strange become familiar. To understand the changes, Mills (1959:10–11) maintains that we are 'required to look beyond them' and to be aware of wider social structures to trace 'linkages among a great variety of milieux'. The interplay of a variety of social environments within Club X became more apparent when I experienced emotional negativity during and after the sexually explicit performance. However, it was initially hard to engage in a careful analysis of these interplays, despite being aware of the centrality of the subcultural imagination in sociological ethnography. This includes exploring how biography intertwines with the outcomes of research. As Mills argues (1959:14) 'The use of the imagination is central to the best work that they might do, that by failing to develop and use it they are failing to meet the cultural expectations that are coming to be demanded of them'; then it is important to always recognise the social and political opportunities that arise in the tensions experienced in research.

Although it is vital to always know your place and purpose in the field (Hammersley and Atkinson 1995) the development of roles within the field make the researcher's subjectivity multifaceted and complex, just like research participants' identity. During and after the performance, I temporarily felt physically and emotionally disconnected from research participants around me. The entertainment was painful for me to watch and to think about. My visual observations of research participants laughing at the performance made me feel different from them, making my presence as 'researcher' becomes more pronounced and my other roles fading in relevance. The research setting was newly illuminated as a subcultural space of difference, where my initial celebratory views were questioned by the presence of complex and multitude perspectives, sexualities and kinks. Poewe (1999:203) discusses reciprocal illumination as significant in seeing 'those special (experiential) moments when an aspect of one's personal life illuminates a research problem and vice versa'. This allows the researcher to see culture, society, ourselves and our pasts as 'newly illuminated or rethought in terms of this experience' (Poewe 1999:204), but only if the researcher is committed to being open and honest, even if careful reflexivity on an experience takes time. This also includes the researcher understanding the issues and implications associated with moments when your role is reduced to that of the researcher only. I felt an outsider inside a community that I had felt affinity to, but this was momentary and the feelings of difference did not follow me to other nights at Club X or, indeed, other research settings. This complicates MacRae's (2007) insight of the 'insider-in' approach in critically exploring the subjectivity of the researcher in field analysis through the researcher already having a connection with the community they are studying. The issue here is feeling let down by your research participants, like you would a close friend who had offended you. To some extent, reflexivity was initially hard to activate when memories and stories converged with how I felt about the performance.

Despite knowing the performers and liking them, the performance itself connected to various taboo subjects both in the mainstream and within the subculture. These taboo subjects will now be explored through a close examination of two topic examples in the performance: military and sexual violence. *First,* not only did the performance feel distasteful, it can be read as disrespectful. In other clubs, such as Club Lash, there was a ban on certain military outfits that could cause offence or could be viewed as politically insensitive or socially and culturally disrespectful. There were notices in several clubs, by the entrance and by bars, which stated certain uniforms should not be worn out of respect. Seeing images of kinky uniforms outside of the contexts and complexities of club spaces can make outsiders easily presuppose a negative psychological profile of research participants, instead of being aware of how certain uniforms are taboo and unacceptable in some club contexts. At another club space, other patrons stopped a performance as they felt the political and racial context of the play-scene was too distasteful. With research participants stopping or seeing an activity as 'offensive', demonstrates that 'human diversity' is only recognised in specific ways and through specific value systems that validate certain forms of expression, and disavow others. Stopping a scene also highlights an ethics of care and responsibility, which operate in subcultural spaces. In general, interrupting a scene is a big taboo, but this example demonstrates how wider socio-historic and socio-political attitudes are still present in subcultural club settings, resulting in research participants feeling the need to stop something they felt was politically insensitive.

Second, what the performers were unaware of was that during my research fieldwork some participants had told me about their experiences of sexual abuse (outside the community). Their confidential accounts have not left me. Their moments of suffering became my moments of reflexive despair. Being with living breathing people and seeing their tears and hearing their accounts made me realise that field research connects itself to you emotionally (Ellis 1991a, 1991b; Ellis and Flaherty 1992; Brak-Lamy 2012; Carroll 2012; Coles et al. 2014; Kirby and Corzine 1981). The feelings of distress and hate towards the perpetrators that I felt when I heard the stories, mirrored my feelings towards those laughing and applauding at the end of the show. The intensity of emotions – of anger, disconnection, loneliness and despair – grew in the days and months after the performance. The reality of the scene continued to be alive in my head. I felt sick, alone and helpless, highlighting that research and debates do become located bodily (Carroll 2012; Coles et al. 2014). Consequently, the many realities research participants experience are not devoid of affective qualities, nor are experiences, our sense of belonging or detachment clinically disconnected from other aspects of our lives. Coles et al. (2014:98) explore how it is important for a 'researcher management' of personal trauma, and this connects with Blackman's (2007) account on feeling hate towards domestic abusers after hearing survivor stories.

Care, rules and differences in the field

Research management is vital, specifically as stories and feelings follow you beyond the spaces of 'research' (Blackman and Commane 2011; Brak-Lamy 2012; Carroll 2012; Coles et al. 2014; Kirby and Corzine 1981). Therefore the spaces and exchanges in the research setting are not isolated from personal, political and wider social systems that give meaning to how the world presents itself to us. Acknowledging how these intersect is key, specifically when re-presenting the diversity found in the field, but also maintaining commitment to sustaining the agency of research participants. This also demonstrates that the researcher is still reflexive when they are feeling disempowered for a temporary period of time.

Wanting to make a difference or wanting to re-present a marginalised subculture, in its many contexts and forms, kept me committed in working through my own conflicting emotions in the field. Disclosing stories and emotions from fieldwork exchanges, therefore, allows the research setting to be analysed through the various contexts that intersect. The emotions of the researcher are important to analyse, as this enables the researcher to see how social forms and discourses operate, interact and influence one another at the personal level. This also opens out analysis to how we can see interactions, personal troubles and public issues, socially (Mills 1959), thus developing a holistic and multidirectional perspective of social phenomena. The emotional reactions of the researcher become what Reger (2015:91) calls 'data indicators', which should be drawn upon *throughout* the research process instead of disclosing 'when the coast is clear' (Kleinman and Copp 1993:17). Although the researchers emotions are important, there are sticking points in sociological enquires, where researchers may not feel comfortable disclosing feelings or being honest about their 'bias' because of the impact on their career or not being seen as professional enough. This has an impact on the clarity and integrity of fieldwork accounts, emotions and encounters.

Honesty and how we tell stories from within field research gives integrity to fieldwork accounts and the dilemmas the researcher may feel they are facing. Although Coles et al. (2014:107) state, 'I feel that the way in which we tell our stories can be powerful in dealing with the trauma we experience in the field', it is important to adapt this telling and honesty in accounts of the research process. The visibility of hidden parts of your ethnography (Blackman 2007) enables the researcher to understand and feel that the location of the field is not a set space; instead it intersects within all aspects of the researcher's life. Common norms, expectations and habits within the researchers discipline (Savin-Baden and Howell Major 2013) can be damaging to the creativity and intellectual freedom of the researcher, but also inhibits the researcher disclosing emotional accounts that enable them to see ethnographic research as complex, multifaceted and affective. Thus, 'the field' is multifaceted, multispatial and not fixed to one location as differences exist in personal values, backgrounds and life experiences. Although I experienced temporary reflexive disempowerment, the holistic setting of the ethnography enabled regenerations of research commitment. With this, it is important to highlight that all three of the performers involved in the fantasy were against sexual violence. The club was a safe space, where individuals were looked after and where BDSM play was performed and enacted via the safe, sane and consensual mantra. In terms of care, I observed, read and overheard stories about how new patrons would be welcomed by the management and would be looked after by staff and clubbers alike to make them feel comfortable. This is supported by Lindemann (2013) on BDSM as therapy and reducing stress, but also Williams and Storm (2012:6) highlighting that the relationships found within the BDSM community 'may contribute to physical, social, emotional, and cognitive health'. The emotions and knowledge's produced through exchanges with research participants build a fuller picture of the field, which includes the careful assessment of the feelings of upset, excitement, joy and pain you may experience when engaged in fieldwork.

Researcher positionality and working through negative fieldwork

Understanding researcher positionality, as fieldwork relationships and familiarity develop, is an area where reflexivity allows the researcher to have critical distance. Critical distance can be difficult when the researcher is immersed in the research setting for a long period of time. However, researcher positionality and the accounts of the researcher may become research objects in themselves. The principles of autoethnography highlight that the researcher is researchable, especially when the lens of analysis turns around and faces the ethnographer when they are reflecting on their position, feelings and emotions in the field (Cole and Knowles 2000; Hammersley and Atkinson 1995; O'Reilly 2005). This enables the researcher to actively move beyond reflection to reflexivity and become more critically aware of their personal stance and positionality, thus allowing, and not suppressing, alternative interpretations (Savin-Baden and Howell Major 2013:79). Building upon this complexity is the multitude of roles the researcher has in their exchanges within the research setting and with different research participants. In the research, my roles included being a friend, a punter and someone who was, like some research participants, discovering parts of who I am. My roles were neither static, nor clinical and without feeling. I loved the friends I made in the research setting; I was and still am, protective of them. I also understood my place and purpose in the field, but this did not reduce the care or value of the friends that I made, who are still my friends now, after the research ended. Jorgensen (1989:61) highlights that the researcher has many roles in the field and that the 'multiple roles offers the distinct advantage of providing access to different standpoints and perspectives. The researcher gains a more comprehensive and accurate picture of what is happening.' I found myself talking to gender fluid, queer and kinky people, sex workers and other professionals with whom I would not have socialised or interacted in particular ways if the research had not been conducted. These interactions opened my eyes to the everyday realities of research participants, and also to a range of perspectives about gender, sexuality and identity.

Despite my negative feelings and traumas in the field, it was important to understand that when researching sexualised subcultural spaces it can be easy for outsiders to think that you are fully defined by those you study (Kirby and Corzine 1981), when in fact differences and variability's with research participants allow greater complexity, nuance and clarity to what is studied, felt and lived. In the context of my research – conducted in subcultural, minority and taboo settings – I have found that 'outsiders' may try to unravel, undermine and challenge difference through implying general social and moral concerns (Blackman and Commane 2011; Commane 2010, 2012; Sumner 1994; Weeks 1991). This connects with Williams and Storm's (2012:3) findings on how individuals may not disclose their involvement with the BDSM community to 'outsiders', because of fearing being mislabelled or being seen as 'psychopathological' due to engaging 'in unconventional practices that are, unfortunately, not understood but feared within our society'. I often encountered C. Wright Mills' split between scholarship and biography, where some academics and others outside my friendship circle (beyond the research) prejudged me and mocked my research participants resulting in agency being removed. I have been subject to labelling such as 'disgrace to my sex', and my participants and I being perceived as 'up for it' or 'damaged goods' because of having an identity associated with an apparent deviancy.

With all of the above in mind, it was essential to understand the range and conflicting emotions I had felt days and months after the performance, as these emotions were not a full reflection of the care and support I observed in the ethnography. These emotions made me disempowered, but critical distance enabled me to work through negative fieldwork and be more emotionally attuned to the needs of participants. Although some of the memories from fieldwork exchanges and encounters have been painful for me; writing honestly about my subjectivity in the process of fieldwork has enabled me to understand how the researcher can feel and become as disempowered as research participants can be. Rather than see temporary reflexive disempowerment as a weakness, I found that being aware of the fragility of subjectivity within contexts of research and its physical and emotional locations, increased empathy for my research participants. This connects with the concept of overcoming 'hidden ethnography' (Blackman 2007), which highlights the issues of researchers tending to hide their emotions from the field in written accounts, rather than seeing them as valid and central to how research outcomes are achieved. This enabled me – as the researcher – to be more sensitively attuned to the complexities that fieldwork presents throughout the research process allowing you to see a bigger picture (Trautner and Borland 2013). Feeling is transformative and powerful, which means there is value in the researcher being honest about the processes of emotions in research and how these can shape the ways in which research participants, and their sense of identity, are re-presented in written accounts. This also gives depth and nuance to the multiple and changeable ways in which research participants can feel, express and be. Working through and reflecting upon these negative but important emotions, enables me to gain a deeper understanding of the complexity of any community, and the ease to which anyone could use the performance as a way to demonise research participants for political or personal means. Thinking through emotions therefore matters and, as Alford Young (2012:51) states, 'the visibility that researchers experience is a unique and particular quality of the craft of ethnography', then the researcher has to acknowledge the craft of emotional reflexivity in affective research. Thus, evoking yourself and reflecting upon this enables greater empathy and nuance that thickens descriptions and makes a multitude of realities present in the 'field' of research.

Conclusion: temporary reflexive disempowerment and the subcultural imagination

This chapter has explored the interplay of dilemmas, emotions, relationships and exchanges in field research in BDSM and fetish clubs, through the notion of *temporary reflexive disempowerment* after viewing a sexually explicit performance. The incident observed changed my approach to research, particularly with understanding the *value* of the researcher disclosing emotion, and the *implications* on the subjectivity and representation of individuals within subcultures. The value and place of emotions in research provoke points of contestation, highlighted by Mills through the split between biography and scholarship. Acknowledging this has enabled me to develop a multidirectional and holistic approach that encourages alternative interpretations and space for the researchers' subjectivity. Despite me being aware of wider social structures and tracing what Mills (1959:10–11) argues as the 'linkages among a great variety of milieu', emotional rawness is still present. My route back to reflexivity – through the sociological imagination – created an opportunity to understand the processes the researcher has to go through to carefully and critically unpack the political ramifications of researcher positionality, particularly when researching marginalised subcultures. Reflexivity and working through temporary reflexive disempowerment, is something you have to go through and feel. Recognising the affective qualities of communing and developing relationships with participants and the subculture, calls attention to the fragility of the researcher's subjectivity and, indeed, the subjectivity and the existence of others.

References

Anderson, T. (2009) *Rave Culture: The Alteration and Decline of a Philadelphia Music Scene*. Philadelphia, PA: Temple University Press.

Blackman, S. (2007) '"Hidden ethnography": crossing emotional boarders in qualitative accounts of young people's lives', *Sociology*, 41(4): 699–716.

Blackman, S. and Commane, G. (2011) 'Double reflexivity: the politics of friendship, fieldwork and representation within ethnographic studies of young people'. In Heath, S. and Walker, C. (eds) *Innovations in Youth Research*. London: Palgrave, 229–247.

Brak-Lamy, G. (2012) 'Emotions during fieldwork in the anthropology of sexuality: from experience to epistemological reflexions', *Journal of Human Sexuality*, Annual, Vol. 15. (www.ejhs.org – accessed 10 October 2015).

Carroll, K. (2012) 'Infertile? The emotional labour of sensitive and feminist research methodologies', *Qualitative Research*, 13: 546–561.

Cresswell, T. (2004) *Place: A Short Introduction*. Oxford: Blackwell Publishing.

Coffey, A. (1999) *The Ethnographic Self*. London: Sage.

Cole, L. and Knowles, G. (2000) *Doing Reflexive Life History Research*. Walnut Creek, CA: AltaMira.

Coles, J., Astbury, J., Dartnall, E. and Limjerwala, S. (2014) 'A qualitative exploration of researcher trauma and researchers' response to investigating sexual violence', *Violence Against Women*, 20(1): 95–117.

Commane, G. (2012) 'The transfigured body: fetish, fashion and performance'. Unpublished PhD Canterbury Christ Church University.

Ellis, C. (1991a) 'Sociological introspection and emotional experience'. In Denzin, N. (ed.) *Symbolic Interaction*. Greenwich, NY: JAI Press, 14(1): 23–50.

Ellis, C. (1991b) 'Emotional Sociology'. In Denzin, N. (ed.) *Studies in Symbolic Interaction*, Greenwich, NY: JAI Press, 12: 123–145.

Ellis, C. and Flaherty, M. (eds) (1992) *Investigating Subjectivity: Research on Lived Experience*. Newbury Park, CA: Sage.

Foucault, Michel (1977) *Discipline and Punish: the Birth of the Prison*. New York: Pantheon Books.

Gelder, K. (2005) *The Subcultures Reader*. New York: Routledge.

Hammersley, M. and Atkinson, P. (1995) *Ethnography. Principles in Practice*. London: Routledge.

Hillier, B. and Hanson J. (1984) *The Social Logic of Space*. Cambridge: Cambridge University Press.

Jackson, P. (2004) *Inside Clubbing. Sensual Experiments and the Art of Being Human*. Oxford: Berg.

Jorgensen, Danny (1989) *Participant Observation: A Methodology for Human Studies*. London: Sage.

Kirby, R. and Corzine, J. (1981) 'The contagion of stigma: fieldwork among deviants', *Qualitative Sociology*, 4(1): 3–20.

Kleinman, S. and Copp, M. A. (1993) *Emotions and Fieldwork*. Newbury Park, CA: Sage.

Lefebvre, H. (1991) *The Production of Space*. Oxford: Basil Blackwell.

Lindemann, Danielle (2013) 'Health Discourse and within-group stigma in professional BDSM', *Social Science and Medicine*, 99, 169–175.

MacRae, R. (2007) '"Insider" and "Outsider" Issues in Youth Research.' In Hodkinson, P. and Deicke, W. (eds) *Youth Cultures: Scenes, Subcultures and Tribes*. New York: Routledge, 51–62.

Massey, D. (2005) *For Space*. London: Sage.

Mills, C. Wright (1959) *The Sociological Imagination*. New York: Oxford University Press.

O'Reilly, K. (2005) *Ethnographic Methods*. London: Routledge.

Poewe, Karla (1999) 'Afterword. No hiding place: reflections on the confessions of Manda Cesara.' In Markowitz, F. and Ashkenazi, M. (eds) *Sex, Sexuality and the Anthropologist*. Chicago, IL: University of Illinois Press, 197–206.

Reger, Jo (2015) 'The story of a slut walk: sexuality, race and generational divisions in contemporary feminist activism', *Journal of Contemporary Ethnography*, 44(1): 84–112.

Savin-Baden, M. and Howell Major, C. (2013) *Qualitative Research: The Essential Guide to Theory and Practice*. London: Routledge.

Sumner, C. (1994) *The Sociology of Deviance*. Buckingham: Open University Press.

Trautner, M. and Borland, E. (2013) 'Using the sociological imagination to teach about academic integrity', *Teaching Sociology*, 41: 377–388.

Weeks, J. (1991) *Against Nature. Essays on History, Sexuality and Identity.* London: Rivers Oram Press.

Wilkins, A. (2008) '"So full of myself as a chick": goth women, sexual independence, and gender egalitarianism', *Gender & Society*, 18(3): 328–339.

Williams, D. and Storm, E. (2012) 'Unconventional leisure and career: insights into the work of professional dominatrices', *Journal of Human Sexuality*, Annual, Vol. 15. (www.ejhs.org – accessed 10 October 2015).

Young, A. (2012) 'Uncovering the hidden "I" in contemporary urban ethnography', *The Sociological Quarterly*, 54: 51–65.

Part III
Epistemologies, pedagogies and the subcultural subject

8 Understanding nightlife identities and divisions through the subculture/post-subculture debate

Robert Hollands

Introduction

Subcultural theory and analysis has played a crucial role in the history of understanding cultural activity, consumption, and leisure within the field of youth studies. While the concept of subculture generally has a longer and more complicated history (see Blackman 2014), in terms of the study of young people, one of the main starting points for debate is the work of the Centre for Contemporary Cultural Studies (CCCS) (Hall and Jefferson 1976). Over time however, the concept of 'youth subcultures' as espoused by CCCS has increasingly been criticised for its lack of applicability in understanding the complexity of youth consumer and leisure identities in the contemporary period (Bennett 2000; Hodkinson and Deicke 2009; Muggleton 2000; Redhead 1998). Moreover, the idea that we were now in an era of 'post-subcultural' identity and activity increasingly became a dominant paradigm in the youth studies field (Bennett and Kahn-Harris 2004; Huq 2006).

Despite the dominance of post-subcultural approaches, there has been a call to re-examine, reconceptualise and revitalise aspects of subcultural theory (Hodkinson 2012, 2002; Blackman 2005; Shildrick and MacDonald 2006; Nayak 2006), as well as a growing chorus of critiques of post-subculture in terms of its explanatory power and empirical basis (Blackman 2014; Hesmondhalgh 2005; Hollands 2002). For example, within nightlife research, some studies have launched counter-critiques of post-subcultural approaches due to their over-emphases on 'agency-based' consumption choices, and a failure to recognise continuing leisure divisions here, including class-based ones (see Chatterton and Hollands 2003; Hollands 2002). Post-subculturalists themselves have begun to reassess the impact of the 'cultural turn' in youth studies (Bennett 2011), including suggesting that attempts need to be made to bring together studies of youth cultural analyses, identity and belonging, with ideas around transitions and inequalities (Woodman and Bennett 2015).

The aim of this chapter will seek to explore this history and shift in perspective from subculture to post-subculture in more detail with specific reference to some of my (joint) empirical work on nightlife and virtual youth cultures (Chatterton and Hollands 2003; Hollands 2002; Greener and Hollands 2006). It begins by arguing that we all have our own subcultural imagination based partly on our own experiences of them, as well as the kind of research we have conducted on young people, and in what era and traditions of youth studies our work has been located. The chapter then turns to theoretical debates about subculture and post-subculture, arguing that postmodern notions of 'club-cultures' (Redhead 1998) and 'neo-tribes' (Bennett 1999) do not encompass the full array of nightlife identities and groupings, nor do they explain significant class divisions. The chapter concludes by returning to discuss the fate of the subcultural imaginations in the present period.

Talking about 'my generation'?: the subcultural imagination, personal experience and researcher positionality

Ideas about subculture are always 'relative' to both one's own generational cohort when we might have experienced them directly or researched them 'second-hand' (see Hollands 2003). In the same way that C. Wright Mills (1959) talked about the sociological imagination as a product of history, structure and biography, the subcultural imagination is also influenced by these factors. For example, my current student's understanding of youth subcultures historically comes primarily from documentary evidence (films and photos), and academic representations, disagreements and debates of subculture in the literature that I present to them, and is filtered through their own generational experience. Similarly, those old enough have their own personal recollections and experiences of historical styles and focal concerns – this is why subcultures have undergone so many revivals and re-appropriations over the years – and why some youths appear to have hung on to aspects of these identities into middle age (Bennett and Hodkinson 2012).

For instance, my own subcultural imagination is affected by geographical, temporal and national identity issues. While I may very well have been (or like to think I would have been) a 21 year-old punk had I lived in the London metropolitan region in 1977, my youth cultural proclivities growing up in small town rural Canada were instead expressed through involvement in a form of 'jock' culture in high school and university, a phenomenon studied by a number of authors (Miller 2009; Ortner 2002; Eckert 1989). Yet reading accounts of this subculture today, as a sociologist, do not really match up with my previous experience of it. While current research on jock culture has largely negative connotations (arrogant, self-centred, 'muscle brains' engaged in negative behaviours associated with bullying, misconduct, heavy drinking, sexism and hegemonic masculinity (http://smhp.psych.ucla.edu/pdfdocs/youth/jocks.pdf; also see Miller et al. 2006; Miller 2009)), more historical research (closer to my era) paradoxically saw jocks as popular, 'socialite conformists', with high cultural (class) capital, making up a high school subculture which markedly contrasted with other non-conformist cultures like 'druggies' and 'burnouts' (Eckert 1989; Ortner 2002).

Yet, in much the same way that Richard Linklater represents in his somewhat autobiographically inspired film *Dazed and Confused* (1993) (especially through one of the main characters, quarterback Randall 'Pink' Floyd), rather than being segregated from other student subcultures and involved in a 'militaristic, masculine, rah-rah', jock culture, I remember being equally at home among the drug-taking hippy element in high school, and I was certainly not unique in the crossover. Additionally, I was certainly not popular but actually rather shy and aloof in high school, and I had fairly low cultural capital coming from a working class family. Neither was I a political conformist, which might also help explain my trajectory from being a physical education student at university, to becoming engaged in 'radical' sport sociology (see Hollands 1984, 1988) and then moving into the politically charged world of cultural studies (ironically, considering we are talking about youth subcultures here, doing a PhD at the Centre for Contemporary Cultural Studies at the University of Birmingham, Hollands, 1990), and eventually ending up working in academia as a sociology professor. The message here, I guess, is that academic representations of subcultures do not always chide well with one's actual experience of a subcultural grouping, and this is another factor which may affect one's own subcultural imagination and memory.

Temporally, I myself had also 'missed' the 'golden age' – or what was at least thought of as the golden age – of British subcultures, having arrived in the UK in 1983, both in terms of either experiencing it directly or researching it. While remnants of punk subculture persisted into the 80s, they were largely parodies and pastiches of the original culture, and while two-tone, reggae and some aspects of post-punk culture were clearly evident to me when I lived and studied at the University of Birmingham, the primary youth concern at that time was with youth unemployment and the labour market (i.e. youth transition studies were largely dominant then (see Banks et al. 1992) – hence my PhD was on cultures of work and training rather than styles of leisure and musical identity (Hollands 1990). Subcultures, when they were mentioned by YTS trainees at all, tended to be imitations and revivals of past youth cultural styles and musical taste (Hollands 1990: 140–1), rather than significant examples of identity and resistance. Yet ironically, near the end of my PhD, Britain suddenly experienced what was probably the last big youth cultural phenomenon – rave culture or acid house (Reynolds 1998). However, rather than being viewed as a subculture, in the traditional sense, sociological models for understanding it in this way had moved on (Redhead 1993; Hollands 1995). In the next section of this chapter I look at the theoretical and social/cultural transformations that occurred during this period, before turning to examples from my work on nightlife consumer identities, and a study of the psytrance dance culture, as a way of examining the changing fate of my own subcultural imagination.

Theoretical trajectories: from subculture to clubcultures, 'neo-tribes' and back

While the term subculture existed prior to, and had a much longer history in the US (including work on American youth – see Blackman 2014; Williams 2007), many agree that research into British youth cultures really began in the 1970s when the Birmingham Centre for Contemporary Cultural Studies (CCCS) began investigating modern youth groupings (Hall and Jefferson 1976; Willis 1978; Hebdige 1979). Initially, it is important to note that there were indeed significant variations between different CCCS writers such as Dick Hebdige's more semiotic work *Subculture* (1979) (and his consideration of more mixed working and middle-class (art school) subcultures such as punk), Paul Willis's (1978) more ethnographic and 'homology' based study of middle class hippies and working class bikers, and John Clark's and Tony Jefferson's more orthodox studies of skinheads and Teddy Boys respectively (Clarke 1976; Hall and Jefferson 1976). While sometimes misrepresented, CCCS did choose to focus the *majority* of their studies on local, marginal and working-class youth subcultures such as the Teddy Boys (Hall and Jefferson 1976) and skinheads (Clarke 1976), developing their neo-Marxist theory of class-based subcultures which were tightly bound around a homology of style, argot, territory, music and other focal concerns.

Although they did not claim that their sub-cultural paradigm was intended to be a model which explained youth cultures in their entirety, Hall and Jefferson's (1976) work clearly demonstrated that there were very different sub-sets of youth sub-cultural styles, expressions and meanings, rather than a general and homogenous 'youth culture'. And while it was also true that CCCS concentrated on male, white working class cultures, even their early work contained one of the initial discussions of the absence of young girls (McRobbie and Garber 1976) and the impact race and ethnicity had on white subcultures (Hebdige 1979). A more careful reading of *Resistance Through Rituals* also reveals some discussion of middle class youth cultures and how they might be more differentially understood (pp. 57–71). In particular, Hall and Jefferson (1976: 60) prophetically hinted at the 'individualisation thesis', a dominant theme in 1990s youth sociology (see Furlong and Cartmel 2007). In fact, some of the youth subcultures CCCS looked at involved working class youths borrowing from media-based, middle class cultures, punk being the most exemplary (see Hebdige 1979).

However, CCCS subcultural theories came under considerable criticism in the 1980s (some of the early criticism coming from within their own ranks – see McRobbie and Garber 1976; also Griffin 1993). In general, their reliance on Marxist theory led to critics commenting that subcultural researchers were romanticising spectacular working-class youth and were ignoring mainstream and middle-class youth cultures (Griffin 2011; Hodkinson 2012; Hodkinson and Deicke 2009; Williams 2007), so that subcultural findings and cases fitted within their own political ideologies (Bennett 1999). Additional criticisms included the well know gender critique and male bias (McRobbie and Nava 1984), issues around ethnicity (Griffin 2011), and a developing critique based on more postmodern notions of youth culture in the 1990s (see Redhead 1993). As such, there was a decline in youth cultural analyses in the 1980s, and subcultural theory appeared somewhat moribund through to the millennium (Muggleton 2000).

As Cohen and Ainley (2000: 86) argue, by 'the early 1990s the textualization of cultural studies was complete' and by implication, the study of youth cultures was decidedly influenced by postmodern thinking exemplified by a somewhat diverse set of writings around 'clubcultures' (Redhead 1998), and 'neo-tribes' (Bennett 2000). Youth sub-cultures were viewed as in terminal decline, replaced by more loose, fragmented, hybrid and transitory global cultures 'of avoidance', with the first real alternative youth cultural paradigm to challenge the notion of subcultures from CCCS coming out of Steve Redhead's postmodern inspired work (see Redhead 1993, 1998). Redhead's position can best be summed up by the assertion that class subcultures – if they ever indeed existed (Redhead, 1993) – have now been surpassed by 'clubcultures' (Redhead 1998); loose, globally based youth formations grounded in the media/market niches of contemporary dance music, and the regulation and indeed criminalisation of youth cultures characterised by a kind of 'hedonism in hard times' (Redhead 1993).

The concept of dance cultures as 'tribes' and 'neotribes' has also been used to describe post-subcultures (Maffesoli 1996; Bennett 1999). This is based around the idea that in the postmodern there is such a fragmentation of homogeneous culture that it is no longer be possible to have subcultures, so even smaller groups or tribes/ neo-tribes, with shared lifestyles or interests, form and reform (Maffesoli 1996). Similarly, some of the recent writing on youth cultures and drug cultures, suggests that the spread of certain substances across youth groups and evidence of poly-drug use (multiple substances), implies that drug use is now 'postmodern' rather than subcultural in character (see Parker, Aldridge and Measham 1998; although see Blackman (2010) for a critique of this idea). Bennett (1999) claims that the concept of 'neo-tribes' recognises how a person may belong to a number of different groups, switching from one musical style to another, suggesting a much more transient and hybrid form of consumption identity (Bennett 2005). Muggleton (1997: 98) has taken some of the ideas of club culture and neo-tribe even further, in his discussion of 'post-subculture', where he states that: 'Post-subculturalists no longer have any sense of subcultural authenticity, where inception is rooted in particular socio-temporal contexts and tied to underlying structural relations.'

The postmodern position perspective has been accompanied by ideas about the role of globalisation and fragmentation of identities (Hall 1997), the rise of individualism (Furlong and Cartmel 2007), and shifts in class structure and identification (Furlong, Woodman and Wyn 2011), all reasons why identifiable youth subcultures have perhaps faded in contemporary society. However, a counter argument has been that aspects of subcultural approaches have perhaps been written off too easily or misunderstood (see MacDonald and Shildrick 2006; Blackman 2005) and that post-subcultural approaches themselves are inadequate in terms of simply inverting past perspectives rather than providing adequate evidence themselves (Hesmondhalgh 2005), as well as failing to explain the persistence of youth leisure divisions, class being among them (see Hollands 2002). These new concerns with hybridity, tribes and post-subculturalist forms, although interesting, have often meant that 'en route questions of class trans/formation were rather left to one side' (Cohen and Ainley 2000: 84). Even theorists like Bennett (2011) in his analyses and defence of the impact of the 'postsubcultural turn' has admitted that such approaches emphasising 'pick and mix' styles have been compromised by relying on quite small data sets, and that questions of inequality in youth culture have not disappeared.

Clearly, there are examples of contemporary postmodern youth cultural activity to be found. Yet, the same question that plagued earlier theorists of youth subcultures remains: are postmodern examples any more representative or empirically demonstrable among the young than minority sub-cultures were (Hesmondhalgh 2005)? The problem with post-subcultural theorising and methodology here is that they do not appear to find inequalities or stratified youth cultures partly because they are not looking for it. Recent research on clubbing and music festivals in the UK and dance consumer identities abroad (i.e. Ibiza), appears to refute 'pick and mix' culture by demonstrating the continuing impact class taste and labelling has on constructing boundaries and difference (Bhardwa 2014). Additionally, postmodernism does not possess a theoretical framework that allows them to explain social division within the leisure sphere, differentiate young people on the basis of their economic or domestic situation, or to account for the role locality plays in youth culture (Hollands 1995). In the next section, we take a closer look at how youth cultures in the night-time economy are not just fragmented, but are also segmented and divided.

Researching nightlife: from subculture to class segmentation

Postmodern approaches to youth culture through the guise of terms such as 'club-cultures', post-subculture and ideas about 'neo-tribes' (Redhead 1993, 1999; Muggleton 2000; Bennett 1999), combined with the fact that night-life cultures are changing so quickly and frequently through increased individualisation, fragmentation and globalisation, has supposedly fuelled a complex array of youth nightlife. Subculture and class, in this framework have either disappeared altogether, or appear much less significant as explanatory tools. However, counter approaches to understanding nightlife consumption and further research in this area, suggests a much closer link between transitions in the work and production sphere (Hollands 2002; Ball et al. 2000), and socially segmented sets of youth consumption spaces, identities and groupings (Chatterton and Hollands 2003). While minority elements of 'neo-tribal' and hybrid forms of youth identity and consumption clearly exist in the night-time economy ('cultural omnivores'), we argue that the main focus for the development of nightlife is a more 'mainstream' commercial form which exploits existing social, economic and cultural cleavages in the population, segregating young adults into particular spaces and places. This is an active process, fuelled partly through an internal competition among youth groups to maintain social and status distinctions (Thornton 1995), but which also reflects wider class elements in terms of style and types of nightlife venues consumed (Bourdieu 1984).

Contrary to either a free-floating, individualised, 'pick and mix' story of postmodern youth cultures or a simple 'class correspondence' subcultural model of leisure, our research on nightlife activity in three UK cities involving interviews and focus groups with around 80 young adults (Chatterton and Holland

2003; Hollands 2002) is instead characterised by hierarchically segmented consumption groupings and spaces in cities, which are highly structured around drinking circuits or areas each with their own set of codes, dress styles, language and tastes (Bourdieu 1984; Thornton 1995). Despite postmodern assertions that hybrid eclectic styles today make it more problematic for young people to distinguish between themselves and other youth cultures (Muggleton 1998: 199), many of our respondents had no such difficulty in identifying class-based nightlife groupings based on appearance and style. For example, within what we call commercial mainstream nightlife spaces there was a clear dichotomy recognised by nightlife revellers between more mobile and middle-class gentrified youth and working class or 'townie' youth. For example see the 'style-based' (clothing, behaviour, demeanour) identifiers of local working class youth nightlife consumers below:

> They're down there in their Ben Sherman's and their black polished shoes looking very smart, but acting like wankers.
>
> (Paul, 23 years old, Leeds)

> People who wear Rockport and the like cause trouble ... they're scallies.
>
> (Chain bar owner)

> Simon: They wear Ben Sherman shirts and they go out and get pissed.
> Jane: ...   have a shag and have a fight ...
> Simon: Shag, fight and a kebab, very loud.
>
> (Comments from Newcastle focus group 3)

> The queue is full of large groups of boys in luminous Ben Sherman shirts and spiky hair and girls in tiny tops ... There is a stage where those celebrating special occasions get up to show off and which, tonight, is occupied by a girl wearing a plastic sash reading 'the party starts here' and four of her friends in bikini tops and paste tiaras.
>
> (Brockes 2000)

Here, emphasis is on particular clothing brands (Ben Sherman, Rockport shoes), styles (spiky hair, revealing tops, hen party tiaras) and behaviour (loud, aggressive, promiscuous) work as codes for the expression of class-based consumption, styles and behaviours (Skeggs 1997). Unsurprisingly, in a cultural climate of blame and social exclusion (Shildrick and MacDonald 2006), some young people openly expressed quite scathing views about more marginalised youth (invoking not only class but gender and ageist stereotypes), in our research:

> Nasty, horrible creatures of society, who crawl out from under their stone on Thursday 'cos its dole day. They put on the same frock every week 'cos they don't wanna buy a new one until they get too fat.
>
> (Mark, 20 years old, Leeds)

Similarly, there were equally derogatory feelings about more middle class up-market nightlife consumer (though the 'symbolic violence' in the first quote is perhaps more imaginary than real):

> Some of them are just really stuck up. Some of the times that I've been in this Quayside bar, when I come out of there I just want to drop a bomb on it you know... there is a dress code sort of thing ... and people in there think they are something different.
>
> (Dave, 31 years old, Newcastle upon Tyne)

> They're all like posh blonde birds who go round in puffa jackets and things like that. They've got rich daddies and you can tell, because they usually have a Moschino bag or something, and they walk around with these silly handbags.
>
> (Ben, 20 years old, Leeds)

> Sarah: People who are dressed in all the designer stuff.
> Steve: Pretentious people on a Saturday.
> Steve: I hate to see these beautiful perfect people with their perfect make up and their perfect hair.
>
> (Comments from Newcastle focus group 2)

These were not simply opinions and ideas, but social differences that created real barriers and boundaries, even when the clientele of a particular venue was more mixed. As one woman (Jackie, 23 years old, Leeds) commented to us about visiting a new 'up market city centre bar':

> Everybody inside was all tarted up and I was wearing trainers and looking a bit scruffy ... It's just the way they make you feel once you're in there. The people who sort of sneer at you and you think I don't feel comfortable here because I can't relax when everyone else is sort of preening ...

Of course, there were examples of more mixed and hybrid nightscapes and groupings. Rachel, who fitted into the consumption typology of a 'cultural omnivore' ('Me I go everywhere and get on with everyone') as well as examples of working class youth trying to elevate their cultural status on nights out through consumption (Jane: 'Me, I'm a cocktail person') also occurred. However, cultural mixing here was the exception rather than the rule, and as Roberts (1997) has argued engaging in the same leisure activity does not mean that differences in class meaning simply disappear. As such there is little evidence here for the fragmentary 'pick and mix' culture expressed by postmodern approaches. And while subculture in the traditional sense does not exactly apply to such nightlife consumption groupings, particularly in the sense that such identities are created through 'labelling' by others, rather than by affiliation, class notions of style and taste remain below the surface here. The applicability of subculture and post-subculture is further empirically tested below by applying these ideas to the characteristics of a virtual dance culture called psytrance.

Beyond subculture and post-subculture? The case of virtual psytrance

In a second research study, we define 'virtual psytrancers' as young adults who enjoy 'psychedelic trance', a particular form of computer generated dance music, and who keep in contact through internet discussion forums as well as participate in dance events both in their own country and in some cases, world-wide (Greener and Hollands 2006). Unique for a youth cultural study, we utilised an internet-based online questionnaire, and created a large international sample of 569 virtual psytrancers from over 40 countries, assessing the shared attitudes, cultural elements, global spaces and international connections of the group.

By definition, virtual psytrance would appear to be a quintessential postmodern culture. Formed out of the fusion of travelling party-goers to Goa in India, the import of 'acid house music' from Britain's rave scene, and the introduction of electronic equipment capable of producing strange psychedelic effects, 'psytrance' was born (Mathesdorf 2003). Additionally, its postmodern character is exemplified by the fact that it has become, through the internet, a global culture, consumed by young people around the world. The fragmentary character of its origins and its global consumption through the internet would appear to suggest that the culture would have a fleeting ephemeral quality in which people of different cultures and classes could temporally engage in and modify to their needs. For example, the vast majority of its proponents keep in touch with it virtually, suggesting that there is a choice when to engage, or even a lack of social obligation to participate (Galston 2000). And with over 40 different types of drugs consumed at psytrance parties, such multiple or 'poly' drug use (see Parker et al. 1998) again would appear to be at odds with more subcultural homologies of style and drug taking (Willis 1976).

However, despite these initial postsubcultural elements, the research revealed some deeper and more paradoxical aspects which appeared to be more subcultural in character. First, nearly 80% of survey respondents claim to view themselves as 'belonging' to a psytrance community, reminiscent of subcultural identification and affiliation. Similarly such bonds are shown to be strong and stable with 85% of respondents being involved with psytrance for 4 years or more, with nearly 20% involved for over 10 years. Terms employed include 'family', 'community', 'friends' and 'tribes', which indicate the existence of extremely strong feelings of kinship and solidarity between psytrancers.

Second, like many youth subcultures before them, music and drugs helped create an important common affinity between virtual psytrancers. Over 90% of respondents believe that music is the most important as aspect of a psytrance party (US respondent: 'Being a psytrancer is about being one with the music'). Within the psytrance scene, drugs are quite a significant aspect of the experience with nearly 90% of respondents claiming that they have used drugs at a psytrance party. While we mentioned the use of a variety of different drugs was widespread, the main drugs of choice were split between three choices – ecstasy, LSD, and cannabis – all three homologous with the main elements of the culture (dance/spirituality, mind alteration and relaxation).

Finally, even an internet-based subculture such as psytrance, appeared to need physical and face-to-face contact between members. As such, meeting up at physical locations for communal dances or 'parties' is important to virtual psytrancers, as it presents a means of developing and reinforcing their shared 'virtual' culture, as well cultivating friendship and community. Ninety-seven per cent of virtual psytrancers had attended parties in physical locations, with nearly 30% congregating every two to three weeks, and with the vast majority attending dance events in their own country. With 84% of psytrancers engaging with their culture via the internet every 2 to 5 days, as well as regularly meeting in temporary physical locations, also shows that the connections between psytrancers are extremely stable, rather than transient and superficial as suggested by postmodern thinking (Bennett 1999).

In our view this group epitomises a 'postmodern subculture' – a global, internet-based grouping (hence seemingly postmodern), yet whom also share temporary physical spaces (i.e. attend psytrance events in one or more countries), and are characterised by a strong attachment to a particular form of music, and a common set of values, practices and belief systems (i.e. aspects of what we think of as subculture).

Conclusion

Recently I attended a first year seminar on the topic of youth subcultures as a 'peer observer' to one of my teaching assistants on a module I run called 'Comparing Cultures'. The students were extremely well prepared and spoke animatedly about youth subcultures, its elements and theory behind it, differences between UK and US models, and discussed the current state and future of youth culture. What I found so revealing about the seminar was the passion and excitement with which they discussed youth subcultural studies from the past (almost as a form of youth 'nostalgia'), which contrasted markedly with a kind of resignation that they no longer appeared to exist in the present day, at least not in the same (identifiable) way. Ideas about the role of the internet, globalisation and the rise of individualism, combined with the fragmentation of identities (including class) in the present period, were all muted as reasons why identifiable youth subcultures were not a feature of contemporary society. In their place, students discussed a more 'pick and mix' and agency-based model of youth styles and identities, where 'alternative' seemed to mean just another slightly different consumer choice, rather than a 'resistant' subculture.

One might be tempted to stop here and accept that we are indeed in a post-subculturalist landscape. Yet, returning to the idea of the subcultural imagination, this situation might also be saying something important about this generation of students own social backgrounds, consumer experiences, and belief in individual agency. For a largely middle class group, engaged heavily in the global cultures of the internet, and surrounded by a seemingly endless array of consumer goods, styles, music and nightlife, youth cultural choices must indeed seem endless (with class influences supposedly disappearing along with identifiable subcultural styles). Yet, when pushed to discuss their own nightlife venue choices, it quickly becomes apparent that even here there are significant class (fraction) differences both within the student population, as well as outwith. For instance, there are clear 'taste differences' in where more upper class and privately educated university students (the 'rahs' – see Mountford 2012) have been known to socialise, as opposed to state school students, or those that see themselves as 'alternative' or more political (i.e. such as those engaged in the 2010 student occupation, see Reinghans and Hollands 2013). Additionally, many students avoided certain venues as they were seen as 'common' (class-loaded term) including eschewing the city centre of Newcastle altogether on the weekend as it was 'full of locals' (also see Hollands 1995). Similarly, students were quick to identity working class 'townies' or 'chavs' in subcultural terms, with reference to clothes, style and demeanour (Nayak 2006; Hayward and Yar 2006).

This of course does not imply that subculture as a concept can or should be resurrected in its earlier form. Many of the conditions mentioned above have impacted on aspects central to its original formulation, meaning that future subcultures will probably not develop in the same way as the CCCS envisaged, or at all. The narcissism of social media culture may mean that young people today are far too busy 'representing themselves' virtually (see Robards 2014), to revolt, shock or resist in real life. Or, it may mean that any future subcultures will probably all have a 'virtual' and global element like the example of psytrance discussed earlier. A key point however, is not to throw out the impact of class on young people's identities and transitions 'baby' with the subcultural 'bath water'. There is also a view that, in the right circumstances, the young will always seek to shock, to question, to revolt or resist in some fashion – and youth subcultures have always been a way of expressing this. In Don Lett's excellent *Subculture* film series, Pauline Black (2012), former band member of the two-tone group *The Specials*, argues: 'Subculture is alive and well, but not as we know it, because we will be surprised, there is something coming, we just don't know what it is.' On the other hand, it could be argued that we have perhaps entered an extended period of 'status quo' when it comes to youth subcultural challenges to the prevailing consumerist and neo-liberal social order. In the meanwhile, I think there is value in revisiting the relevance of youth subcultures, if only to advance our future collective 'subcultural imagination'.

References

Ball, S., M. Maguire and S. Macrae (2000) *Choice, Pathways and Transitions Post-16: New Youth, New Economies in the Global City.* London: Routledge/ Falmer.
Banks, M., I. Bates, G. Breakwell and J. Bynner (1992) *Careers and Identities.* Buckingham: Open University Press.

Bennett, A. (1999) 'Subcultures or Neo-Tribes? Rethinking the Relationship between Youth, Style and Music Taste.' *Sociology* 33(3): 599–617.

Bennett, A. (2000) *Popular Music And Youth Culture: Music, Identity And Place.* Basingstoke: Macmillan.

Bennett, A. (2005) 'In Defence of Neo-Tribes: A Response to Blackman and Hesmondhalgh.' *Journal of Youth Studies* 8(2): 255–259.

Bennett, A. (2011) 'The Post-subculturalist Turn: Some Reflections 10 Years On.' *Journal of Youth Studies* 14(5): 493–506.

Bennett, A. and K. Kahn-Harris (eds) (2004) *After Subculture: Critical Studies in Contemporary Youth Culture.* Basingstoke: Palgrave.

Bennett, A. and P. Hodkinson (2012) *Ageing and Youth Cultures: Music, Style and Identity.* Oxford: Berg.

Bhardwa, B. (2014) 'The Construction of Dance Consumer Identities: An Exploration of Drug Use, Digital Technologies and Control in Three Dance Settings.' PhD in Sociology, Lancaster University, September.

Black, P. (2012) 'Beaten Generation', *Subculture* film (Don Letts) at: https://www.fredperrysubculture.com/film/7299/beaten-generation.

Blackman, S. (2005) 'Youth Subcultural Theory: A Critical Engagement with the Concept, Its Origins and Politics, From the Chicago School to Postmodernism.' *Journal of Youth Studies* 8(1): 1–20.

Blackman, S. (2010) 'Youth Subcultures, Normalisation and Drug Prohibition: The Politics of Contemporary Crisis and Change?' *British Politics* 5: 337–366.

Blackman, S. (2014) 'Subculture Theory: An Historical and Contemporary Assessment of the Concept for Understanding Deviance.' *Deviant Behavior* 35(6): 496–512.

Bourdieu, P. (1984) *Distinction: A Social Critique of the Judgement of Taste.* London: Routledge.

Brockes, E. (2000) 'Yorkie Bars.' *The Guardian*, 4 March, p. 16.

Chatterton, P. and R. Hollands (2003) *Urban Nightscapes: Youth Cultures, Pleasure Spaces and Corporate Power.* London: Routledge.

Clarke, J. (1976) 'Skinheads and the Magical Recovery of Community'. In: S. Hall and T. Jefferson (eds) *Resistance Through Rituals: Youth Subcultures in Post War Britain.* London: Hutchinson, 99–102.

Clarke, J., J. Clarke, S. Hall, T. Jefferson and B. Roberts (1976) 'Subcultures, Cultures and Class.' In: S. Hall and T. Jefferson (eds) *Resistance Through Rituals: Youth Subcultures in Post War Britain.* London: Hutchinson, 9–74.

Cohen, P. and P. Ainley (2000) 'In the Country of the Blind?: Youth Studies and Cultural Studies in Britain.' *Journal of Youth Studies* 3(1): 79–95.

Eckert, P. (1989) *Jocks and Burnouts: Social Categories and Identity in the High School.* New York: Teacher's College Press.

Furlong, A. and F. Cartmel (2007) *Youth and Social Change.* Milton Keynes: Open University Press.

Furlong, A.D. Woodman and J. Wyn (2011) 'Changing Times, Changing Perspectives: Reconciling "Transition" and "Cultural" Perspectives on Youth and Young Adulthood.' *Journal of Sociology* 47(4): 355–370.

Galston, W. A. (2000) 'Does the Internet Strengthen Community?' *National Civic Review* 89(3): 193–202.

Greener, T. and R. Hollands (2006) 'Beyond Subculture and Post-subculture? The Case of Virtual Psytrance.' *Journal of Youth Studies* 9(4): 393–418.

Griffin, C. (1993) *Representations of Youth.* Cambridge: Polity.

Griffin, C. (2011) 'The Trouble With Class: Researching Youth, Class and Culture Beyond the "Birmingham School".' *Journal of Youth Studies* 14(3): 245–259.

Hall, S. (1997) 'The Local and the Global: Globalization and Identity.' In: A. King, (ed.) *Culture, Globalization and the World System: Contemporary Conditions for the Representation of Identity.* Minneapolis, MN: University of Minnesota Press, 19–39.

Hall, S. and T. Jefferson (eds) (1976) *Resistance Through Rituals: Youth Subcultures in Post War Britain.* London: Hutchinson.

Hayward, J. and M. Yar (2006) 'The "Chav" Phenomenon: Consumption, Media and the Construction of a New Underclass.' *Crime, Media, Culture* 2(1): 9–28.

Hebdidge, D. (1979) *Subculture: The Meaning of Style.* London: Methuen.

Hesmondhalgh, D. (2005) 'Subcultures, Scenes or Tribes?: None of the Above.' *Journal of Youth Studies* 8(1): 21–40.

Hodkinson, P. (2002) *Goth: Identity, Style and Subculture.* Oxford: Berg.

Hodkinson P. (2012) 'Beyond Spectacular Specifics in the Study of Youth (Sub)Cultures.' *Journal of Youth Studies* 15(5): 557–572.

Hodkinson P. and W. Deicke (ed.) (2009) *Youth Cultures: Scenes, Subcultures and Tribes.* London: Routledge.

Hollands, R. (1984) 'The Role of Cultural Studies and Social Criticism in the Sociological Study of Sport.' *Quest* 36(1): 66–79.

Hollands, R. (1988) 'English Canadian Sports Novels and Cultural Production.' In: J. Harvey and H. Cantelon, eds. *Not Just a Game: Essays in Canadian Sport Sociology.* Ottawa: University of Ottawa Press, 213–234.

Hollands, R. (1990) *The Long Transition: Class, Culture and Youth Training.* London: Macmillan.

Hollands, R. (1995) *Friday Night, Saturday Night: Youth Cultural Identification in the Post-Industrial City.* Newcastle: Newcastle University.

Hollands, R. (2002) 'Divisions in the Dark; Youth Cultures, Transitions and Segmented Consumption Spaces in the Night-time Economy.' *Journal of Youth Studies* 5(2): 153–172.

Hollands, R. (2003) 'Double Exposure: Exploring the Social and Political Relations of the Ethnographic Youth Research.' In: A. Bennett, M. Cieslick and S. Miles, eds. *Researching Youth.* Basingstoke: Palgrave, 157–169.

Huq, R. (2006) *Beyond Subculture.* London: Routledge.

McRobbie, A. and L. Garber (1976) 'Girls and Subcultures: An Exploration.' In: S. Hall and T. Jefferson, eds. *Resistance Through Rituals: Youth Subcultures in Post War Britain.* London: Hutchinson, 209–222.

McRobbie, A. and M. Nava (1984) *Gender and Generation.* London: Macmillan.

Maffesoli, M. (1996) *The Time of Tribes: The Decline of Individualism in Mass Society.* London: Sage.

Mathesdorf, K. (2003) 'History of Psychedelic Trance.' *Isratrance* [online]. Available at: http://forum.isratrance.com/viewtopic.php?topic=13979&forum=1&3 [accessed 24 November 2004].

Miller, K., M. Melnick, M. Farrell, D. Sabo and G. Barnes (2006) 'Jocks, Gender, Binge Drinking and Adolescent Violence.' *Journal of Interpersonal Violence* 21: 105–120.

Miller, K. (2009) 'Sport-related Identities and the "Toxic Jock".' (Report). *Journal of Sport Behavior* http://www.southalabama.edu/psychology/journal.html.

Mills, C. W. (1959) *The Sociological Imagination.* New York: Oxford University Press.

Mountford, V. (2012) 'Everyday Class Distinctions in Higher Education'. PhD in Sociology, School of Geography, Politics and Sociology, Newcastle University.

Muggleton, D. (1998) 'The Post-subculturalist.' In: S. Redhead, J. O'Conner and D. Wynne, eds. *The Clubcultures Reader*. Oxford: Blackwell, 167–185.

Muggleton, D. (2000) *Inside Subculture: The Postmodern Meaning of Style*. London: Berg.

Muggleton, D. and R. Weinzierl (eds) (2004) *The Post-Subcultures Reader*. Oxford: Berg.

Nayak, A. (2006) 'Displaced Masculinities: Chavs, Youth and Class in the Post-Industrial City.' *Sociology* 40(5): 813–831.

Ortner S. (2002) 'Burned Like a Tattoo: High School Social Categories and "American Culture".' *Ethnography* 3(2): 115–48.

Parker, H., J. Aldridge and F. Measham (1998) *Illegal Leisure*. London: Routlege.

Redhead, S. (1993) *Rave-Off: Politics and Deviance in Contemporary Youth Culture* . Aldershot: Avebury Press.

Redhead, S. (1997) *Subcultures to Clubcultures*, Oxford: Blackwell.

Redhead, S. (ed.) (1998) *The Club Cultures Reader.* Oxford: Blackwell.

Reynolds, S. (1998) *Energy Flash: Journey Through Rave Culture and Dance Music*. London: Picador.

Rheingans, R. and R. Hollands (2013) '"There is No Alternative?": Challenging Dominant Understandings of Youth Politics in Late Modernity Through a Case Study of the 2010 UK Student Occupation Movement.' *Journal of Youth Studies* 16(4): 546–564.

Robards, B. (2014) 'Mediating Experiences of "Growing Up" on Facebook's Timeline: Privacy, Ephemerality and the Reflexive Project of Self.' In: A. Bennett and B. Robards, eds. *Mediated Youth Cultures: The Internet, Belonging and New Cultural Configurations*. Basingstoke: Palgrave, 26–41.

Roberts, K. (1997) 'Same Activities, Different Meanings: British Youth Cultures in the 1990s.' *Leisure Studies* 16: 1–15.

Shildrick, T. and R. MacDonald (2006) 'In Defence of Subculture: Young People, Leisure and Social Divisions.' *Journal of Youth Studies* 9(2): 125–140.

Skeggs, B. (1997) *Formations of Class & Gender: Becoming Respectable.* London: Sage.

Thornton, S. (1995) *Club Cultures: Music, Media and Subcultural Capital.* Cambridge: Polity Press.

Williams, J. P. (2007) 'Youth-Subcultural Studies: Sociological Traditions and Core Concepts.' *Sociology Compass* 1(2): 572–593.

Willis, P. (1976) 'The Cultural Meaning of Drug Use.' In: S. Hall and T. Jefferson, eds. *Resistance Through Rituals: Youth Subcultures in Post War Britain*. London: Hutchinson, 106–118.

Willis, P. (1978) *Profane Culture*. London: Routledge.

Woodman, D. and A. Bennett (eds) (2015) *Youth Cultures, Belonging and Transitions: Bridging the Gap in Youth Research*. Basingstoke: Palgrave.

9 Feminism, subculture and the production of knowledge

Developing intersectional
epistemologies amidst the reflexive turn

Michelle Kempson

This chapter presents a framework for engaging with subculture through feminist methodology. Drawing upon research into the production of feminist zines in the UK, the chapter explores how some grassroots feminists negotiate their subcultural status as knowledge produces, and asks how a researcher might explore the collective aspects of grassroots feminism without promoting their own feminist values. The central objective of the chapter is to explore how researchers can avoid prioritising certain knowledge paradigms over others, while acknowledging how different 'versions of feminism' co-exist within zine subculture (Kempson, 2015a). To do this, the chapter (re)engages with C. Wright Mills' (1959) explanation of how history, biography, and social structures intersect, and argues for the development of 'intersectional epistemologies' that are equipped explain how a researcher can engage reflexively with an internally diverse subcultural environment.

From C. Wright Mills to feminist methodology

This chapter develops a feminist engagement with the work of C. Wright Mills' in order to suggest the need for a 'multi-focus', reflexively tuned, approach to the study of subculture. First, however, it is important to acknowledge that C. Wright Mills was writing at a time when structural inequalities were not high on the sociological agenda. Although 'social movements shattered the consensus sociology of the 1950s' (Burawoy, 2008:366), it took a while longer for the voices of women, and gendered critiques of social structures, to become integrated within the discipline (Komarovsky, 1991). Certainly C. Wright Mills' reflections on elitism and class structures (1956 [1970]) contributed a new type of knowledge to sociological enquiry; however, his depiction of women, in *White Collar: the American middle classes* (1951 [1956]) for example, has received criticism for its derogatory representation of the female research participants. Preceding Simone de Beauvoir's *The Second Sex* (1949), the paradigm of Western philosophical thought (reproduced through the intellectual elitism that C. Wright Mills (1956 [1970]) warned us about) had offered no substantive account of how gender inequality is sustained. Following this, antagonism between biological determinism and social constructivism emerged, with feminists explaining how the latter can account for the way in which gender roles become constituted through culture and history (Oakley, 1985).

The acceptance of gender roles as socially (re)produced opens up the possibility for the (re)negotiation of historical depictions of women. From around the 1960s, feminist scholars have pointed out the problems with positivist research traditions that do not write the researcher into their own research (Cook and Fonow, 1986). Specifically, feminist research is credited as championing qualitative enquiry that engages in detail with the biographical narratives of women (although it should be noted that some contemporary writings on feminist method also recognise the potential of quantitative enquiry to shape feminist discourse – see Cohen and Hughes, 2012). In recent decades, feminist methodology has re-ordered understandings of 'autonomy' (Abrams, 1998) via the introduction of 'intersectional' analysis (Crenshaw, 1989); a framework through which feminists have begun to explain how the oppression of women is constituted not only via gendered, but also racial, identifications. This framework has been used to explain how people manage the 'meeting point' of their different identities (Crenshaw, 1991; Yuval-Davis, 2006) and how structural inequalities are experienced.

The process of 'history making' is deeply structural, and is shaped by dominant knowledge economies that serve to amplify certain voices, while muting others. We cannot, therefore, realise C. Wright Mills' call for sociologists to 'zoom-out' from micro-focus research agendas in order to develop broader historical understandings of the social world, without first critiquing the dominant discourses that distort the process of 'history making'. For example, intersectional analyses have highlighted how white, western, feminist thought dominates the feminist movement (Carby, 1982; Mohanty, 1988), and have engaged with racial and class inequalities that are rendered invisible by some feminist discourse. Mohanty (1988) and Davis (2008) argue, though, that such analyses can prevent the possibility of achieving a *unified* feminist movement. This critique, explored in the context of subcultures research later on in this chapter, highlights a problem with the underlying political project of feminism that looks increasingly more fragmented with each 'splintering off' of various intersections of the movement. This chapter acknowledges these drawbacks, while advocating a continued engagement with the concept that is equipped to address how the coordination of history and biography (Mills, 1959) might improve subcultures research. It argues that the intersections between feminist theory, queer studies, and anti-racist movements provide subcultures researchers with a means of relocating the subcultures debate away from the 'subculture vs. post-subculture' discourse, and towards an engagement with processes of historicity that shape current understandings of the 'subcultural subject'.

Feminism and subculture

When the negotiation of subjectivity is discussed in relation to subculture, it is often done so by presuming that particular social groups are either oppressed within the subcultures within which they interact, and so are relegated to the peripheries of such spaces (McRobbie and Garber, 1975), or that they cultivate *separate* spaces in order to avoid such oppression (Blackman, 1998; Halberstam, 2005; Harris, 2003; Monem, 2007; Taylor, 2010). For McRobbie and Garber (1975) in the 1970s, girls negotiate a different kind of 'risk' than their male peers, meaning that their subcultural expressions take place within 'bedroom culture', rather than on the street; a reflection that was later connected to girls' use of the internet to forge social connections (Aaragon, 2008; Garrison, 2000; Harris, 2008). Further accounts of the relationship between feminism and subculture focus on distinct forms of feminist organising that isolate feminist subcultures from 'masculine' subcultural formations. The most prominent of these is the Riot Grrrl subculture, which is often interpreted as a rejection of dominant modes of femininity (Rosenberg and Garofalo, 1998; Monem, 2007). Such accounts often construct a version of Riot Grrrl that emphasises its separatist aspects.

Other accounts of girls' participation in subculture focus instead on how girls and women negotiate 'already formed' male subcultures. For instance, Leblanc's (2005) ethnographic study of girls in a punk subculture illustrates the way in which girls negotiate, and subvert, femininity, within a punk community dominated largely by male musicians and male-oriented fandom. She offers an alternative perspective on girls and punk, arguing that girls enter the punk subculture because it provides them the possibility of subverting dominant conceptualisations of femininity. This chapter also explores the benefits of recognising that subcultures, rather than constituting fixed spaces within which feminists must somehow situate themselves, can be transformed by the presence of feminist sensibilities.

Recent calls to acknowledge the structural aspects of subculture (Shildrick and MacDonald, 2006) have not only highlighted that subculture and dominant culture have a messier relationship than has often been presumed, but also that structural inequality is present *within* subcultures themselves, in ways that are not always made visible in subcultures research. Furthermore, people access subculture from a variety of entrance points, and may experience 'insider' and 'outsider' status simultaneously within a given subcultural space (Kempson, 2015b). Dunn and Farnsworth (2012) offer a more nuanced analysis by pointing out that the 1970s punk scene 'was extremely diverse, drawing in males, females, transgendered individuals, straights and homosexuals' (137) but that through time it became a masculinised space. They go on to suggest that while Riot Grrrl was once motivated by the possibility of 'reclaiming the multi-gendered spaces of the initial punk movement' (138) it became a women-centred space with a central manifesto of resistance to the masculinised punk subculture. This point is important because it does not characterise punk as an essentially masculine space, or indeed view Riot Grrrl as a straightforward challenge to this. This inspires questions about the way in which feminist historicity develops, and how marginal feminist perspectives become eclipsed by dominant 'versions' of feminist history (Hemmings, 2011; Kempson, 2015a). Furthermore, it highlights that,

> popular perceptions are no safe guide to the actual magnitude of a social problem. Ill-understood but partly known processes of social perception

involve patterned omitting, supplementing, and organizing of what is selectively perceived as the social reality

(Merton and Nisbet, 1971:811)

For example, Halberstam (2005) argues that subculture is usually engaged with through the lens of heteronormative 'life-span' narratives; a particular knowledge paradigm that marginalises alternative experiences of the 'life-course'. In this way subcultures research can claim to challenge structural inequalities, while also reinforcing them, if insufficient attention is paid to the possibility of (re)producing these dominant discourses within research methodology. This chapter argues that 'intersectional epistemologies' (a means of embedding an awareness of the above process into research design) not only uncover the ways in which a participant's biography is constituted through the version of social history they have accessed, and have a knowledge of, but it also allows a researcher to critique the ways in which they ascribe meaning to their data. It is important that feminist research finds ways of engaging with the subcultural investments of people without defaulting to dominant discourses of 'femininity' or 'girlhood' to inform their methodological choices. The chapter now moves on to address these ideas via engagement with a specific subcultural example: the creation of feminist zines in the UK.

The research context: negotiating researcher subjectivity

Zines are paper creations (Piepmeier, 2009) containing artwork, autobiographical writing, and political commentary that are circulated via subcultural networks. Zines are difficult to define in terms of genre (Poletti, 2008); they do, however, form an important part of grassroots feminist spaces. There is a modest field of scholarship emerging that defines the zine in a variety of ways: as a form of resistance to conditions of modernity (Harris, 2001, 2003, 2008), as autobiographical accounts of contemporary 'girlhood' (Piepmeier, 2009; Schilt, 2003), as an empowering cultural production practice (Kearney, 1988) and as an important communication practice within DIY subcultural networks (Kempson, 20145a). The zine is, therefore, a product of multiple modes of historicity that have relevance within a variety of cultural fields (such as punk and DIY subcultural contexts, DIY media production, and autobiographical writing).

Having written for zines, I wanted to conduct research into the surrounding subculture in the UK because I had questions about how feminist zines perform activism, and about how the 'feminism' in these zines is constructed and situated in relation to the rest of the zine subculture. I had initially believed that such a disparately located community of zine producers did not constitute a subculture. However, as the interviews and ethnographic work progressed I began to understand the space as an internally heterogeneous, but also relatively *cohesive*, politicised cultural field that had a lot in common with contemporary conceptualisations of subculture (Hodkinson, 2002, for instance). Engagement within the wider subcultural context of zine exchange prompted me to consider whether 'feminist zine subculture' was indeed a tangible social space, or whether it might be more accurately understood as a wider zine subculture through which feminist articulations are negotiated. It also became clear that zine subculture is influenced by a variety of other cultural fields, and that it overlaps with other subcultural environments that contribute to its characterisation.

History is constituted through the politics of 'place' and vice versa, meaning that the historical context of a subculture can only be understood once it is *located*. The feminist zines analysed appear to circulate via a variety of geographical and spatial contexts (including squatting networks and university campuses). Engagement with such diverse contexts presents an opportunity gain a multi-dimensional perspective of the internal character of a subculture that 'zooms out', as C. Wright Mills advised, to the broader geo-political and historical contexts of a social phenomenon, while not losing sight of the micro-negotiations that locate the individual within them. However, often, no distinction is made between the participants' differing statuses *within* subcultural spaces, meaning that C. Wright Mills' call for sociologists to acknowledge the complex relationship between individual biographies and collective cultural histories has yet to be fully realised in subcultures research. In fact, many participants within this research negotiate marginal positions in relation to zine subculture, which influences the way they make sense of their participation (Kempson, 2015b). Furthermore, as mentioned above, there are complicated overlaps between the subcultures with which zine creators engage, to the extent where individuals and collectives can relate within multiple subcultural contexts, and can identify with numerous labels (punk, queer, feminist, anarchist, vegan, for example) at various times and to varying degrees. The majority of participants within this study report having more than one subcultural investment:

> I think I'm in the punk community coz I've been kind of a part of it now and quite involved in it because I've been squatting and living with the punks and I go to the gigs all the time and maybe I'm sort of more a part of that scene and the queer ... scene is not really aligned with the punks coz that's not really their scene so it's like this other queer thing. I walk in two different scenes ... other people ... I know, like, other scenes where, there's this girl – I've never spoken to her – but she's real punk looking, you know, like the black jacket and the studs and stuff and then I see her around at ... shows or the queer bands, and I'm like 'Who are you?' like I'm usually the only punk here!
>
> (Kathy, interviewed in January 2010)

Talking with Kathy, it became evident that she negotiates her participation within multiple subcultural environments, including: zine subculture, the South London punk scene, queer culture in two large global cities (one of which she remains involved with via the internet), and DIY feminist culture. In the above account, Kathy suggests that the queer and punk subcultures in London are relatively separate spaces. This does not, however, prevent her from identifying with both subcultures simultaneously, and *authentically*. This means that the researcher must be careful not to presume that a participant's affiliation to one subcultural environment is more significant and legitimate than another, by taking into consideration the participant's 'whole life' (Omel'Chenko and Pilkington, 2013), rather than researching one subculture in a vacuum. Understanding the place of subculture in the lives of young people, and the possibility of capturing subcultural behaviours via research, means asking epistemological questions about how researchers interpret the biographical, but mainly *performative*, snapshots 'collected' during fieldwork.

Twenty-nine in-depth interviews were conducted with people I met as I became familiar zine culture in the UK. These interviews were designed to find out about the participants' experiences of the subculture and motivation for creating or distributing zines. However, since 'interviewees *and interviewers* work to construct themselves as certain types-of-people in relation to the topic of the interview' (Rapley, 2001:303), researchers must find ways of reading the subtext of the discussion. The word 'feminist', for example, may evoke different images for different people, which poses a problem when researchers come to analyse their data. This does not render interview data invalid and unusable, though, and can produce interesting information about how both parties perform the self within the context of the research topic. This performative element of interview data formed the main focus of enquiry here. I conducted an intuition-led analysis that allowed room to explore the influences of latent content on the interview situation, and the option of re-engaging with the participants at a later date in order to build upon the initial conversations. Nevertheless, interviews are not conducted to find 'truth', and can sometimes result in contradictions that are difficult to analyse. However, 'interpretive social scientists listen beyond, between, and underneath participants' words to understand the social conditions that produce apparent contradictions in their accounts' (Power, 2004:858).

Several of the participants suggested that I conduct the initial interview with them at zinefests[1] they had organised. This meant that I began to attend zinefests in order to interact with participants of the zine subculture in 'context'. Throughout the research period I attended six zinefests: Brighton Zinefest, 2010; Women's Library Zinefest 2010; Bradford Zine Fayre 2010; Brighton Zinefest 2011; London Zine Symposium, 2011; and Women's Library Zinefest 2011. I began to meet people at zinefests who expressed an interest in the research and asked whether I would like to interview them. My attendance at these zinefests, coupled with the interviews I conducted, required an exploration of my own researcher subjectivity, and its influence upon the character of the resulting data. Upon commencing the research, I was concerned that my actor shift (from zine reader and writer, to academic researcher) would be an uncomfortable transition to make. My main concern was that my capacity as an academic researcher would result in the move from an 'insider' to an 'outsider' within the space, and I worried that my 'academic gaze' would make zine creators wary of the interview process. However, face-to-face communication invites further conversation and 'small talk', which often resulted in me being asked whether I created my own zine. I always replied that I never had, but that I had written for other zines. This response was worth a certain amount of subcultural capital (Thornton, 1995) because it meant that I had legitimised my presence there. However, I met a lot of zine creators who are also involved in academia at various levels, and so these fears were probably unwarranted, and I attribute them to my preconception that zine centred events are privy to certain processes of 'border-control' (Kempson, 2015b). Further reflection allowed me to see that 'zine writer' and 'academic researcher' are not mutually exclusive subject positions (Poletti, 2008). In fact, my history as a zine contributor and reader was especially beneficial when selecting zines for analysis because I knew how to access them, and what the protocol was for this. It also meant that I knew whom I should approach in the zine community for interviews, and how best to approach them.

Although many people involved in DIY spaces are not concerned by the way in which academics may represent their involvement with zines, there is a certain suspicion about the use of zine content by academics. Specifically, at the time of the interviews, the reproduction of zines without the permission of the zine creator was a strong topic of debate within the subculture. As a result of this, I was asked several times at zinefests whether I agreed that zine content should be reproduced, and profited upon, without the express consent of the zine creator. This questioning did not appear to be targeted at 'sussing out' my position as an academic, but as part of the collective dialogue of the subculture at the time. Indeed, having knowledge of the issues receiving attention in the subculture became a useful means of instigating communications with people in that space. I learned that zine creation and academia cross over into one another (many feminists find themselves politically active while at university and, for several of the participants, zine creation becomes intertwined with this activism). However, feeling accepted within a social space does not automatically grant a researcher knowledge about how participants' own biographies intersect with that subculture; a complex question that, this chapter argues, requires an epistemological engagement with intersectionality.

Developing intersectional epistemologies

The zines themselves indicate the importance of engaging with plural feminisms and with behaviours and identifications that might not be instantly interpreted as feminist, or which reside on the margins of the feminist movement. As a genre, feminist zines are representative of new versions of feminist subjectivity that are responding to the pluralities of the movement. Many of the participants in this study report feeling disenfranchised from the more 'visible' dimensions feminism in the UK and are especially critical of feminist wave theory because of its domination over feminist 'history making' (Kempson, 2015a). In order for a researcher to capture this process, and to locate the character of their own interpretations within this research context, the development of multi-position awareness is necessary. Lykke (2005) argues that an intersectional approach can support a researcher's ability to situate themselves critically within the knowledge they produce; a process that this chapter argues would benefit scholarly engagements with subculture.

As mentioned earlier, there are concerns that a pluralistic reading of feminism will result in the fragmentation of the movement, to the point where no consensus about what a 'feminist' is can be reached (Mohanty, 1988). Disagreement about what constitutes 'feminism' within the zines demonstrates the paradoxes that characterise contemporary feminism, and begs the question of whether feminists can ever mobilise cohesively within subcultural contexts.

There was a distinct sense within the interview data that the participants consider feminism to be a relatively unified movement, despite its internal heterogeneity. This, however, poses a distinct analytical problem because it can be presumed that the researcher and participant, as two feminist-identified individuals, share an unspoken knowledge about feminism. I therefore found that I had to press the interviewees to expand on their understanding of feminism when they assumed that this elaboration was not necessary. Rather than identifying with the 'third wave', many of the research participants prefer to see themselves as part of the 'DIY' (do-it-yourself) feminist movement that is not necessarily bound to third wave narratives (Kempson, 2015b). This means that the methodological logic of the project was reliant on me looking deeper into the feminist biographies of the research participants instead of presuming that 'feminist' means the same thing to everyone. At the heart of this issue are questions about the possibility of developing more intersectional readings of feminist identity that account for the varying experiences of 'feminism in subculture'.

C. Wright Mills (2008) argued that sociology needed to find ways of addressing 'problems of biography, of history and of their intersections with social structures' (143). However, Back and Puwar (2012) warn us that widening the scope of analysis might result in totalising representations of societal groups, or historical epochs, that do the very opposite of what C. Wright Mills invited. This invites questions about how to realise such an ambitious call without flattening the complexities of agency. This chapter argues that a recognition of how different histories are written and accessed, and how visible they are, and to whom, marks a sensible point from which to commence the design of subcultures research. Many of the participants in this study, for instance, grapple with understandings of their own gender and sexual identification. This impacts how they negotiate subjectivity within subcultural contexts and how this negotiation is influenced by their personal histories. But more than that, these accounts allude to a complex paradigm shift whereby the zine creators are challenging heteronormative life-course expectations (as explored above). It also challenges wider modernist assumptions about what constitutes 'progress', and 'success'. Furthermore, a rhetoric of 'like-mindedness' tends to punctuate accounts of subcultural and feminist engagement alike, which eclipses inequalities *within* these spaces. For example, Brah and Pheonix (2004) question the validity of a 'global sisterhood' on the grounds that such a vision masks unequal power relations. They go onto state that: 'A key feature of feminist analysis of "intersectionality" is that they are concerned with "decentring" of the "normative subject" of feminism" (78). In this vein, intersectional research methodologies allow the researcher to become conscious of the need to subvert the reproduction of dominant knowledge paradigms that marginalise certain voices, while placing others at centre stage.

Discussions of gender and ethnicity within the zines analysed are not always situated within third wave discourses (even though 'third wave' was originally intended to highlight black women's relationship with women's emancipation initiatives (Walker, 1995). Instead, these discussions are located within a complex habitus (Bourdieu, 1984) that draws upon a number of subject positions and collectivisms that are each connected via marginalised (DIY) feminist subjectivities. Such collectivisms include, but are not limited to; Riot Grrrl, bohemia, racial activism, transgender activism, squatter movements, and mental health awareness. Within these contexts, several themes emerge surrounding the negotiation of black feminist subjectivities. In *Cooking Hearts up on the Stove* zine, for instance, the author discusses the rejection of the 'feminist' label within her family because feminism is seen as a predominantly white identification. Likewise, *Race Revolt* zine details several instances of racism from within feminist spaces, referring to an incident whereby several white feminists organised a workshop centred on 'racism within feminism' in order to discuss this issue collectively. The zine states that the white feminists present at the discussion appeared to feel entitled to centre the discussion on the 'guilt' of white feminists, rather than focusing on first-hand experiences of racism. This account provokes questions about the central concerns of some areas of feminist organising. It highlights the intersectional inequalities that remain within feminist communities that presume that all women should relate their experiences of oppression to *feminist* discourses exclusively. Many of the zines analysed challenge these forms of orthodoxy by constructing narratives that subvert dominant conceptualisations of what feminism should look like. Although racism and homophobia were condemned within the zines, they were not always related to as 'feminist' issues. There are implications here for the ways in which feminism and subculture might be linked to one another, and for the ways in which feminist histories are constructed. For instance, many of the participants dispel any overly simplistic readings of feminist subcultural participation that might view alternative spaces as being somehow immune to oppressive narratives:

> I think that zinefests should come up with explicit policies of anti-oppression and state outright that it will not tolerate zines (or zinesters) which are racist, sexist, homophobic, transphobic, ableist, xenophobic, classist, etc. to participate. I think there is a lot of resistance to this as people are often, especially in anarchist circles, afraid of censorship. While I can appreciate that censorship has with it its own set of dangers, I think that it's important to acknowledge the inherent hierarchies that are reproduced in alternative media spaces. We are not all equals just because we say we want to be that way, in a society of deep inequality, unless we do something to actively challenge these inequalities they are merely replicated in alternative spaces.
>
> (Mandy, interviewed online in September 2011)

There is an important lesson in the above testimony about the internal contractions of some subcultural environments. Researchers should, therefore, be wary of flattening internal hierarchies within these spaces by presuming that the participants all share the same values, or that their experiences of social structures lead to the same biographical imprints. For Christensen and Qvotrup Jensen (2012), intersectional analysis is not possible unless the researcher *critiques* the social categories they inscribe onto the participants, and finds ways of linking these to individuals' biographies. Intersectional analysis, therefore, becomes a *dynamic* process that can capture 'stories we can tell about ourselves in relation to social categories like gender, class, and ethnicity' (114). This approach also highlights the importance of engaging with participants' own reflections on their relationship with social structures. These reflections can then be contextualised, but not *overwritten*, by the researcher.

This might mean continuing to develop more integrated, and participatory, research methodologies that consult participants on issues of data collection and interpretation. It might also mean finding innovative ways to triangulate data collection in order to arrive upon more dynamic approaches to feminist research than the 'subject/object' methodological cul de sac (Cook and Fonow, 1986). In the case of zines, attention to the character of emerging data (zine content and interview transcripts) becomes the means by which methodological boundaries are established and negotiated. Data collection then becomes dynamic, collaborative, and non-linear; a process that is to be re-defined and revised throughout the entire research process, rather than constituting the static 'end result' of a period of fieldwork.

Conclusion

The objective of this chapter has been to suggest the benefits of applying 'intersectional epistemologies' to the study of subculture in order to realise C. Wright Mills' call to examine how the history of a society, and the collective discourses surrounding this, intersect with individual biographies. It is suggested that this can be achieved by developing integrated methodological strategies that view methodology and reflexivity as ever-evolving processes that respond *dynamically* as the research unfolds. This study did not, therefore, seek to present a definitive definition of 'feminist zines', but rather to comment on their potential as subcultural artefacts.

C. Wright Mills called for broader focus on how a researcher could develop intellectual craftsmanship [sic] which, for Burawoy (2008), evokes an image of a solitary sociologist conducting research, and failing to maintain an intellectual investment in the discipline as a whole. This concept can, though, be adapted to the contemporary context by emphasising its requirement that researchers engage at a deeper level with the methodological choices they make, and how these choices either illuminate, or discount, various participant subjectivities. This idea has been drawn upon within this chapter in order to argue that 'intersectional epistemologies' can be employed to reengage with the 'lost voices' of subcultures, by challenging the knowledge paradigms through which a researcher makes sense of their data. It is at this point that a researcher can recognise how their own 'subcultural imagination' might not only impact the outcomes of their own study, but how it might help to shape the 'history making' of subcultures from a broader perspective. Furthermore, any re-engagement C. Wright Mills' work should not be singularly concerned with furthering knowledge of the 'individual', but should also acknowledge that the way in which individuals make sense of their own biographies tells us many things about the broader practice of 'history making'.

Finally, reflexivity in the context of research means more than simply developing an awareness of how your own identity impacts the research outcomes. It also provides researchers with the opportunity to reflect that the intersections between social structure and history might not look the same for each participant. Recasting intersectionality as an *epistemological* consideration, as well as a theoretical framework, supports a more dynamic approach to research design that speaks to C. Wright Mills' call for sociology to break away from orthodox processes of knowledge production.

Note

1 Zinefests are independently run 'market places' that facilitate the sale and trade of zines and other DIY cultural production.

References

Aaragon, J. (2008) 'The "Lady" Revolution in the Age of Technology', *International Journal of Media and Cultural Politics* 4(1): 71–85.

Abrams, K. (1998) 'From Autonomy to Agency: Feminist Perspectives on Self-Direction', *William & Mary Law Review* 40(3): 805.

Back, L. and Puwar, N. (eds) (2012) *Live Methods*. Oxford: Blackwell.

Beauvoir, S. de (1949) *The Second Sex*. New York: Vintage Books.

Blackman, S. (1998) '"Poxy Cupid": An Ethnographic and Feminist Account of a Resistant Female Youth Culture – The New Wave Girls'. In *Cool Places: Geographies of Youth Cultures*, Skelton, T. and Valentine, G. (eds) London: Routledge, 207–228.

Bourdieu, P. (1984) *Distinction: A Social Critique of the Judgement of Taste*, Cambridge, MA: Harvard University Press.

Brah, A. and Phoenix, A. (2004) 'Ain't I a Woman? Revisiting Intersectionality', *Journal of International Women's Studies* 5(3): 75–86.

Burawoy, M. (2008) 'Open Letter to C. Wright Mills', *Antipode* 40(3): 365–375.

Carby, H. (1982) 'White Woman Listen! Black Feminism and the Boundaries of Sisterhood.' In *The Empire Strikes Back: Race and Realism in 70s Britain*, The Centre for Contemporary Studies (ed.) London: Hutchinson, 212–235.

Christensen, A. D and Qvotrup, Jensen S. (2012) 'Doing Intersectional Analysis: Methodological Implications for Qualitative Research', *NORA – Nordic Journal of Feminist and Gender Research* 20(2): 109–125.

Cohen, R. and Hughes, C. (2012) *Feminism Counts: Quantitative Methods and Researching Gender*. Oxford: Routledge.

Cook, J. A. and Fonow, M. M. (1986) 'Knowledge and Women's Interests: Issues of Epistemology and Methodology in Feminist Sociological Research', *Sociological Inquiry* 56: 2–29.

Crenshaw, K. (1989) 'Demarginalizing the Intersection of Race and Sex: A Black Feminist Critique of Antidiscrimination Doctrine, Feminist Theory, and Antiracist Politics', *University of Chicago Legal Forum* 14: 538–554.

Crenshaw, K. (1991) 'Mapping the Margins: Intersectionality, Identity Politics, and Violence against Women of Color', *Stanford Law Review* 43(6): 1241–1299.

Davis, K. (2008) 'Intersectionality As Buzzword: A Sociology of Science Perspective on What Makes a Feminist Theory Successful', *Feminist Theory* 9(1): 67–85.

Dunn, K. and Farnsworth, M. S. (2012) '"We ARE the Revolution" Riot Grrrl Press, Girl Empowerment, and DIY Self Publishing', *Women's Studies: An Interdisciplinary Journal* 41(2):136–157.

Garrison, E. (2000) 'U.S. Feminism – Grrrl Style! Youth (Sub)cultures and the Technologies of the Third Wave', *Feminist Studies* 26(1): 141–170.

Halberstam, J. (2005) *In a Queer Time and Place: Transgender Bodies, Subcultural Lives.* New York: New York University Press.

Harding, S. (1987) *Feminism and Methodology: Social Science Issues.* Bloomington: Indiana University Press.

Harris, A. (2001) 'Revisiting Bedroom Culture: Spaces for Young Women's Politics', *Hecate* 27(1): 128–138.

Harris, A. (2003) 'gURL Scenes and Grrrl Zines: Girlhood, Power and Risk Under Late Modernity', *Feminist Review* 75: 28–56.

Harris, A. (2008) 'Young Women, Late Modern Politics, and the Participatory Possibilities of Online Cultures', *Journal of Youth Studies* 11(5): 481–495.

Hemmings, C. (2011) *Why Stories Matter: The Political Grammar of Feminist Theory.* Durham and London: Duke University Press.

Hodkinson, P. (2002) *Goth: Identity, Style and Subculture.* Oxford: Berg.

Kearney, M.C. 1998. 'Don't Need You Rethinking Identity Politics and Separatism from a Grrrl Perspective'. In *Youth Culture: Identity in a Postmodern World*, J. S. Epstein (ed.) Oxford: Blackwell, 148–188.

Kempson, M. (2015a) 'My Version of Feminism: Subjectivity, DIY and the feminist zine', *New Feminisms in Europe: Special edition of Social Movement Studies* 14(4): 459–472,

Kempson, M. (2015b) 'I Sometimes Wonder Whether I'm an Outsider': Negotiating Subcultural Belonging at Zinefests', *Sociology* 49(6): 1081–1095.

Komarovsky, M. (1991) 'Some Reflections on the Feminist Scholarship in Sociology', *Annul Review of Sociology* 17: 1–25.

LeBlanc, L. (2005) *Pretty in Punk: Girls' Gender Resistance in a Boys' Subculture.* New Brunswick, NJ: Rutgers University Press.

McCall, L. (2005) 'The Complexity of Intersectionality', *Signs* 30(3): 1771–800.

McRobbie, A. and Garber, J. (1997) [1975] 'Girls and Subcultures'. In *The Subcultures Reader*, Gelder, K. and Thornton, S. (eds) London: Routledge, 112–120.

Mills, C. W. (1951) [1956] *White Collar: The American middle classes.* New York: Oxford University Press.

Mills, C. W. (1956) [1970] *The Power Elite.* New York: Oxford University Press.

Mills, C. W. (1959) [2000] *The Sociological Imagination.* New York: Oxford University Press.

Mohanty, C. T. (1988) 'Under Western Eyes: Feminist Scholarship and Colonial Discourses', *Feminist Review* 30: 61–88.

Monem, N. K. (2007) *Riot Grrrl: Revolution Girl Style Now*. London: Black Dog Publishing.

Oakley, A. (1985) *Sex, Gender and Society: Towards a New Society*. London: Ashgate.

Omel'chenko, E. and Pilkington, H. (2013) 'Regrounding Youth Cultural Theory (In Post-Socialist Youth Cultural Practice)', *Sociology Compass* 7(3): 208–224.

Piepmeier, A. (2009) *Girl Zines; Making Media, Doing Feminism*. New York: New York University Press.

Poletti, A. (2008) *Intimate Ephemera: Reading Youth Lives in Australian Zine Culture*. Melbourne: Melbourne University Press.

Power, E. M. (2004) 'Toward Understanding in Postmodern Interview Analysis: Interpreting the Contradictory Remarks of a Research Participant', *Qualitative Health Research* 14(6): 858–865.

Rapley, T, J. (2001) 'The Art(fulness) of Open-Ended Interviewing: Some Considerations on Analysing Interviews', *Qualitative Research* 1(3): 303–323.

Rosenberg, J. and Garofalo, G. (1998) 'Riot Grrrl: Revolutions from Within', *Signs: Journal of Contemporary Women's Culture* 23(3): 809–841.

Schilt, K. (2003) 'I'll Resist With Every Inch and Every Breath: Girls and Zine Making as a Form of Resistance', *Youth & Society* 35(1): 71–97.

Shildrick, T and MacDonald, R. (2006) 'In Defence of Subculture: Young People, Leisure and Social Divisions', *Journal of Youth Studies* 9(2): 125–140.

Taylor, J. (2010) 'Queer Temporalities and the Significance of "Music Scene" Participation in the Social Identities of Middle-Aged Queers', *Sociology* 44(5): 893–907.

Walker, R. (1995) *To Be Real: Telling the Truth and Changing the Face of Feminism*. New York: Anchor.

Yuval-Davis, N. (2006) 'Intersectionality and Feminist Politics', *European Journal of Women's Studies* 13(3): 193–210.

Zobl, E. (2009) 'Cultural Production, Transnational Networking, and Critical Reflection in Feminist Zines', *Signs: Journal of Women in Culture and Society* 35(1): 1–12.

10 Bulgarian post-transitional subcultures

Insider ethnographic research of the underground scene

Vihra Barova

Introduction

This chapter is focused on the application of ethnographic methods in the study of marginalized subcultural participants and their protective responses and tactical actions of subcultural resistance, which are shaped and provoked by the social and economic changes in Bulgaria after 1989. I will explore the transformation of post-transitional subcultures in their social and historical context and also through comparative reading of CCCS subcultural theory (Clarke 1976; Cohen, P. 1972 [1980]; Hall and Jefferson 1976; Hebdige 1979) and the post-subculturalist critique (Bennett 2002; Muggleton 2000). I will approach the underground scene as a specific kind of space, which is socially constructed and opposed to mainstream spatial practices (Lefebvre 1991). I want to suggest that there is a specific transformation of the "westernized" and "spectacular" subcultures of the 90s into a "hidden" underground post-transitional subculture nowadays whose main traits can be best understood through the ethnographic methods and reflexivity. I also want to argue that there are two main trends in the contemporary subcultural development – on the one hand, it is the loss of music and stylistic definiteness, but with an emphasis on the ideological commitment, and on the other hand, it is the "secretion" of the subcultural signs by replacing them with new "secret" code in a conscious attempt to remain separate from the mainstream and to minimize consumption.

The main methodological question I wish to pose in the second part of the chapter is how to make ethnography about such a culture, whose participants desire to remain hidden and demand their signs are not academically translated. In terms of research positionality, if you are a subcultural participant, how could you, at the same time, be the one who observes and do the research? As a subcultural insider I wanted to make my contribution to the sociological ethnographic imagination by employing auto-ethnography and other ethnographic techniques that give priority to the research subjects. Consequently, I will focus on the participant/researcher relations and the emotional boundaries of research (Blackman 2007, 2010). I will explore the emotional and moral boundaries, through one personal document gathered in the field – a reverse interview with one of the participants. The ethnographic interview generated intensely personalised feelings and reflections, generating an academic challenge for reflexivity – for example, is the researcher allowed to show her or his human, non-academic side on the field, and what is her or his main reason to investigate? Finally, I will discuss these issues in relation to C. Wright Mills' promise of the social sciences and his appeal for intellectual craft (Mills [1959] 2000).

Social and historical context: Bulgarian subcultures

At the same time as ethnographically studying the subcultural actions of resistance, I will also pay attention to the structure of power, the historical knowledge, keeping in mind the promise of the social sciences as formulated by Wright Mills (Mills [1959] 2000: 3–24, 53) – for the local responses of the examined subcultures also depend on the historical changes of the existing social structure.

Subcultures of the so-called "Transition" in the Eastern bloc are actually products of a radical and sudden social and economic change, which is carried out in a very short span of Eastern Europe history. The Bulgarian case represents the same processes of transformation and new social stratification. The subcultures first labelled as "westernized" including punks, Goths, bikers, etc. appeared in the country in the late 1980s. A variety of subcultural lifestyles, which were products of quite different social and economic processes in the West, were "imported" into Bulgaria all at once. Transplanted into Bulgaria, these subcultural identities took on rather different meanings for Bulgarian youth. During the first years after the Fall, punks and other subcultural characters became favourites of the media and thus became visible to the public. During the late socialist era the attitude towards them was quite ambivalent. On one hand, they were regarded as an embodiment of the new democratic processes and as an expression of the desired pluralism (Pilkington 1994: 82–3), and on the other hand, they were regarded as antisocial movements. In a 1991 interview with a first generation Bulgarian punk (born around 1970), the following question was posed to the young man: "What do you want to see changed in society?" He replied:

> Everyone should feel free. I want to be a part of society. It has not thrown me out; it's me that has thrown myself out of it. I do not want to look grey, to melt into the crowd, to be put in a mould and wear the label: made in somewhere. [Skortcheva, L. 1991. Punks hate order and drabness (in Bulg.). 'Club 15' 9: 3]

At the beginning of the transition, people like him were turned into celebrities of the Change. They were actually exploited by the media as examples, though marginal ones, of the desired social and political change. Their voices were heard, or at least they were allowed to speak openly. However, after this first subcultural boom in the late 80s and 90s, a period of gradual marginalization followed. Slowly but constantly the subcultural participants lost their significance and became an invisible and unwanted part of the post-socialist social structure. The media interest towards them lessened and the public attitude towards them changed accordingly. The constant loss of personal status influenced group identity. As a result, the outward appearance and behaviour of the subcultural members nowadays are less fashionable and less provocative, while their practices form a protective response of subcultural resistance that denies the mainstream values of the newly built society (e.g. consumerism, competitiveness, individualism). In short, this is the how the westernized "spectacular"[1] subcultures of the 90s were gradually transformed into a post-transitional underground scene.

Post-transitional subcultures

At the present time, the main carrier of the subcultural agency is the generation of those born in the late 80s and early 90s. This generation builds its identity after the years of political and economic transition in Bulgaria and faces structural problems unfamiliar to the previous generations (including unemployment and the consequent labour migration, isolation from the public urban space, unequal access to education and other social inequalities). During the period of transition not only the subcultural activists changed because of the age limits in the youth movements. Moreover, the social class, from which the subcultural youths are recruited, has changed itself. I argue that youth subcultural styles inherited from the short "transition" period as "westernized" (i.e. local imitations of western subcultural patterns) and somewhat "elitist" (due to their prevalence in the cities, the capital and elite high-schools) are undergoing rapid transformation and take new forms embracing ideologies characteristic of the working class, and accordingly change their expression tools and symbols. The subcultures of the "ghetto", the suburbs and the small town's periphery come to take their place with new imagery, ideology and symbols. They are invisible, they are isolated, but yet they exist; for example, the small underground scenes of *anarcho-punk*, *straight edge hardcore*, also the groups of *graffiti writers*, *ravers* and the relatively bigger factions of football *casuals*. This post-transitional transformation is interconnected with the changing dominant attitude towards subcultural agents, who were once discerned as *agents of change*, but afterwards labelled as agents of deviance, which is partly due to their social class. This new subcultural positioning became increasingly observed through sensitive ethnography and reflexivity. The subcultural/underground participants have built their own culture as one secret culture with clear boundaries that often require ethnographic insider research.

From the basis of researcher positionality I am writing about culture and society under reconstruction, where the subcultural theory, which has more explanatory potential, is that of the CCCS. In the 70s and 80s of the twentieth century authors of the Birmingham School made an attempt to explain the emergence of youth subcultures and also to free them from the label "deviant" by applying a "complex Marxist theory" (Hall 1980: 25), that consists of Levi-Strauss' structuralist theory of bricolage, an Althusserian theory of ideology, Barthes' semiological analysis and Gramsci's idea of cultural hegemony. They came to the conclusion that the post-war youth subcultures should reflect the occurrence of significant changes in the social and economic situation in the parental class (Cohen, P. 1972 [1980]; Willis 1981). The post-war British youth subcultures *were identified as* working class and it is possible to notice similarities with the post-socialist subcultures in Bulgaria. As the working class, once put at the top of the socialist ideology, has gradually lost its significance for the post-socialist society, it is now suffering significant changes in its social and economic situation. Consequently, these changes reflect in the subcultural imagination of the post-socialist working-class youth.

The Birmingham School approach paid attention exclusively to the collective actions of resistance, common background and the subcultural styles as products of youth's imagination and not of cultural industries (Clarke 1976; Cohen, P. 1972 [1980]; Hall and Jefferson 1976; Hebdige 1979; Willis 1981). The post-subculturalist theory as postmodern and anti-heroic actually doubts the subcultural potential for resistance, which is replaced by the individual consumption of "life-styles" (Bennett 1999: 605), which are equally competing with one another at the global market of cultural industries, in the absence of a dominant culture and social struggle. As Blackman (2014: 505) states: "Post-subculturalist theory wants us to view subcultures more creatively, liberating identity from the subordination of oppression." In fact, many post-subcultural theorists argue that the subcultural identity increases fluidity in relation to dress-code and music preferences, which blurs the boundaries between subcultures and finally leads to their gradual extinction (Bennett 2002; Hesmondhalgh 2005; Muggleton 2000). In contrast, as a subcultural insider who is personally and socially engaged with the youth subcultures, I argue that there are two main trends in the contemporary subcultural development – on the one hand, it is indeed the loss of music and stylistic definiteness, but with an emphasis on the ideological commitment (e.g. political activism), and on the other hand, it is the "secretion" of the subcultural signs by replacing them with new "secret" code thus creating "unspectacular" subcultures, who are in fact difficult for direct observation. These "unspectacular" groupings do not lack the feeling of belonging and their lifestyles are not "for sale". Nowadays the subcultural boundaries might be blurred and their styles – not homological, but they are not simply by-products of the cultural industries and they still reflect social divisions and inequalities. This is one of the reasons for me to choose the unifying term "underground scene", as it describes both the fluidity and subcultural transgression of the researched groups. The underground is a field, where different subcultures live together and mix with one another, although not in a random "stylistic game" (Muggleton 2000: 47) but under strict rules. Moreover, this field includes a particular kind of space (real and imagined) that is occupied by the subcultural participants. The "underground" space is under the surface of the "hyper-reality" and beyond the competitions for upward social mobility.

This underground space is also a social sub-product of new social relations. It is subject to the post-socialist reconstruction of urban public space. As stated by Lefebvre (1991: 26), "the space thus produced also serves as a tool of thought and of action, in addition to being a means of production it is also a means of control, and hence of domination, of power". In this sense, the space left at subcultures' disposal is the space that is of no value for the mainstream society. In the beginning of post-socialism the available spaces of no value and consequently no surveillance were the memorials of the socialist past. These can be the former Chinese embassy (used as a squatting house until 2005–6) or an abandoned factory. Other gathering places have included the former mausoleum of Bulgaria's first communist leader Georgi Dimitrov (destroyed by the authorities in 1999) and the garden around the monument of the Soviet Army. The cultural centre of the past has been slowly turning into the commercial centre of today, with its own new rules. Thus the subcultural participants of the post-transitional period, once visible in the city centre, were no longer able to dwell in it and were gradually pushed out to non-commercialised parts of the city. The backyards of houses in the centre that were favourite places for subcultural gatherings can no longer be used because their new owners have put up fences and cameras, and locked doors. Therefore, the young people have begun searching for new places to gather in relatively independent locations, where they could reside freely and unwatched. Unofficial small clubs in the basements or remote play spaces in the suburbs came to replace the old gathering places that were located in the main public urban spaces. This post-transitional trend is yet another reason to call the new subcultures "hidden" and "underground". I also see them as "dispossessed inheritors" of the urban space they once inhabited, and subjects to spatial segregation. On the other hand, the underground space has its advantages that are in contradiction to the commercial mainstream values, since as socially constructed, it is also able to shape spatial practices, based on values and the social production of meanings (Lefebvre 1991). The gradual spatial movement of subcultures to the periphery of the urban commercialized landscape provides for several subcultural actions of resistance: they avoid surveillance, they minimize consumption, and they create their own ground that affirms their feeling of belonging and solidarity. I argue that subcultural lifestyle is built through several specific practices that are accomplished in the peripheral urban underground space (e.g. soft drugs consumption, which is part of the night-time economy of the informal youth clubs, second-hand trade and exchange of subcultural commodities, and different "do-it-yourself" practices like DIY music and clothing production as well as the organization of semi-illegal pubs, clubs and tattoo studios). All these spatial and consumer practices have an ideological dimension pointed at the commercialized mainstream and shape the subcultural identity of a particular group, according to its particular desires and constraints. The "hidden" semi-illegal nature of these practices predetermines the need for ethnographic approach and reflexivity.

Making the auto-ethnography and subcultural commitment

In the second part of this chapter I'd like to focus on the sociological imagination and to be more precise, to write about the intellectual craft, the moral engagements of the researcher, and the limits and possibilities of "human nature". In this part of the study I will focus on the participant/researcher relations and the emotional boundaries of research. I will explore the emotional and moral problems, which the researcher meets in a situation when he/she shares a common background or values with the researched. Access issues and gaining confidence in the researched groups will be also discussed. The main methodological question I wish to pose is how to make ethnography about such a subculture, whose vulnerable members desire to remain hidden and demand their signs not to be translated.

The ethnographic insider research becomes particularly prevalent in contemporary youth studies. Paul Hodkinson (2005) and Andy Bennett (2002, 2003) argue that such an approach needs further methodological elaboration, since insider knowledge is controversial and it brings both advantages and difficulties to the research. Hodkinson suggests cautious reflexive analysis of the insider researcher's position, while Bennett argues that the advantages of such kinds of "native" research are only realized when insider status is combined with a variety of generic social and research skills (Bennett 2003). Insider knowledge shouldn't be taken for granted, but should be taken only as additional tool of the ethnographic equipment. I argue that it could also be used as a tool for making the "hidden ethnography" more transparent (see Blackman 2007: 701).

While thinking about researcher positionality and the role of the researcher, who is at the same time an insider in the researched group, I was inspired to write down a story about a young researcher from the first transitional generation (i.e. me) studying young adults from the second (post-transitional) generation, who share similar values with her, but suffer different social and spatial divisions. I argue that such a native way of research has its advantages concerning the possibility to create an authentic story in a dialogic form. I call myself "an insider", in order not to advocate the insider knowledge, but to reveal the extent of my own emotional engagement in the study of several youth subcultural groups in Bulgaria, whose boundaries are already very blurred, but yet they are united by a common emic term – "the underground", its connotation including deviance as well as social and spatial separation from the mainstream. The underground members sometimes also call themselves "a family" stressing the sameness between each other and on the informal relations that dominate over the formal ones, which makes their circle close and intimate. The subcultural bond between me and the other subcultural participants brings many advantages to my research including deeper knowledge about the researched participants, but at the same time problems such as the possible risk of double exclusion of the researcher both from the academic and the subcultural circles. Sometimes the subcultural characters accused me of "betrayal", i.e. that "I'm not subcultural anymore since I'm writing a scientific book". Sometimes my academic colleagues criticized me for not trusting enough in my own authority. I was forced to take sides – subcultural or academic, underground or elitist. And that was something I couldn't comply with as it might take the researcher into an endless circle of power relations and subordination. The only thing I could do in this case was to follow Howard Becker's (1967: 247) argument and to "satisfy the demands of our science by always making clear the limits of what we have studied, marking the boundaries beyond which our findings cannot be safely applied". Consequently I engaged myself in a "one-sided" study, in which my "insider" knowledge served as additional method for my ethnographic research of subcultural actions and youth's creative agency. I found the Chicago School's urban fieldwork studies through "lived experience" as a guiding example for the experimentation with research methods that is "driven by the passion to develop sociology to challenge social inequality" (Blackman 2010: 196). I tried to accomplish this task through the application of an "ethnographic mosaic" that relates to Nels Anderson's approach ([1923] 1967, 1983) and combines past personal experience and deep commitment to the research subjects. Concerning the emotional side of my unusual long-term participant observation, I also found support in the works of Clifford Shaw ([1930] 1966) and Frederic Thrasher ([1927] 1963).

Being aware of the social vulnerability of the researched subcultural participants, I chose the ethnographic methods and reflexivity as central in my study. In my attempt to protect them from prejudice, I found initial inspiration in the early Chicago School methods and approach that understands deviance on the basis of social factors, in its cultural and community context, thus emphasizing its normality (Blackman 2014: 498). As Blackman (2010: 195) states: "Sociological researchers at the Chicago School were experimentally employing some of the key empathetic strategies which would later define urban ethnographic practice, through the use of narrative, biography, autobiography, personal documents, dialog, participation, observation, life stories, rapport and voice." These methods marked the beginning of the sociological ethnographic imagination (Blackman 2010: 196). As subcultural insider I would like to make my contribution to the ethnographic imagination and its empathetic potential by employing auto-ethnography and a variety of ethnographic techniques that give priority to the researched subcultural participants.

Auto-ethnography is a reflexive method that differs both from the ethnography of others and the insider ethnography of a native researcher. Carolyn Ellis (2004: xix) defines it as "research, writing, story, and method that connect the autobiographical and personal to the cultural, social, and political". It allows researchers to avoid detachment and indifference towards the researched participants. Auto-ethnography combines various genres and voices that may "vary in their emphasis on the writing and research process (*graphy*), culture (*ethnos*), and self (*auto*)" (Reed-Danahay 1997: 2). However, auto-ethnography is also seen as problematic and controversial, even narcissistic. Amanda Coffey (1999) suggests critical awareness of the ethnographic self, instead of taking it for granted. In other words, researcher's interaction with social and cultural reality should be made explicit.

In my research the ethnographic self is revealed in order to express the researcher's commitment to the subcultural participants and auto-ethnography is advanced in order to emphasize shared values. In this particular case, the ethnographic self overlaps with the subcultural self with an emphasis on subcultural (*ethnos*), and not on self (*auto*). By analogy with the feminist ethnography (Skeggs 2001), it might be defined as subcultural ethnography, in which, for exclusively ethical reasons, the researcher is also a participant, and the participants are enabled "to establish research agendas" (Skeggs 2001: 426). Moreover, the focus on subcultural biography and autobiography concerns the researcher's personal experience in the much broader and holistic meaning. It is related to C. Wright Mills' concept of the sociological imagination that joins together life experience and intellectual work in order to successfully "build up an adequate view of a total society and of its components" (Mills 1959: 211). Hence, subcultural ethnographic imagination is part of the researcher's "elaborate interplay" that deals both with the private troubles and the public issues and seeks the links between individual milieu and social structure.

What I was actually doing in the field looked like a constant interplay between me as subcultural participant and me as "the researcher". In terms of researcher reflexivity I was concerned about misinterpreting the facts. Very often I was in doubt about whether I would help or do harm to my group through this research, since fieldwork might also represent "an intrusion and intervention into a system of relationships ... (and) the potential treacherousness of this relationship seems inescapable" (Stacey 1988: 23). Most of all I wanted to create an authentic story in a dialogic form that is reflexive and at least partially subcultural. I tried different ethnographic techniques in order to accomplish this task. I participated and I observed, I gathered life-stories and I talked about mine, I interviewed the participants (individually and collectively) and I let them interview me. The final result was one emotional participant observation full of ups and downs, a contribution to the "reflexive turn" (Bourdieu and Wacquant 1992). Blackman (2007: 701) argues that, "Through the writing process the ethnographer decides how much to reveal", and "that to reveal what is usually hidden is to cross emotional borders in fieldwork accounts". In this sense, I tried to put in use all the naturalistic data gathered on the field. I was also aware that my group is very sensible about revealing their "secret" culture and contrary to expectations the "hidden ethnography" was rather better approach than an objective description of the subcultural environment. I certainly made several descriptions of subcultural dress-codes and gathering places, but I was keen to create a story about the shared experiences, fears and problems of social exclusion. During the fieldwork, I repeatedly regretted that the presentation of me being a researcher, i.e. holding a PhD degree automatically placed a barrier between my respondents and me. The theoretical insight caused by this ethnographic discomfort occurred to me at the time when I discovered that one of the participants also had a higher education, but he was zealously *hiding* that fact in his desire to please me and keep his street-punk identity "intact". I knew I wanted to do the same thing, because we both shared the subcultural mistrust of the white-collared world and the "claim for illiteracy" Hebdige described about punk (1979: 19). However, there are more positive cases in which my biography served as an effective example to follow. During our participant/researcher relationship one of my key respondents radically changed her way of life. She was a hardcore-punk girl, 12 years younger than me, who had a dead-end job and whose leisure activities were dominated by soft drugs consumption. She was an intelligent young woman who became highly interested in my research. I did the fieldwork in her town in the spring of 2012 and I returned there in autumn. She hadn't told me the good news, but I met her in the university, during her first term as a sociology student. She hadn't changed her style, but she told me she had reduced drug taking. Later on she visited my first lecture on youth subcultures at the same university. We discussed the issue of drug use and subcultures in front of the other students as equals. We shared the pride of being both subcultural and academic. At the same time I realized that our conversation in front of the students was another piece of the reflexive "ethnographic mosaic". It was also a piece of my auto-ethnography.

For Bourdieu, the "reflexive turn" is about power and risk because the sociologist exposes their origins, biography, locality and "intellectual bias" (Blackman 2007: 700). Yet, this risk must be taken if we stay true to C. Wright Mills' promise. In my case I used my own life-story as a complex tool for interaction with the other research participants. For Merrill and West (2009: 5) it is something implicit, since "we cannot write stories of others without reflecting our own histories, social and cultural locations as well as subjectivities and values". I didn't want to underestimate this fact, so in this study I tried to expose openly my origins (a subcultural insider), values and biases. I did it in order to point out the similarities and differences between me and the other participants. I did it also in an attempt to show that there are some collective rather than individual values and constrains that unites all the life-stories gathered in the fluid but yet common subcultural field.

Subcultural participants and the dual role of the ethnographer

Fieldwork carried out in 2012 explored the underground space of one Bulgarian city in the South. The participants in this research actually come from different subcultural styles, but are interdependent through their personal informal relations. Every subculture has its core and periphery. The core members of the subcultural groups are usually 10–20 people, who share stronger beliefs and deeper knowledge about the origins, music, style and ideology of their subculture. Boys slightly prevail in numbers, but girls' presence is not just peripheral. The age group is in the range of 15 to 30 years, and the most active at present is the generation born between 1986 and 1990. The main identity tag – the group affiliation – includes three major subcategories – *punk, hardcore and casual* – that is interconnected through the participants' actual relations as well as their physical presence in one and the same spatiality. Each tag constitutes a distinct subculture, with its own history and discernible practices, but at the same time all the participants take part in the larger underground group of the "folk devils" set up in opposition to the mainstream (Cohen, S. 1972).

The feeling of being different, shared by all with whom I have spoken, makes the subcultural members quite careful when they choose who they can trust. Trust is achieved mainly in the circle of people sharing the signs of the subculture. These signs are based on a secret knowledge within the particular groups. Being *"genuine"* and not a *"poser"* means that you master the secret code which makes you part of the *"family"*. It means that you know the intimate zone of the group. *A key methodological issue for sociological researcher is if you know the code, how could you at the same time be the one who observes and do the research?* Being aware of my dual position in this research, I tried not to make a comprehensive description but a selective sensitive ethnography with biographical reflection. I wanted to employ the sociological craft in order to produce a morally engaged work, through what Mills sees as an elaborate interplay. Mills ([1959] 2000:

161) argues, "To understand biography of an individual, we must understand the significance and meaning of the roles he has played and does play." I took the risk to involve the subcultural "secret code" into the craft and even to change places with the researched when it is necessary, thus "blurring any distinction between the roles of scientist and non-scientist on the social level and scientist and human on the personal level" (Kerr about Mills – Kerr 2009: 119).

A reverse interview: the challenge of reflexivity for insider research

The specifics of research were determined by one more crucial factor: how to gain access into the groups and how to win their trust. The research problem was related to the marginalization of some members of the groups due to accusations related to hooliganism, politically incorrect views, clashes with the police and drug use. Even though I used my knowledge of the underground spaces, they still felt suspicious of my intentions. Their distrust of me was fully justified because the responsibility for maintaining their anonymity was left entirely in my hands. Sometimes I was even blamed for leaks of information – "espionage" or "treason" – and began to call my own identity in question. In all cases, winning their trust required hard and delicate work on my part, and often my loyalty was tested within the group in different ways. In order to show the process of initiating the researcher into the group, I'd like to cite here part of an interview with one of my key informants (Loko, a 22 year-old boy, a subcultural character who is also an active participant in one of the local football firms) as an illustration of how my intentions towards the groups have been checked. The following interview was also first in chronological order (recorded on 10 March 2012) and many of my future contacts and conversations, as well as some of my failures, were dependent on it. This interview will be called a *reverse interview*; in this case the respondent asked the questions and the researcher responded:

Loko: What do you think of subcultures in Bulgaria?
Vihra: (jokingly) I think I'm the one who should ask questions.
Loko: No, I want to see the opinion of the ordinary people about the subcultures.
Vihra: Yeah, right, but I am now in the role of researcher.
Loko: And researchers are not people?
Vihra: When you step into the shoes of researchers, you remain somewhat detached.
Loko: So does that mean a researcher is not a human?
Vihra: Well, you become an observer. I am now an entity, who observes.
Loko: What do you want to watch?
Vihra: You.
Loko: All right, what's the point of these interviews and the whole thing? Does it make sense to you, the things that you're doing?
Vihra: For me – yes, but I fear that may not make sense to the people whom I write about. I'll try that it makes sense for everyone, but it's another

topic of conversation. I mean, there's an idea that these studies should be done so that my voice is ... not over yours, meaning to give to others to talk, but not only talk, but also being heard.

Loko: And do you think to manipulate that book somehow?

Vihra: Well, I hope not, but I will give my opinion in the end; I have to say what I think.

Loko: Do you cut out the words of people in such a way, so that they sound different and are taken out of the context of their conversation and sound in another way?

Vihra: No, I do not do that. We're not talking about direct quotations at all, like "the man said this and that", and not citing his full name, age, occupation, not at all!

Loko: And will those objects of your research remain anonymous?

Vihra: You will remain anonymous, of course. This is part of the research ethics. It is, in fact, mandatory. Unless someone told you, "I want to be presented."

Loko: What chance is there to change the facts and present them differently?

Vihra: To whom?

Loko: The general public, who will read the book.

Vihra: But why? Why do I have to show it otherwise?

Loko: So, when you write a book you have a sort of benefit from it, don't you? So, one type of benefit is to show things that you think and show what life is; if you do this, it will be satisfying to you and to your beliefs; on the other hand, another reason to write a book is the financial goal to earn some money. And in order to make money, you would want to appeal to wider audience. So, in your case here, the subculture topic, would you decorate it with facts that will attract people?

Vihra: (after a long pause, but flatly) No. Furthermore, I must say, though why I should say it to you I don't know, but I do not study subculture as something interesting, exotic and mainly based on music. My research is actually quite a sociological one and seeks some class characteristics in those things.

Loko: So you're not doing a book that can be read by the ordinary people and be understood by the teens?

Vihra: It will be read by the people, but it won't be a teenage bestseller.

Loko: Yes, but subcultures are supported mostly by people under 25 years.

A lot of methodological issues are intertwined in the interview with Loko. For a start, I will point out just few of them. First of all – *is the researcher allowed to show her or his human, non-academic side on the field*; second – *does the researcher intend to sell her or his research or have another reason to investigate*; third – *does the researcher know for certain that she or he won't change or decorate the facts for the purpose of creating proper academic text?*

I will discuss these issues in relation to C. Wright Mills' promise of the social sciences and his appeal for intellectual craft (Mills [1959] 2000). The reflexive approach which is central in C. Wright Mills' work is an approach fuelled with deep emotional commitment to the subjects studied and to the social problems of young adults. The answers to these questions follow the logic of the intellectual craft – they express the need for personal involvement in the research and for "everyday empiricism" in which "the most admirable thinkers within the scholarly community ... do not split their work from their lives" (Mills [1959] 2000: 195); the demand for moral and political autonomy of the researcher (ibid.: 226) and the appeal for intelligibility (ibid.: 218–221).

In relation to Loko's assertions and my researcher positionality I will put forward three responses to the subcultural questions. First subcultural question – *Is the researcher human?* My answer to Loko should be – *Yes, she is; it is her right and her responsibility*, since through their imagination, researchers become part of the whole structure, history and culture. They are not alone in their research. I'll try to illustrate this through one of the emic subcultural terms – "family". Being part of the family makes me an insider, but it doesn't mean that, as a member of this informal family, I am not allowed to be slightly different from the others – for example, the more educated one. And if my family accepts me as a scholar, I'll be even more useful to them because of my skills and knowledge. Because "the social scientist is not only an 'ordinary man'. It is his very task intellectually to transcend the millieux in which he happens to live" (Mills [1959] 2000: 184). On the other hand, as an outsider, who is making the research, I'll be more efficient if I try to "show my human face", i.e. to share and compare my own biography with the participants in order to understand the similarities and differences between us and eventually to solve shared structural and moral problems of exclusion.

Second subcultural question – *What is the reason for doing the research? Who will benefit from it?* The answer should be – *The benefits are for you and me only. I am autonomous in my research.* This question is linked to the subcultural distrust to those in power, and the answer is directly related to the demand for moral and political autonomy of the researcher. Mills ([1959] 2000: 226) states, "Above all, do not give up your moral and political autonomy by accepting in somebody's else's terms the illiberal practicality of the bureaucratic ethos or the liberal practicality of the moral scatter." The question and answer are also linked to the desire for academic status and the subcultural suspicion that the academic status has already become more important for the researcher than their subcultural biography. Or even worse, that the desire to sell their book will dominate, thus making the researcher morally indifferent to the subcultural milieu.

Third subcultural question – *What chance is there to change the facts and present them differently?* The answer should be – *No, I won't change or decorate the facts for the purpose of creating proper academic text.* This dialogue also concerns the desire for academic status and it concerns language itself as "a tool and component of the scientific method" (Kerr 2009: 127). It is clearly stated by Mills:

> Desire for status is one reason why academic men slip so readily into unintelligibility. To overcome the academic *prose* you have first to overcome the academic *pose*. It is much less important to study grammar and Anglo-

Saxon roots than to clarify your own answers to these three questions: (1) How difficult and complex after all is my subject? (2) When I write, what status am I claiming for myself? (3) For whom am I trying to write?

(Mills [1959] 2000: 218–19)

The last questions cited are interconnected in my case, because the specific kind of people I am trying to write about have influenced my past and thus formed my own voice, even the language in which my thoughts are shaped. And this resulted in my expectations of status. It resulted in the fact that I am actually suspicious of formal social status and formal institutions in general and sometimes I hide my own social status as some of the other subcultural participants do in order to be more "subcultural", which sometimes overlaps with the idea of being more "human". In this "elaborate interplay" I took the role of translator of subcultural meanings as well as a spokesperson of a particular group – because, as Mills said, "Your past plays into and affects your present, and it defines your capacity for future experience" (Mills [1959] 2000: 196).

Conclusion

According to C. Wright Mills ([1959] 2000: 134), "Social science is the study of biography and of history, and the problems of their intersection within social structure." Moreover, "historical transformations carry meanings not only for individual ways of life, but for the very character of the human being" (ibid.: 158). Such an approach poses the problem – what is to be human? Mills contends that the:

chief danger today lies in the unruly forces of contemporary society itself, with its alienating methods of production, its enveloping techniques of political domination, its international anarchy – in a word, its pervasive transformations of the very "nature" of men and the conditions and aims of his life.

(ibid.: 13)

The latter statement is of great significance for an "insider" researcher such as me, who is studying subcultural deviance and is seeking for its explanation.

In this search for an explanation I have intertwined the underground scene and its participants, the historical and social transformation they and myself went through – an "elaborate interplay" of the subcultural imagination. I explored transformations and subcultural deviance as interdependent problems and I took the CCCS theory as a starting point for my argument because, as Blackman (2014: 508) argues, it possesses "explanatory potential to account for young people's subcultural activities across different countries at different historical and political conjunctures". Consequently, I studied subculture from outside, through the existing social structure and its spatial dimensions, and I studied it from within – through grounded ethnography with a reflexive approach. The key focus of my work became the ethnographic craft that is related to researcher's position in the field as well as his or her moral engagements to the researched participants. I made explicit my insider position in order to draw the attention to certain shared values. Accordingly, I employed auto-ethnography with an emphasis on culture (*ethnos*) rather than on self (*auto*) – (see Reed-Danahay 1997). As a moral engagement to the researched, I made an attempt to produce *subcultural ethnography* that enables participants to take part in the process of writing the subcultural story. During this process, I changed roles with one of the subcultural participants and through his "voice" I was enabled to pose the main research questions: *Is the researcher human, what is the reason for doing the research, and how (and to whom) the research will be presented?*

The answers that followed ought to reveal the precise position of the researcher in her dual role of mediator and translator of subcultural meanings as well as her intentions for the realization of one ethical ethnographic project concerned with youth subcultures and social inequalities. This project suggests personal commitment to the social problems of youth, moral and political autonomy and cautious dealing with the ethnographic data gathered in the subcultural field. It deals with the "human variety" and problems of cultural difference and social exclusion. In conclusion, I will suggest that subculture might be a fluid phenomenon, but it is permanent as a process. Youth subcultures have the potential to offer changes to the mainstream culture. Naturally, this is not a linear process, and multiple subcultures can coexist. What matters, though, is that the nature of the subculture is to counter, thus keeping a symbolic balance in a given social order. After all, subcultures submit the necessary difference, they import the "wild" into the "cultural", by renouncing the social prestige: this subcultural potential is helpful to insider researchers to do their studies in an independent way.

Note

1 By analogy with the term of Dick Hebdige (1979)

References

Anderson, N. (1967/1923) *The Hobo: The Sociology of the Homeless Man.* Chicago, IL: University of Chicago Press.

Anderson, N. (1983) Stranger at the Gate: Reflections on the Chicago School of Sociology, *Urban Life* 11(4): 396–406.

Becker, H.S. (1967) Whose Side Are We On?, *Social Problems* 14(3): 239–247.

Bennett, A. (1999) Subcultures or Neo-Tribes. Rethinking the Relationship Between Youth, Style and Musical Taste, *Sociology* 33(3): 599–617.

Bennett, A. (2002) Researching Youth Culture and Popular Music: A Methodological Critique, *The British Journal of Sociology* 53(3): 451–66.

Bennett, A. (2003) The Use of Insider Knowledge in Ethnographic Research on Contemporary Youth Music Scenes. In A. Bennett, M. Cieslik and S. Miles (eds) *Researching Youth.* London: Palgrave, 186–99.

Blackman, S. (2007) 'Hidden Ethnography': Crossing Emotional Borders in Qualitative Accounts of Young People's Lives, *Sociology* 41(4): 699–716.

Blackman, S. (2010) 'The Ethnographic Mosaic' of the Chicago School: Critically Locating Vivien Palmer, Clifford Shaw and Frederic Thrasher's Research Methods in Contemporary Reflexive Sociological Interpretation. In C. Hart (ed.) *The Legacy of the Chicago School of Sociology.* Kingswinsford: Midrash Publishing, 195–215.

Blackman, S. (2014) Subculture Theory: An Historical and Contemporary Assessment of the Concept for Understanding Deviance, *Deviant Behavior* 35(6): 495–512.

Bourdieu, P. and Wacquant, L. (1992) *An Invitation to Reflexive Sociology.* Cambridge: Polity Press.

Clarke, J. (1976) The Skinheads & The Magical Recovery of Community. In S. Hall and T. Jefferson (eds) *Resistance Through Rituals: Youth Subcultures in Post-war Britain.* London: Routledge, 99–102.

Coffey, A. (1999) *The Ethnographic Self.* London: Sage.

Cohen, P. (1972 [1980]) Sub-cultural Conflict and Working Class Community. *Working Papers in Cultural Studies.* No.2. Birmingham.

Cohen, S. (1972) *Folk Devils and Moral Panics.* London: McGibbon & Kee.

Ellis, C. (2004) *The Ethnographic I: A Methodological Novel About Autoethnography.* Walnut Creek, CA: AltaMira Press.

Hall, S. (1980) Cultural Studies and the Centre: Some Problematics and Problems. In S. Hall, D. Hobson, A. Lowe, and P. Willis (eds) *Culture, Media and Language*, London: Hutchinson, 15-48.

Hall, S. and Jefferson, T. (eds) (1976) *Resistance Through Rituals: Youth Subcultures in Post-war Britain.* London: Routledge.

Hebdige, D. (1979) *Subculture: The Meaning of Style.* London: Methuen & Co.

Hesmondhalgh, D. (2005) Subcultures, Scenes or Tribes? None of the Above, *Journal of Youth Studies* 8(1): 21–40.

Hodkinson, P. (2005) Insider Research in the Study of Youth Culture, *Journal of Youth Studies* 8(2): 131–150.

Kerr, K. (2009) *Postmodern Cowboy: C. Wright Mills and a New 21st Century Sociology.* East Boulder, CO: Paradigm Publishers.

Lefebvre, H. (1991/1974) *The Production of Space.* Oxford: Basil Blackwell.

Merrill, B. and West, L. (2009) *Using Biographical Methods in Social Research.* London: Sage.

Muggleton, D. (2000) *Inside Subculture: The Postmodern Meaning of Style.* London: Berg.

Mills, C. Wright (2000/1959) *The Sociological Imagination.* New York: Oxford University Press.

Pilkington, H. (1994) *Russia's Youth and Its Culture: A Nation's Constructors and Constructed.* London: Routledge.

Reed-Danahay, D. (1997) *Auto/ethnography: Rewriting the Self and the Social (Explorations in Anthropology).* Oxford: Berg.

Shaw, C. (1966/1930) *The Jack-Roller: A Delinquent Boy's Own Story.* Chicago, IL: University of Chicago Press.

Skeggs, B. (2001) Feminist Ethnography. In P. Atkinson (ed.) *Handbook of Ethnography.* London: Sage, 426–442.

Stacey, J. (1988) Can There Be a Feminist Ethnography?, *Women's Studies International Forum* 11(1): 21–27.

Thrasher, F. (1963/1927) *The Gang: A Study of 1,313 Gangs in Chicago.* Chicago, IL: University of Chicago Press.

Willis, P. (2009/1981) Learning to Labour. In M. Hechter and C. Horne (eds) *Theories of Social Order.* Stanford, CA: Stanford University Press, 204–215.

11   Connecting personal troubles and public issues in Asian subculture studies

J. Patrick Williams

In comparison to research in western societies, it is fair to say that the Asian youth subculture studies literature is relatively limited. Oftentimes, studies deal with western cultural phenomena, such as music or fashion, that have been imported to Asian societies and/or appropriated by small groups of Asian youths via mass and social media flows (e.g., Liew and Fu 2006; Quader and Redden 2014; Wallach 2008). Less often, studies focus on specific Asian cultural phenomena, such as Japanese "Otaku," that have circulated internationally (e.g., Ito, Okabe and Tsuji 2012). Rarer still is comparative research that includes both western and Asian subcultural groups (e.g., Hannerz 2015).

Also rare in the Asian subculture literature are discussions of reflexivity regarding the relations between researchers and what they study. In most cases, the literature is quite traditional and conservative, following the tracks laid out by the Chicago or Birmingham traditions of subculture studies. In those traditions, scholars treated subcultures with a mixture of anthropological reverence for the exotic and parochial concern for the disenfranchised. Chicago School ethnographers may have gone farther than Birmingham semioticians in describing individuals' day-to-day lives, yet both traditions imposed external definitions and identities on those they studied as they described cultural processes and phenomena in realist terms. Since the 1990s, more "insider" research (e.g., Andes 1998; Driver 2011; Hodkinson 2005), as well as critical and evaluative work on traditional subcultural studies (e.g., Bennett 2011; Blackman 2014) has been published, functioning as a type of counterweight to traditional scholarship, yet this kind of introspection cannot be easily found in studies of Asian youth subcultures.

This chapter attempts to fill this gap by reporting on the process of writing with, rather than about, youths and their cultural interests. Drawing from two research projects with Singaporean university students, I reflect on doing collaborative ethnographic subcultural studies in Asia. As I describe below, each project was different, with unique interests and goals. Yet, what they had in common was the students' development of "the sociological imagination" (Mill 1959:5). By comparing these two projects, I hope readers can learn something about how the sociological imagination affected our research and how the relationship among the students, ethnography, and the cultural topics they studied resulted in the distinct research reports that we produced (Williams and Jauhari bin Zaini 2016; Williams and Ho in press).

Research and the sociological imagination

When I moved to Singapore in 2008, I was a stranger in a strange land. One thing I quickly realised was that I could not enter into youth subcultural worlds with the ease I was used to in western societies. In a region with a history of policies that have repressed or limited the growth of alternative youth cultures, the young people who do participate are often leery of adults who show interest in their practices or beliefs. My "elite" position as a university professor, alongside my race and age, worked against me and I found it difficult to interact meaningfully with many young people whom I didn't know and who didn't know me. I've dealt with this by creating opportunities to interact with local students on the topic of alternative or opposition cultures through an undergraduate sociology course on youth cultures and subcultures, and by having those students go out and collect data themselves. Throughout the course, students interact with the subculture studies literature, collect or create data having to do with a topic of their choice, and write weekly analytic notes that tie data to theories or concepts from the literature (see Williams 2008).

To help empower students in their research, I encourage them to choose from almost any aspect of youth culture or subculture that they would like to study, so long as the topic fits within Polsky's idea of "viewing society as a problem for the [subculturalist] rather than the other way round" (Polsky, cited in Williams 2011:4). I intend this constraint to guide students towards social justice issues. One of my major pedagogical goals is thus to help students develop a sociological imagination about alternative cultures. As Mills (1959:5) states,

> [t]he sociological imagination enables its possessor to understand the [social world] in terms of its meaning for the inner life and the external career of a variety of individuals. It enables him[/her] to take into account how individuals, in the welter of their daily experience, often become falsely conscious of their social positions. Within that welter, the framework of modern society is sought, and within that framework the psychologies of a variety of men and women are formulated.

Through the study of group cultures that exist contra to or otherwise distinct from mainstream culture, I hope that students will develop more nuanced understandings of how and why alternative cultures exist (see also Williams and Hannerz 2014). Such a goal conflicts in some basic ways with the educational tenets that guide learning among Asian youths. In Confucianist societies across East and Southeast Asia such as Singapore, education systems place a premium on performance via standardised testing (Mee 1998) and students are preoccupied with the end product of learning (e.g., exams), even in learning contexts where teachers do not measure performance in that way (Anderson and Weninger 2012). In a course like mine, where I task students with making connections between the inner lives of individuals and larger social structures (with no single, correct way of describing those connections) rather than learning how to memorise and then regurgitate abstract theories or information from past studies, students often have problems coping, even when they are personally interested in the course topic.

The hierarchical nature of Confucianism (Englehart 2000), Singapore's emphasis on meritocracy (Ng 2008), and the subsequent feeling that they must produce the "right" answer to be rewarded, make it difficult for some students to feel that they have a valid voice when it comes to describing social life. For this reason, I have designed my course in a way that gives students more responsibility for their own learning. I "force them to choose" what to study, based on what they consider personally interesting or worthy. Their job becomes to connect the personal to the social by engaging in the sociological analysis of data they collect. The goal is to facilitate the active production of knowledge that connects them and their immediate social milieu to the larger social world. This aligns well with Mills' promise that "the individual can understand his[/her] experience and gauge his[/her] own fate only by locating him[/her]self within [the social world]" (Mills ibid.).

It is sometimes the case that students choose topics in which they have a passing or academic interest only, but there are also students in the course who investigate topics that are deeply personal to them. These are, to me, very promising projects because of the potential for students to experience research in a way that may have long-lasting effects. Many projects do not involve "personal troubles," or students fail to study them in depth. However, there have been instances in which students have conducted projects that exemplify C. Wright Mills' sociological imagination. This chapter deals with two such projects. In one study, a student sought validation for her fan culture experiences against a backdrop of mixed popular sentiment from peers and adults. In the other study, a student worked to retrieve a sense of meaning and self-worth after years of being labelled a trouble-maker in school. I recognised the connection of their personal troubles with larger public issues and wanted to help ensure that these students' voices were heard beyond the classroom. Once the course was over and grades were no longer a barrier between us, I invited each student to discuss the possibility of developing their projects to a point where the results could be published for the larger community of cultural scholars to read. I now turn to each study— one on negotiating deviant fan identities and the other on rescuing a meaningful subcultural self—to consider some connections between personal troubles and public issues.

Validating youth cultural experiences

With a highly rationalised industry that spans the breadth of cultural production and diffusion, Korean popular culture ("K-pop") has had immense international success via music, television, and other entertainment channels, with a correspondingly massive following of consumers and fans across East and Southeast Asia (Chua 2004, 2010; Fu and Liew 2005). Along with the diffusion and consumption of these media products comes the objectification of K-pop identities, for both the artists and fans. These identities are not necessarily positive. In particular, there is a relatively new type of "extreme" fan called sasaeng, who are overtly interested in the private lives of K-pop idols. So-called sasaeng fans in Korea have been reported to engage in a variety of deviant and criminal activities, including installing tracking devices on K-pop stars' cars, sending their favourite stars love letters written in menstrual blood, harassing their friends and families, and even attacking them in public in order to capture their full attention.

Many Singaporean youths are avid K-pop fans, yet are hesitant to admit it because they fear the negative connotations associated with the sasaeng label. When Samantha, a sociology student and diehard K-pop fan, began her research on K-pop identities, there was no academic research published on the sasaeng phenomenon, and only brief observations suggesting its recent emergence. Having spent significant time and money immersing herself in K-pop fan culture, Samantha wanted to take the opportunity to deal explicitly with the stigma attached to K-pop fan identities through research. Though a sociology student, she had also studied Korean language at university, taken an exchange semester in Seoul, and gotten a job in the K-pop industry thanks to her English-language skills—all admittedly because of her intense commitment to K-pop music culture. However, there were a couple of instances during her time in Korea in which her own behaviours were questioned by others in the scene. This made her question her relation to, and identity within, K-pop culture. After returning to Singapore from her exchange programme, she enrolled in my course and knew from the beginning that she wanted to critically analyse (and hopefully validate) her own choices and experiences as a fan.

> On a personal level, I was convinced that I was not a sasaeng fan based on the fact that I was very much sane and would never mean any harm to the idols I supported, and that I would not cross the line in invading their personal space. But ... I began to doubt my own fan identity. Was I sasaeng? What about the others who, like me, went on student exchanges to Korea and did the same things as I did, chasing after stars, were they sasaeng? What exactly is sasaeng? I had to get to the bottom of it.
>
> (Samantha, reflexive memo)

During the semester, it was clear to me that her commitment to the project was extraordinary. With guidance and feedback, she explored the sasaeng identity through ethnographic content analysis (Altheide 1987) and field research, including participant observation and in-depth interviewing. After the semester ended, our collaborative goal became to see how sasaeng fans were characterised in the Singaporean media, and then to compare those findings with observational and interviewee data from Singaporean K-pop fans. In short, we found that Singaporean youths carefully trod a narrow path between appearing excessive in their fandom (at which point they risked being labelled as sasaeng fans) and appearing insufficiently committed to K-pop (at which point they risked being labelled as inauthentic fans or passive consumers).

Samantha's concerns with how people viewed her fandom seemed clear in the bits of data she collected from mass and social media sources. She initially sought out instances in which random netizens posted their opinions about K-pop fandom on news media sites. People wrote things like, "there're a lot of crazy stupid K-pop fans around" and "all this K-pop is a divergence and detrimental to one's sanity". The negative tone set in these examples was representative of a far-reaching antagonism toward excessive fandom. This antagonism, spread virally through both mass and social media, had become a public issue in Mills' sense of the term—the problematic behaviours of a few had become detrimental to the many. Thus the sasaeng label was seen as a problem for passionate fans like Samantha, who wanted to consume K-pop beyond "passive" mainstream means, but were unwilling to risk a spoiled identity. The sasaeng label was therefore a threat to her sense of self.

To connect her own "personal troubles" to the larger public issue surrounding K-pop fandom, Samantha spent time talking to teenage fans and rode with them in rented vans as they "stalked" Korean pop stars around Singapore. Using our sociological imaginations, we analysed how those fans established semantic boundaries between themselves and the behaviours in which so-called sasaeng engaged. We also looked at how fans avoided being seen as entirely normal and developed a working theory about how fans worked to neutralise threats to self from two directions at once. In the end, Samantha came away with a very sociological understanding of her experiences within K-pop fan culture. She became cognisant of the means by which identities were created, circulated, and negotiated, and the resources individuals and groups used in identity work. In her words,

> The project was definitely a means of validating my own experiences as a fan. I came to learn that, despite the mass-mediated image of the extreme fan, each fan has their own definitions which can be elastic. A certain action, considered to be a sasaeng act by one, may not be so in the eyes of another fan, who will find reasons to justify his/her fan identity as not sasaeng. Discovering this defensive mechanism of sorts gave me insight in my own fan identity and how I shaped it over the years, and the academic analysis of the K-pop industry will remind me time and time again to be more aware of mass-mediated images and news reporting styles, to look beyond the glitz and glamour that I was first blinded by and to stay grounded in reality which can easily slip away from the mind amidst the amazingly good looks, the perfected choreographies, the juicy scandals and the downright dirty exposés.
>
> (Samantha, personal correspondence)

Reflexivity and collaboration in subcultural ethnography

In the correspondence above, Samantha reflected on the problematic nature of K-pop fandom and on how she developed her sociological imagination to make sense of her own fan identity. Writing about their ethnographic work within the vegan subculture, Cherry, Coulter and DeSoucey (2011: 233) note that the nature of identities, "especially when those identities prove contentious, poses special obstacles for researchers. How might our own … practices and identities affect fieldwork? And, flipping the direction of inquiry, how might [our study of subcultural identity] affect us as researchers." These are important questions for "insider" researchers dealing with identities that have been Othered, not least because their own selves are bound up in the self/other dichotomy. Yet reading our published report (Williams and Ho 2016), you do not hear either from Samantha or me explicitly. We assume a rather invisible position, as authors reporting findings. This is not surprising; many scholars do not deal as reflexively with their role in research as they could, and most remain "suspicious of authors' voices outside of prescribed forms" (Charmaz and Mitchell 1996:286), choosing to focus on what they deem analytically appropriate or interesting, while ignoring or glossing over what may be some deeply personal aspects of the research.

Yet ethnography is, on the one hand, a product of interaction between a researcher, whose meanings and understandings are elaborated through interpretation and imagination, and a social world (Atkinson 2006). One the other hand, ethnography is a uniquely intimate research process. The researcher's proximity to individuals' and groups' lived experiences inevitably evokes emotions as researcher and researched interact (Fields, Copp and Kleinman 2007). As ethnographers write, many decide not to report on aspects of fieldwork that are explicitly personal, yet which could clearly connect the researcher to the larger social processes under investigation (see Blackman 2007; Ronai 1995).

Autoethnographers do just that by retroactively and selectively writing about past experiences and especially epiphanies—"remembered moments perceived to have significantly impacted the trajectory of a person's life" (Ellis, Adams and Bochner 2011; see also Denzin 1989; Ellis 1997). Autoethnography can allow researchers to investigate a social phenomenon that has personal significance by re-imagining and then analysing epiphanic moments in her or his life. I rarely find such writing among Asian student-researchers. And so I was surprised at reading the following excerpt, which came from a student named Jauhari, who had also enrolled in my youth cultures and subcultures course, about his chosen topic, Rude Boy subculture:

> I know what it means to choose the path different from the "others"; the subcultural path. I was never that popular kid in school. The circle of friends that I had called themselves the "non-MTV" kids, the ones who were definitely different; the non-mainstream. We were often branded as "troublemakers" by teachers and students alike. But we held our heads up high, wearing the label as a badge of honor of sorts simply because we wanted to be seen as different.
>
> (Jauhari, analytic note)

This excerpt not only illustrated to me Jauhari's interest in identity, it also evoked emotions, memories, and reflections as I read it. I was transported back to my own past, remembered my own feelings of difference, of being labelled by adults, and both the good and bad times that resulted from them. I immediately felt a connection to Jauhari because of what and how he wrote, and so I reached out and encouraged him to continue this form of introspective writing. As the weeks went by and we covered a variety of topics including hegemony and resistance, style and homology, identity and labelling in the course, Jaurahi continued to reflect on past experiences and to connect these to the sociological literature. By the end of the semester, his writing had provoked me to write more explicitly about my own subcultural past and to articulate similar events and processes that have often been in my mind, but never published.

A very different collaborative project emerged from my earlier-discussed project with Samantha. In this latter case, I wrote a series of responses to Jauhari's analytic essays, which became the basis for what we have called a "collaborative autoethnography" (Williams and Zaini 2016). Focusing on what we saw as shared experiences, we moved away from the spectacular aspects of subcultures and toward meaning-laden moments. In one example, we discussed experiences in which adults had unilaterally dismissed our tastes and, in doing so, our identities.

Jauhari: I remember the psychiatrist asked me to bring my CD collection to one meeting, saying we could listen and talk about the music. But she just confiscated it all on the grounds that ska music was "dangerous." I vividly recall her shock upon seeing the title of the first track, Gangsters, by The Specials. In retrospect, I realise that the psychiatrist assumed that ska was dangerous since she thought that it was not the usual MTV top-20 music that teenagers listened to. She took the song title at face value, assuming that Gangsters was a valorization of criminal behavior. I highly suspect that she never actually listened to the song.

Me: For me it was my father and not a psychiatrist, but the story was similar. I used his truck one night to drive to the grocery store and accidentally left a Suicidal Tendencies [a punk band] cassette in the tape deck. I'll always remember his reaction the next morning because it seemed so over-the-top to me: "Patrick, do you want to kill yourself?" I knew I wouldn't win a debate with him about lyrical polysemy. Besides, at that point he showed me that he had already pulled all the tape out of the cassette. It hurts to lack the power to properly defend your own interpretation of the music you love.

Both our stories highlight the problematic nature of subcultural identification, and both rely on our use of the sociological imagination. In his final portfolio entry for the course, Jauhari wrote: "Through the project, I became more able to make sense of my subcultural past—wherein making sense goes beyond the mere process of comprehending a past reality and validating it using the academic toolkit."

Through our collaboration, Jauhari was able to reconcile problematic, often painful subcultural experiences from his youth. Indeed, he described the reliving of these experiences as "emancipatory". It was equally significant for me. Connecting events in my own biography—events that were instrumental in sparking the sociological imagination in me more than a decade before being introduced to the writings of C. Wright Mills—to events students have experienced is also part of "reflexive teaching" (Warren 2011). Writing with Jauhari pushed me to broaden my own understandings both of what may count as relevant knowledge in social science scholarship and how the act of teaching becomes consequential in multiple ways (see Liew 2013). This is akin to what Cammarota and Fine (2008: 9–10) call "Youth Participatory Action Research" insomuch as our project was "collaboratively negotiated and co-constructed" and "represents a systematic approach for engaging young people in transformational resistance, educational praxis, and critical epistemologies, [where young people] create their own sense of efficacy in the world and address the social conditions that impede liberation and positive, healthy development" (p. xx). This is, to me, the core of the sociological imagination.

Conclusion: reflexivity in the classroom

These two cases are not just about subcultural ethnographies in Asia; they also express the significance of the sociological imagination within the context of teaching about youth culture and subculture. In the case of K-pop fan culture, Samantha and I produced a traditional, analytic ethnographic account of the sasaeng fan identity. In the case of Rude Boy subculture, Jauhari and I more explicitly embraced our respective standpoints, reflections, and personal feelings in the research process; things that are often confined to "prefaces, separate treatises, novels, convention rooms, and departmental hallways" (Richardson 1995:191). While one study was more or less traditional sociology, the other was relatively antithetical to conventional social-scientific standards. Looking at what the students had to say about their studies, it is clear that each project offers insight into the significance of the sociological imagination for student learning. I argue that a reflexive approach to research, which "allows researchers to link milieu with individual experience while at the same time resolving [some of] the tensions between subjectivity and objectivity" (Warr 1999:21) becomes a key aspect of activating that imagination alongside the support of teachers/advisors/mentors.

The classroom is more than a space where static bits of knowledge are passed down or around, where students are trained to conduct scientific research and to report their findings in accordance with socio-scientific norms. It was in the classroom that subcultural affiliations are (re)enacted and embodied each week as participants bring together pedagogy, theory, and subjectivity (Paulus, Woodside and Ziegler 2010). In some cases, the classroom itself becomes a field site where data are created. In my course, research projects are more than just coursework; they (potentially, at least) embody critical pedagogy rooted in the sociological imagination and Mills' focus on social justice. For students who are dealing with "personal troubles", these research projects can be therapeutic insofar as they provide deeper and more nuanced understandings of the injustices students feel or perceive. But therapy is not all—the sociological imagination ties these personal troubles to public issues in ways that can change the students' very outlook on life, affecting future beliefs and actions. Working together, the ethnographic process can become a series of moments that are as subjectively empowering as they are pedagogically instructive.

C. Wright Mills' sociological imagination encourages us not to accept the dominant narratives handed down through mainstream culture (Giroux 2007). Instead, it opens up alternative explanations for how and why we live the lives we do. In the cases discussed here, the sociological imagination exposed a different reality about what it means to participate in alternative youth cultures in Asia in the early 21st century. This relates not only to research, but to teaching and learning as well. In the classroom, students took the chance to critically assess the nature of social and cultural hierarchies within which they live. For Asian students, many of whom feel a constant pressure to conform to traditional measures of academic achievement, the process of researching alternative youth cultures can be simultaneously stressful and rewarding. To achieve the latter, it first requires reflexivity regarding how their identities affect the process of fieldwork (Finlay 2002; Reinharz 1997). The degree to which reflexivity is visible within research reports still varies, but overall there remains relatively little transparency in the relationship between scholars and the topics they study. The salience of reflexive thinking in ethnographic accounts, however, may be less important than the development of a "political imagination" that extends the sociological imagination outward from the classroom and into everyday life (Burawoy 2008), empowering students and other scholars to make real changes in the way we use sociological knowledge.

References

Altheide, D. (1987) "Ethnographic Content Analysis." *Qualitative Sociology* 10(1):65–77.

Anderson, K. T. and Weninger, C. (2012) "Tracing Ideologies of Learning in Group Talk and Their Impediments to Collaboration." *Linguistics and Education* 23(3):350–360.

Andes, L. (1998) "Growing up Punk: Meaning and Commitment Careers in a Contemporary Youth Subculture." In J. Epstein (Ed.), *Youth Culture: Identity in a Postmodern World* (212–231). Malden, MA: Blackwell.

Atkinson, P. (2006) "Rescuing Autoethnography." *Journal of Contemporary Ethnography* 35(4):400–404.

Bennett, A. (2011) "The Post-Subcultural Turn: Some Reflections 10 Years On." *Journal of Youth Studies* 14(5):493–506.

Blackman, S. (2007) "'Hidden Ethnography': Crossing Emotional Borders in Qualitative Accounts of Young People's Lives." *Sociology* 41(4):699–716.

Blackman, S. (2014) "Subculture Theory: An Historical and Contemporary Assessment of the Concept for Understanding Deviance." *Deviant Behavior* 35(6):496–512.

Burawoy, M. (2008) "Open Letter to C. Wright Mills." *Antipode* 40(3):365–375.

Cammarota, J. and Fine, M. (2008) "Youth Participatory Action Research: A Pedagogy for Transformational Resistance". In J. Cammarota and M. Fine (Eds) *Revolutionizing Education: Youth Participatory Action Research in Motion.* New York: Routledge, 1–11.

Charmaz, K. and Mitchell, R. (1996) "The Myth of Silent Authorship: Self, Substance, and Style in Ethnographic Writing." *Symbolic Interaction* 19(4):285–302.

Cherry, E., Colter, E. and DeSoucey, M. (2011) "Food for Thought, Thought for Food: Consumption, Identity, and Ethnography." *Journal of Contemporary Ethnography* 40(2):231–258.

Chua, B. H. (2004) "Conceptualizing an East Asian Popular Culture." *Inter-Asia Cultural Studies* 5(2):200–221.

Chua, B.H. (2010) "Korean Pop Culture." *Malaysian Journal of Media Studies* 12(1):15–24.

Denzin, N. (1989) *Interpretive Biography*. Thousand Oaks, CA: Sage.

Driver, C. (2011) "Embodying Hardcore: Rethinking 'Subcultural' Authenticities." *Journal of Youth Studies* 14(8):975–990.

Ellis, C. (1997) "Evocative Autoethnography: Writing Emotionally about Our Lives." In W. G. Tierney and Y. S. Lincoln (Eds.), *Representation and the Text: Re-framing the Narrative Voice* (115–142). Albany, NY: State University of New York Press.

Ellis, C., Adams, T. and Bochner, A. (2011) "Autoethnography: An Overview." *Forum: Qualitative Social Research* 12(1). Available online at http://www.qualitative-research.net/index.php/fqs/article/view/1589/3095

Englehart, N. A. (2000) "Rights and Culture in the Asian Values Argument: The Rise and Fall of Confucian Ethics in Singapore." *Human Rights Quarterly* 22(2):548–568.

Fields, J., Copp, M. and Kleinman, S. (2007) "Symbolic Interactionism, Inequality, and Emotions." In J. E. Stets and J. H. Turner (Eds.), *Handbook of the Sociology of Emotions* (155–178). New York: Springer.

Fine, M. (1994) "Working the Hyphens: Reinventing Self and Other in Qualitative Research." In N. K. Denzin and Y. S. Lincoln (Eds.), *Handbook of Qualitative Research* (70–82). Thousand Oaks, CA: Sage.

Finlay, L. (2002) "'Outing' the Researcher: The Provenance, Process, and Practice of Reflexivity." *Qualitative Health Research* 12(4):531–545.

Fu, K. and Liew, K. (2005) "Hallyu in Singapore: Korean Cosmopolitanism or the Consumption of Chineseness?" *Korea Journal* 45(4):206–232.

Giroux, H. (2007) "Democracy, Education, and the Politics of Critical Pedagogy." In P. McLaren and J. L. Kincheloe (Eds.), *Critical Pedagogy: Where Are We Now?* (1–5). New York: Peter Lang Publishing Inc.

Hannerz, E. (2015) *Performing Punk*. New York: Palgrave.

Hodkinson, P. (2005) "'Insider Research' in the Study of Youth Cultures." *Journal of Youth Studies* 8(2):131–149.

Ito, M., Okabe, D. and Tsuji, I. (Eds.). (2012) *Fandom Unbound: Okatu Culture in a Connected World*. New Haven, CT: Yale University Press.

Liew, K. K. and Fu, K. (2006) "Conjuring the Tropical Spectres: Heavy Metal, Cultural Politics in Singapore and Malaysia." *Inter-Asia Cultural Studies* 7(1):99–112.

Liew, W. M. (2013) "Effects beyond Effectiveness: Teaching as a Performative Act." *Curriculum Inquiry* 43(2):261–288.

Mee, C.Y. M. (1998) "The Examination Culture and Its Impact on Literacy Innovations: The Case of Singapore." *Language and Education* 12(3):192–209.

Mills, C. W. (1959) *The Sociological Imagination*. New York. Oxford University Press.

Ng, P.T. (2008) "Educational Reform in Singapore: From Quantity to Quality." *Educational Research for Policy and Practice* 7(1):5–15.

Paulus, T. M., Woodside, M. and Ziegler, M. F. (2010) "'I Tell You, It's a Journey, Isn't It?' Understanding Collaborative Meaning Making in Qualitative Research." *Qualitative Inquiry* 16(10):852–862.

Quader, S. B. and Redden, G. (2014) "Approaching the Underground." *Cultural Studies*. doi: 10.1080/09502386.2014.937945.

Reinharz, S. (1997) "Who Am I? The Need for a Variety of Selves in the Field." In R. Hertz (Ed.), *Reflexivity and Voice* (3–20). Thousand Oaks, CA: Sage.

Richardson, L. (1995) "Writing-Stories: Co-authoring 'The Sea Monster', A Writing-Story." *Qualitative Inquiry* 1(2):189–203.

Ronai, C. (1995) "Multiple Reflections of Child Abuse: An Argument for a Layered Account." *Journal of Contemporary Ethnography* 23(4):395–426.

Tan, K. P. (2008) "Meritocracy and Elitism in a Global City: Ideological Shifts in Singapore." *International Political Science Review* 29(1):7–27.

Tuck, E. and Fine, M. (2007) "Inner Angles: A Range of Ethical Responses to/with Indigenous and Decolonizing Theories." In N. K. Denzin and M. D. Giardina (Eds.), *Ethical Futures in Qualitative Research: Decolonizing the Politics of Knowledge* (145–168). Walnut Creek, CA: Left Coast Press.

Wallach, J. (2008) "Living the Punk Lifestyle in Jakarta." *Ethnomusicology* 52(1):98–116.

Warr, D. (1999) "Personal Troubles, Public Issues, and the Reflexive Practice of Research." *Health Sociology Review* 9(1):21–31.

Williams, J. P. (2008) "Teaching and Learning Guide for Youth-Subculture Studies: Sociological Traditions and Core Concepts." *Sociology Compass* 2(2):765–774.

Williams, J. P. (2011) *Subcultural Theory: Traditions and Concepts*. Cambridge: Polity Press.

Williams, J. P. and Hannerz, E. (2014) "Articulating the 'Counter' in Subculture Studies." *M/C Journal* 17(6). http://journal.media-culture.org.au/index.php/mcjournal/ article/viewArticle/912.

Williams, J. P. and Xiang Xin Ho, S. (2016) "'Sasaengpaen' or K-Pop Fan? Singapore Youths, Authentic Identities, and Asian Media Fandom." *Deviant Behavior* 37(1):81–94.

Williams, J. P. and Kamal Jauhari bin Zaini, M. (2016) "Rude Boy Subculture, Critical Pedagogy, and the Collaborative Construction of an Analytic and Evocative Autoethnography." *Journal of Contemporary Ethnography* 45(1):34–59.

12 Conclusions

C. Wright Mills, the 'subcultural' imagination, reflexivity and the subcultural subject

Shane Blackman and Michelle Kempson

The sociological imagination is an abstract concept and yet it has been welcomed, adapted and celebrated. Barry Krisberg (1974: 146) uses the words 'hero', 'courage' and 'magic' to capture the meaning of C. Wright Mills' contribution. John Brewer (2004: 318) notes that Mills was a 'champion to a younger generation of social critics outside the discipline and had to die young to become a hero in sociology'. Such an accolade was first put forward in *The New York Review of Books* by Susan Sontag (1963) to describe the anthropologist Claude Lévi-Strauss as 'A Hero of our Time'. It would seem that all disciplines may require an intellectual hero, but according to Clifford Geertz (1988: 26) you can be both appreciative and also remain unconverted to the intellectual. This is clear in Michael Burawoy's 'Open Letter to C. Wright Mills', who develops a biographical and theoretical narrative in his critique, which has the taste of a spurned lover. At first Michael Burawoy (2008: 365) describes *The Sociological Imagination* as an 'initiation rite' both 'inspiring and comforting', assessing C. Wright Mills' work as offering an 'enduring truth'. Quite quickly though Burawoy (2008: 374) accuses C. Wright Mills of elitism, leaving out Gramsci, being both gender and race blind, appearing to follow the notion of false consciousness that left no room for opposition or agency for subaltern groups; in short, 'your vision here is still stuck in the past'.

Unfortunately, intellectual heroes can let you down, as they suffer the fate of 'blind spots' outside of their time as the discipline moves forward and they remain back in the past. Gane and Back (2012: 417–418) and Kemple and Mawani (2009: 228) both raise the issue of 'blind spots' in C. Wright Mills' work in relation to race which is largely undeveloped, and women who are characterised as deceptive and manipulative. The destiny of such intellectual heroes is to be left behind, stuck in a sociological museum. According to Geertz (1988: 48) their 'books seem to exist behind glass'. For Brewer (2013: 219) Mills' ideas have become 'increasingly irrelevant' and for Platt (2013: 19), while acknowledging C. Wright Mills' work as a sociological classic, turns away to argue that in sociology we do not see 'any serious use of Mills' ideas'.

In contrast, Dan Wakefield (2000) in *C. Wright Mills: Letters and Autobiographical Writings*, offers a more personal narrative of Mills as someone who died before his time, unable to reap the rewards of the criticism and analysis he put forward and who failed to witness the activism and rebellion of the 1960s as the legacy he inspired. A year after his death the 53rd Presidential address of the *Annual Sociological Association* in 1963 was given by Everett Hughes, and was titled 'Race Relations and the Sociological Imagination' (890). He argues: 'The kind of freeing the imagination that I am speaking of requires a great and deep detachment, a pursuit of sociological thought and research in a playful mood. But it is a detachment of deep concern and intense curiosity that turns away from no human activity.' C. Wright Mills identifies strength and sensitivity through different approaches, which inform and support the development of sociological theory based on a range of platforms of literature, empirical work and theoretical engagement at a political level. Adrian Holiday (2016: 23) sees the importance of C. Wright Mills, as enabling the ethnographer to locate themselves and their actions critically within a wider community or world scenario. He quotes Mills: 'In a word, by their reflection and by their sensibility, they realise the cultural meaning of the social sciences and of their place within this meaning' (Mills 1959: 14). This challenge according to Gane and Back can be identified in the recent work of Bauman (2008: 234–235), which has the spirit of the sociological imagination, and both Mills and Bauman intersect over their concern for the individual. In fact, C. Wright Mills (1943: 171) was always troubled by sociological approaches, which 'tend to slip past structures to focus in isolated situations … where there is a tendency for problems to be considered as problems of individuals'. For Bauman (2001) the main threat to sociality and freedom is the process of individualisation, described as 'me-centred' networks where people position themselves for maximum personal gain. What we share in our life-worlds according to Habermas (1987: 363) is that we are all becoming targets of colonisation and commodification. The challenge for the sociological imagination is to enhance individual biographies, identify cultural sensitivity and develop C. Wright Mills' understanding of 'critical thinking' skills to show an awareness of the relationship between the individual and wider society. Returning to Everett Hughes we would like to put an emphasis on the word 'playful' and the concept of imagination, which retain the strength of hope and optimism unbounded by, or at least pro-actively *aware* of, methodological restrictions.

In the book many authors locate their research positionality as being influenced by the Chicago School, which established the tradition of researcher familiarity with the setting of fieldwork. Here the purpose of using fieldwork accounts by the Chicago School is to demonstrate theoretical relevance and vitality to produce humanistic and naturalistic understandings (Roberts 2006: 20, Blackman 2010: 212). This is expressed through the interplay of the subcultural imagination between the researchers' biography and the development of rapport with the research participants. At a critical level, the researchers speak of the dual roles created through fieldwork and during the writing up, where they move between being an 'insider' and 'outsider'. Here the key generator of reflexivity is described by Alice Goffman (2014: 229–231) as where 'fieldwork is a humbling one' and you have 'to invest significant time and effort' to realise commitment. It is on this basis that we have sought the ideas of C. Wright Mills where in each chapter the authors specify the role of researcher biography and milieu in their historical context. We recognise as Chris Hart (2010: 16–17) does that C. Wright Mills was hostile towards aspects of the Chicago School's 'liberal practicality' and reformist agenda, but Mills missed how this empirical tradition and his sociological imagination would be applied to intersectional social and political problems as Everett Hughes did in 1963. The chapters on youth subcultures in the book and author engagement with the Chicago School, affirm Lars Mjoset's (2013: 80) argument that the ethnographic tradition of the Chicago School and the movement towards grounded theory as a feature of the sociological imagination are 'living out the "yearning" Mills had longed for'.

The subcultural imagination and reflexivity

Blurred with flashing speed, wearing a leather jacket and working boots, Yaroslava Mills' 1958 photograph of C. Wright Mills riding his BMW motorbike is a visual representation of the subcultural imagination. Dan Wakefield (2009: 1), American novelist and journalist, and one of C. Wright Mills students at Columbia in 1954, states, 'Mills' very appearance was a subject of controversy.' The emergence of the Beat Movement and its anti-establishment stance is defined by Theodore Roszak (1970: 24) as the beginning of the counter culture. He elaborates at an 'intellectual level Ginsberg and the beatniks can be associated chronologically with the aggressively activist sociology of C. Wright Mills'. This image and assertion is consolidated by Tom Hayden (2006) in *Radical Nomad: C. Wright Mills and His Times*. We want to use this photographic representation of Mills engaged in his leisure pursuit to affirm his argument that you 'must learn to use your life experience in your intellectual work' (216). In this book we have sought to take up Mills' central humanistic notion of the sociological imagination at a theoretical and methodological level focusing on young adults within different subcultural groupings. The connection between the sociological and the subcultural imagination is the struggle against conformity and the desire for critique. In the chapters, the 'imaginations' combine the twin attractions of dangerous thought and subversive style in opposition to authoritarian power. For Gunter, Williams and Cohen the sociological imagination is about connecting to cultural political purpose in order to promote movement beyond the personal, into a liminal space between both private and public. For the academic to meaningfully employ the sociological imagination, they must 'zoom out' from both the discipline and the knowledge paradigms within which they are used to working, and consciously cultivate more creative approaches to research. Hebdige (2012: 403) argues that his approach is 'to keep the reader on the move – outside the normative stabilised positions prescribed within the critically condoned literature: the position of the "detached outsider"'. The aim of this book has been to develop sociological understandings, which dare to be playful, sensuous and critical. In the chapters we see how researchers adapt their research tools and understanding in a rigorous and reflexive manner to respond to the inner lives of research participants.

Within this book the subcultural imagination describes the democratic and participatory research practice between researcher and participants. We see

Hollands, Kempson, Colosi and Dimou combine detachment and attachment, sometimes through coolness, but all the field relationships described in the chapters are also based on exchange within a community. The subcultural imagination is shaped by the dynamic interaction within the research relationship enabling the ethnographers to locate themselves in a different space, consider their researcher positionality to be able to think from an alternative position. The space within the research relationship also allows participants the freedom to express themselves. We see that as an observer you become inducted within the subcultural grouping, as an ethnographer you practise reflexivity and together in that moment the subcultural imagination is released. Some of the chapters in the book have identified the subcultural imagination as operating at both a collective and individual level through biography and group experience. We see the subcultural imagination interactively move between researcher and participants as part of a reflexive practice. Here biographical exchange points towards the development of empathetic relations and commitment beyond fieldwork interactions as the sensitivity of research proceeds. The researchers here are engaged through commitment to their research participants, where at times the subcultural imagination developed between them can feel both enthralling and disturbing. C. Wright Mills' sociological imagination beckons an awareness of how people's social and cultural interactions influence one another. The craft of ethnography is particularly relevant here in these chapters, as we see authors develop emotional intimacies in diverse situations and contexts. Specifically, Barova, Commane, McPherson and Blackman struggle with the sociological imagination as research participants challenge their researcher positionality. In these chapters we see authors thread biographical context and feeling into critical understandings of the subjective world of research participants. The subcultural imagination develops a critical sensibility during ethnography as authors' intimate personal experience is connected with wider social forces. Relationships are sustained through the imagination under a humanistic impulse where the ideal of C. Wright Mills' promise is to seek lasting momentary friendship through recognition of shared aspirations in conversation and action.

Subculture and subcultural subjects

It has been our intention within this collection to advance the concept of subculture to show innovative and diverse sensitivities through an exploration of subjectivities belonging to both academic researchers and the research participants. The subcultural subject is interactive at the level of relationships within fieldwork through reflexivity. The ethnographic basis to all chapters serves as a critical map where we identify subcultural subjects in live situations engaging with moments of stress, contradiction or pleasure. The concept of subcultural subjects describes the participants within a subculture and at a methodological level enables biographic reflection by both academic researcher and participants. Subculture remains a highly popular label to identify particular groupings or formations across a multiple number of platforms and locations (Dhoest, Malliet Segaert and Haers 2015). For example, the concept subculture is applied to Christian and Satanic subcultures, to Ku Klux Klan subcultures, nerd subcultures or subcultures of violence, sexual subcultures or straightedge subcultures, furry subcultures, graffiti subcultures, bare backing, BDSM and body subcultures. Subculture is also now a popular title for fictional literature. There are numerous studies on music-based subcultures including punk, skinhead, metal, rave, mod, rocker, Goth and hip hop. Also, the concept of subculture has been applied to historical periods before the concept had been created – for example, *Mother Clap's Molly House: Gay Subculture in England, 1700–1830* by Rictor Norton, and David Worrall's *Theatric Revolution: Drama, Censorship, and Romantic Period Subcultures 1773–1832* (2006).

There is no evidence for a decline in the application of the term or concept of subculture within academic disciplines or literary fiction. First, publishers have been responding to the re-emergence of subcultural studies in a retro sense; we have seen the *Routledge Revivals Series* including Pat Rogers' *Grub Street: Studies in a Subculture* (first published in 1972) and David Downes' *The Delinquent Solution: A Study in Subcultural Theory* (first published in 1966). Second, focusing on the contemporary application of subculture to current cultural styles the Bloomsbury publishing house produced a series of titles including: *Queer* (2012), *Body* (2012), *Fetish* (2013) and *Punk* (2013). A strangely contradictory element to this new academic book series titled *Subcultural Styles* is that the series editor is Steve Redhead (1997: x) who once proclaimed that subculture was 'no longer appropriate' as a concept. Clearly this has changed! For sociology, the debate over subcultural terminology is not a minor issue because the term retains explanatory power at both individual and collective levels of policy and society and it is here that we think the subcultural subject offers reflexivity and individuality.

There have been calls to refocus subcultures research and pay more attention to the 'whole lives' of participants (Omel'Chenko and Pilkington 2013), rather than presenting these social worlds in a vacuum. The epistemological drivers of such an approach centre on the possibilities of engaging with how subculture becomes affiliated with individual biographies, and how people's biographies come to intersect. Several of the chapters in this book grapple with the methodological possibility of this call and highlight the importance of reflecting upon the assumptions we make as researchers about how subcultures become constituted through shared subjectivity. Different chapters in the book explore a diversity of subjectivities that belong both to research participants and authors. For the researcher the movement from insider to outsider is quite a common experience. Here familiarity with the field setting or the type of participant allows access and enables empathy. This is where the humane sensitivity of ethnography has the potential to reduce fears and create warmth within fieldwork. Also, some academics reveal that they moved from being an outsider to being an insider primarily based on the subjectivities created within the research relationship, which promoted immediate social and personal recognition and identity. Through fieldwork the ethnographer is creating history with the research participant. But only through the subjectivity of the research participants towards the academic researcher do we see the live agency of the subcultural subjects. We see authors in the book through their fieldwork engage in collaboration through the immediacy of live sociology.

Moreover, different chapters in the book show that young adults negotiate local, individual, collective, national and international contexts of subcultural participation. We identify both globalisation and the internet as offering new and accelerated forms of contact and communication for subcultural subjects (Bennett and Robards 2014). From the very the start of the 1960s when *Ready Steady Go!* was broadcast on the ITV network across the UK all young people had direct and immediate access to mod fashion, style, music, language, dance, attitude and posture (Osgerby 2004). The emergence of globalized youth subcultures is not a contemporary phenomenon. The proliferation of subcultural types on a global basis (such as the Teddy Boys) had already been noted by Richard Hoggart (1957: 249), and defined as the 'juke-box boys' following 'the debilitating mass-trend of the day'. T. R. Fyvel (1961: 27–34) states that the 'Teddy Boy International is a form of delinquent behavior identified in the US, Russia, Sweden, Austria, Japan, Germany, Paris and Australia each country having its own cultural forms'. History is a vital part of social inquiry for C. Wright Mills and we affirm this enabling tool to grasp history and biography and the relations between the two within society. Young people's participation in subcultures changes and adapts according to milieu but as Ross Haenfler (2014: 135) argues 'subcultures have always been mediated'. For us the sociological imagination focuses on creativity within everyday practices and addresses how individual 'ordinary youth' take up degrees of subcultural identification and at the same time examines the real lives and collective responses of participants in subcultures. Theoretically, subculture is a reservoir of ideas, histories and practices for its bearers to respond to contradictory societal issues of discrimination, gender, ethnicity and social class. However, as has been shown within several of the chapters in this book, the researcher's response to such structural considerations comes with a caveat that requires introspection, and oftentimes, an acknowledgement of privilege. This highlights the importance of developing innovative methodologies that result in true collaborative relationships between researchers and participants. We have further to go within subcultural studies in order to fully realise C. Wright Mills' call to enact reflexivity, and we have argued here that this will entail researchers finding ways to situate themselves subjectively, not just within the fieldwork they design, but also within the resulting knowledge generated.

References

Bauman, Z. (2001) *Community*. Cambridge: Polity Press.

Bauman, Z. (2008) 'Postscript: Bauman on Bauman ProDoma Sua', in Jacobsen, M. and Poder, P. (eds) *The Sociology of Zygmunt Bauman: Challenges and Critiques*. Aldershot: Ashgate, 231–240.

Bennett, A. and Robards, B. (eds) (2014) *Mediated Youth Cultures: The Internet, Belonging and New Cultural Configurations*. Basingstoke: Palgrave.

Blackman, S. (2010) 'The Ethnographic Mosaic' of the Chicago School: critically locating Vivien Palmer, Clifford Shaw and Frederic Thrasher's research methods in contemporary reflexive sociological interpretation', in Hart, C. (ed.) *The Legacy of the Chicago School of Sociology*. Kingswinsford: Midrash Publishing, 195–215.

Brewer, J. (2004) 'Imagining The Sociological Imagination: the biographical context of a sociological classic', *British Journal of Sociology* 55(3): 317–333.

Brewer, J. (2013) 'The Sociological Imagination and Public Sociology', in Scott, J. and Nilsen, A. (eds) *C. Wright Mills and the Sociological Imagination: Contemporary Perspectives*. London: Edward Elgar, 219–221.

Burawoy, M. (2008) 'Open Letter to C. Wright Mills', *Antipode* 40(3): 365–337.

Dhoest, A. Malliet, S. Segaert, B. and Haers, J. (eds) (2015) *The Border of Subculture*. London: Routledge.

Fyvel, T. R. (1961) *The Insecure Offender*. London: Chatto and Windus.

Ganes, N. and Back, L. (2012) 'C. Wright Mills 50 Years On: the promise and craft of sociology revisited', *Theory, Culture and Society* 29(7/8): 399–421.

Geertz, C. (1988) *Works and Lives*. Stanford, CA: Stanford University Press.

Goffman, A. (2014) *On the Run*. Chicago, IL: Chicago University Press.

Habermas, J. (1987) *The Theory of Communicative Action Volume 2*. Boston, MA: Beacon Press.

Haenfler, R. (2014) *Subcultures*, London: Routledge.

Hart, C. (2010) 'Introduction', in Hart, C. (ed) *The Legacy of the Chicago School of Sociology*, Kingswinsford: Midrash Publishing, 1–43.

Hayden, T. (2006) *Radical Nomad: Wright Mills and His Times*. Boulder, CO: Paradigm Publishing.

Hebdige, D. (2012) 'Contemporizing "Subculture": 30 years to life', *European Journal of Cultural Studies* 15(3): 399–424.

Hoggart, R. (1957) *The Uses of Literacy*. London: Chatto and Windus.

Holiday, A. (2016) *Doing and Writing Qualitative Research*, 3rd edition. London: Sage.

Hughes, E. (1963) 'Race Relations and the Sociological Imagination', *American Sociological Review* 28(6): 879–890.

Kemble, T. and Mawani, R. (2009) 'The Sociological Imagination and its Imperial Shadow', *Theory, Culture and Society* 26(7–8): 228–249.

Krisberg, B. (1974) 'The Sociological Imagination Revisited', *Canadian Journal of Criminology and Corrections* 16: 145–161.

Mills, C. W. (1943) 'The Professional Ideology of Social Pathologists', *American Journal of Sociology* 49(2): 165–180.

Mills, C. W. (1959) *The Sociological Imagination*. New York: Oxford University Press.

Mjoset, L. (2013) 'The Fate of the Sociological Imagination: Mills, social science and contemporary sociology', in Scott, J. and Nilsen, A. (eds) *C. Wright Mills and the Sociological Imagination: Contemporary Perspectives*. London: Edward Elgar, 57–87.

Omel'chenko, E. and Pilkington, H. (2013) 'Regrounding Youth Cultural Theory (in post-socialist youth cultural practice)', *Sociology Compass* 7(3): 208–224.

Osgerby, B. (2004) *Youth Media*. London: Routledge.

Platt, J. (2013) 'The Sociological Imagination: "on intellectual craftsmanship" and Millis's influence on research methods', in Scott, J. and Nilsen, A. (eds) *C. Wright Mills and the Sociological Imagination: Contemporary Perspectives*. London: Edward Elgar, 3–28.

Roberts, B. (2006) *Micro Social Theory*. Basingstoke: Palgrave.

Roszak, T. (1970) *The Making of a Counter Culture*. London: Faber and Faber.

Sontag, S. (1963) 'A Hero of our Time', *The New York Review of Books*, November, 1, 7, www.nybooks.com (accessed: 20 September 2015).

Wakefield, D. (2000) 'Introduction', in Mills, K. and Mills, P. (eds) *C. Wright Mills: Letters and Autobiographical Writings*. Berkeley, CA: University of California Press, 1–18.

Wakefield, D. (2009) *C. Wright Mills: Before His Time*, 18 March, www.thenation.com/authors/dan-wakefield (accessed: 20 September 2015).

Index